# MOIR'S GUIDE SOUTH

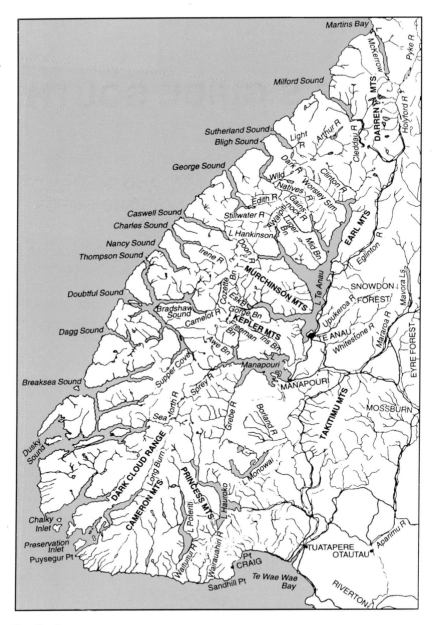

Fiordland

# MOIR'S GUIDE SOUTH

## GUIDE BOOK TO THE TRACKS AND ROUTES OF THE GREAT SOUTHERN LAKES AND FIORDS OF NEW ZEALAND

SIXTH EDITION
(Completely Revised)

EDITED BY
**ROBIN G. M<sup>c</sup>NEILL**

PUBLISHED BY
GREAT SOUTHERN LAKES PRESS

1995

Although every effort has been made to ensure that the information contained in this guide book is accurate at the time of publication the editor and publishers accept no responsibility for any accident, misadventure or injury associated with its use. The sketch maps are for general guidance only and are no substitute for NZMS 1 or NZMS 260 maps.

It would be very much appreciated if errors, omissions or clarifications for the routes are brought to the attention of the editor for incorporation into subsequent editions.

Great Southern Lakes Press
P.O. Box 12-205
Christchurch
NEW ZEALAND

Successor to
"Guide Book to the Tourist Routes of the Great Southern Lakes"
GEORGE M. MOIR, 1925.

*Second Edition:* Edited by W. SCOTT GILKISON and ARTHUR H. HAMILTON under the present title, 1949,1950 (NZAC).

*Third Edition:* Edited by GERARD HALL-JONES (Southern Section) 1959, and PETER M. CHANDLER (Northern Section) 1961 (NZAC).

*Fourth Edition:* Edited by GERARD HALL-JONES (Southern Section) 1969, 1973; PETER M. CHANDLER and RONALD J. KEEN (Northern Section) 1968 (NZAC).

*Fifth Edition:* Edited by GERARD HALL-JONES (Southern Section) 1979, 1986; L.D. KENNEDY (Northern Section) 1977,1984 (NZAC).

*Sixth Edition:* Edited by ROBIN MCNEILL 1995.

ISBN: 0-473-03432-8

Cover Photo: Hugh van Noorden
Maps: Robin McNeill and Mary Strang
Layout & Design: The Caxton Press

# Contents

### Irene Valley, Windward River and Large Burn, 144
Cozette Burn to Irene Valley
Cozette Burn to Robin Saddle
Irene River to Windward River and Gold Arm, Charles Sound
Charles Sound to Nancy Sound
Irene Valley to Large Burn
Lake Marchant
Emelius Arm, Charles Sound to Irene Valley
Large Burn to Kiwi Flat, Doon River

## South of the Murchison Mountains and West of Lake Manapouri

### Camelot River and Cozette Burn, 148
Fowler Pass to Bradshaw Sound via Tuaraki Stream and Camelot River,
Macpherson Pass to Tuaraki Stream via Torre Stream
Awe Burn to Elaine Stream
Cozette Burn

### Gorge Burn, 151
Lake Te Anau to Lake Eva and Macpherson Pass
Lake Boomerang to Fowler Pass
Lake Eva to Hidden Lake, Head of Cozette Burn

### Freeman Valley, 154
Freeman Burn Hut to Fowler Pass
Steven Falls to Iris Burn via Lake Herries and Delta Burn
Delta Burn

### Kepler Track, 157
Control Gates to Iris Burn Hut via Mt Luxmore
Iris Burn Hut to Control gates via Moturau Hut
Side Trips from the Kepler Track

### Mica Burn-Oonah Burn-Awe Burn-Elaine Stream, 160
Mica Burn
Mica Burn Saddle to Oonah Saddle
Oonah Saddle to Awe Burn
Awe Burn
North Branch Awe Burn to Lake Annie
Lake Annie to Camelot River via Anehu Pass and Elaine Stream

### Garnock Burn Area, 164
Pearl Harbour return via the Circle Track
The Monument
Pearl Harbour to Hope Arm

Port Craig to Wairaurahiri, Waitutu and Big Rivers
Big River to Hill E
Hill E to Kisbee Bay, Preservation Inlet via the Inland Route
Hill E to Puysegur Point via the Coastal Route

# East of Fiordland

## Eglinton Valley, 212
Boyd Creek and Henry Creek to Upukerora River
Eglinton East Branch to Cascade Creek and Greenstone Valley
Eglinton Valley to Glade House via Dore Pass
Hut Creek
Hut Creek to Glade Burn via Glade Pass
Mistake Creek to Hut Creek via U Pass
Cascade Creek
Mistake Creek to Falls Creek
Melita Creek to Falls Creek
Key Summit to Greenstone Valley via tops

## Mavora Lakes and Snowdon Forest, 219
Mavora-Greenstone Walkway
Mararoa River to Kiwi Burn Hut from Kiwi Burn swing bridge
Kiwi Burn Swing bridge to Whitestone River via upper Kiwi Burn
Tracks from the South Mavora Swing bridge
Boyd Creek to Upukerora Headwaters
Boyd Creek to Upukerora River via Dunton Swamp
Henry Creek to Upukerora River

## Eyre Mountains, 225
Acton Hut to Cromel Hut
Acton Hut to Cromel Branch Hut
Acton Hut to Islands Hut
Cromel Hut to Cromel Branch Hut
Cromel Branch Hut to Cromel Bivvy
Cromel Branch Hut to Irthing Bivvy
Irthing Stream
Mt Bee Ridge
Windley River
Oreti River
Mataura River to Billy Saddle and Eyre Peak
Mataura River—Lochy River—Long Burn—Robert Creek
Robert Creek
Eyre Creek

# List of Photographs and Maps

## PHOTOGRAPHS
Unless otherwise indicated in the captions, the photographs in this guide book were taken by the editor.

*Front cover:* Lower Clinton River, Milford Track, *Hugh van Noorden.*
*Back cover:* The editor in the Glaisnock Valley, *Bill Barclay.*

## MAPS

# Editor's Foreword

*Moir's Guide* can be likened to Hone Heke's famous axe which had two new heads and three new handles— this sixth edition of *Moir's Guide* is the result of cumulative efforts by eight different editors and countless contributors over a period of 70 years. In this time it has evolved considerably from the guide originally edited by Dr George Moir.

The guide book was first published in 1925, adapted from articles George had written for the Otago Daily Times. It was a thin brown book which described the tourist tracks in the vicinity of what George insisted on calling "The Great Southern Lakes" and was intentionally a "Trampers Guide to the Tracks" rather than a "Climber's Guide to the Peaks". Not only was it the first, and for many years the only, guide book to be published for the area, but the section describing the Milford Track was long considered to be the authoritative text.

After being out of print for many years a largely revised second edition of *Moir's Guide* was published by the New Zealand Alpine Club in 1948, edited by W. Scott Gilkison and Arthur H. Hamilton. George Moir provided a certain amount of assistance. In this edition the coverage was expanded to include a number of off-track routes from the bottom of Fiordland to the head of the Landsborough River. In doing so it became New Zealand's most influential tramping guide book.

Questions concerning the copyright of the guide book arose in 1948 and were concluded with George assigning his copyright to the New Zealand Alpine Club for the purpose of the second edition only. After Gerard Hall-Jones became the next editor in 1957 he resolved informally with George for his assignment to be extended. As no copyrights were reserved by Scott, Arthur or Gerard the subsequent editions of the guide book were published as copyright of the New Zealand Alpine Club. These three author-editors gave their services without charge, on the basis that all profits would be accumulated by the Club to fund reprints, new editions and other publications. For many years the profits were isolated in a separate account, but they were more recently absorbed into the club's general funds with the result that by 1994 no money remained to finance the sixth edition.

In 1957 it was recognised that with the increasing numbers of route descriptions to be included as a result of improved tramping and hunting access the third edition of *Moir's Guide* would have to be divided into two parts. Gerard Hall-Jones edited the first, the Southern Section, covering the regions south of the Hollyford. This part enlarged the second edition considerably by extending into the lesser-known valleys of northern Fiordland and west and south of Lakes

17

Te Anau and Manapouri. His fourth and fifth editions continued the revision and expansion until ultimately every Fiordland valley of any significance was covered with the exception of those in the Murchison Special Area. Gerard had sought widely for route information for all his editions and in doing so firmly established the tradition of users contributing to the guide book.

On Gerard's retirement in 1992, after an editorial term of 35 years, it was timely to review the content and presentation of the guide book. It was decided to expand its scope to include the much underrated Snowdon, Mavora, Eyre and Takitimu areas for which no current guide existed. The opportunity to rearrange and retitle a number of sections was taken along with the inclusion of an index.

While much of the substance of the chapters was essentially correct, changes had occurred since the fifth edition so in 1993 and 1994 a concerted effort was made to contact those who had been into off-track Fiordland in recent years to verify and amend route details. The response was heartening and almost every chapter has benefited from the exercise. Each section now fully acknowledges the new contributors for that section in order to give credit where credit is due and also to provide parties with some idea of the currency of the route information.

Many people have helped me get this edition to print. However, my sincere thanks must go not only to the many people who provided me with assistance and new information for the sixth edition, including Gerard Hall-Jones, but also to those who went before them. In addition I wish to expressly thank Martin Cox, Matt Sillars, Barry Smith and Eugene McNeill for their parts in producing this guide book, Mary Strang for her work on the maps and Bruce Fraser who circulated the draft in Te Anau and who provided many helpful comments.

I want to warmly acknowledge the genuine hospitality my wife Sue and I have enjoyed from members of the Southland Section of the New Zealand Alpine Club and the Southland Tramping Club over many years. Finally, my thanks go to Sue, who has been a wonderful companion on many of my own expeditions into the areas described in this guide book, for her love, encouragement, tolerance, forbearance and practicality.

Robin G. McNeill
39 Hackthorne Road,
Christchurch

July 1995

# INTRODUCTION

# Essential Advice

## ROUTE DETAIL

The amount of detail given in this guide book has been matched to suit the most frequent users of each section. In practice this means that the more popular tracks have been treated rather more generously than the off-track country to the west and south of Lake Te Anau. For these latter areas, the route descriptions are indeed only for guidance and parties will need to rely as much on their own navigational abilities as on this guide book.

While several sources of independent information for the popular and easier routes and tracks have been used in preparing this guide book, this is not true for much of the country infrequently visited. Accordingly, the editor asks that parties who note any errors or sources of confusion in the guide book to advise him and supply correct descriptions. Write to the editor, C/o Great Southern Lakes Press, P.O. Box 12-205, Christchurch.

## CHANGES TO TRACKS AND ROUTES

Parties should be prepared to adapt to changes to tracks, routes and huts subsequent to this guide book going to press. Especially in Fiordland, a week of particularly bad weather can create slips that can form new lakes, destroy huts and tracks, or cause massive avalanches that flatten many hectares of bush. Fords and wire bridges are especially vulnerable to severe flooding.

## TIMES

In this guide book the times given are those which an "average" party for the route or track could under "average" conditions expect to take allowing for appropriate rest periods. There are many factors which give rise to variations in times, such as weather, conditions, fitness, experience, weight of packs, mistakes in route-finding and so on, and allowances should be made for these.

Off-track, a fit party very familiar with the terrain and travelling light can sometimes take less than half the time of even an experienced party new to the area. Also, off-track travel times are sensitive to the deer numbers in the area over the previous few years, along with the party's experience in reading deer trails. Both of these factors are quite variable and all that can be safely said is that it is unlikely that a party new to an area will be faster than the times contained in this guide book. Conversely, parties are unlikely to take more than half as much time again as those quoted.

## WHERE TO GO

Parties who have not previously tramped in New Zealand are very strongly urged to attempt some of the popular tracks first. The Milford, Routeburn and Greenstone-Caples Tracks are ideally suited to first-time trampers, although experienced parties will also find these tracks extremely rewarding.

Parties with some tramping experience will enjoy the Kepler and Hollyford Tracks while those seeking rather more demanding tracks should consider the George Sound and Dusky Sound Tracks. The Takitimu and Eyre Mountains should not be overlooked as they contain good tracks, as well as easy to moderate off-track tramping.

## TRAVELLING SOLO

Only the Kepler, Greenstone-Caples, Hollyford, Milford and Routeburn Tracks are suitable for solo travel. Even the Dusky Sound Track has sufficient difficulties to make it imprudent for solo trampers to attempt it. Excluding those few individuals with many years of off-track experience, travelling away from the tracks without being part of a larger party must be viewed as foolhardy. It should be noted that the range of a Mountain Radio from the bottom of a moraine boulder hole is insufficient to summon help.

## MURCHISON SPECIAL AREA

The habitat of the takahe in the Murchison Mountains between the South and Middle Fiords of Te Anau has been designated as a Special Area and access is allowed only by special permits which are exclusively confined to scientific parties and others engaged in protecting this rare bird. No descriptions are given for this area to dissuade unauthorised parties from entering it.

## WEATHER

It has been joked that there is a definite rainy season in Fiordland— it starts at the beginning of January and finishes at the end of December! However, on average one day in three is fine in Fiordland and travel below the bushline is possible on most days. The winter months tend to be more stable and fine than the summer ones, which is offset by many valley floors being completely devoid of sunshine at this time, making for frigid conditions.

Travelling eastwards, the tributaries of Lake Te Anau tend to have better weather than the west coast catchments, while the Eglinton, Takitimu, Snowdon and Eyre areas are much better still. Indeed, the Eyre Forest has a relatively dry climate. The southern coastal areas tend to be subjected to nearly all the bad weather that reaches New Zealand, while the areas further north follow the typical New Zealand alpine weather cycle of wet nor'-westers with clearing weather after a cold southerly change.

Visitors from overseas are cautioned that New Zealand weather is exceedingly changeable and notoriously unpredictable. It is common for a beautiful fine day to deteriorate in a matter of hours, with plummeting temperatures, heavy rain and possibly snow setting in. The moral is that parties should always be prepared for Hughie, the fancied alpine weather god, to do his worst.

## WINTER TRAVEL

Parties should be aware that winter travel brings about special conditions that must be allowed for. Avalanches provide the greatest hazard and this is especially true in side valleys and even the valley floors in steeper country.

Parties need to ensure that they are properly prepared for winter travel and should include ice axes and crampons for even the tourist tracks, which become very iced up. In addition, deep snow must also be expected which can make travel impossible.

Note that the Milford Road is sometimes closed in winter due to avalanches. As an active avalanche control programme is carried out adjacent to the Milford Road throughout the winter months, parties should ensure their intentions are known by DoC or the avalanche technician. When the road is open the "No Stopping" signs beyond Lyttles Flat should be obeyed to minimise avalanche hazard.

## MOUNTAIN RADIO SERVICE

The Mountain Radio Service provides small, lightweight and easy to use HF SSB transceivers for use by trampers, climbers and hunters. Base stations in Christchurch, Dunedin, Invercargill, and Te Anau establish contact with each field station every evening at scheduled times to give the weather forecast and pass on messages.

The Mountain Radios come equipped with two channels. One is the Mountain Radio Service channel and the other is the DoC field party channel. The DoC channel is usually monitored throughout office hours and should be used initially to summon aid in an emergency. Radios brought down from the North Island may not be fitted with the local DoC channel.

The Canterbury Mountain Radio Service can be contacted at P.O. Box 22-342, Christchurch, phone 0(3)366 5241 and the Southland Field Radio contact is Ray Phillips, phone 0(3)216 3751 (evenings).

# JOIN US NOW
## Help Protect New Zealand's Wild Places

Federated Mountain Clubs (FMC) is New Zealand's national advocate for trampers, walkers, climbers and mountaineers. Membership of FMC is now also available to individuals as well as clubs. We promote the interests of backcountry recreational users and the preservation and extension of our national parks, Wildernesses and other public conservation lands. We have been your voice since our formation in 1931.

Join our 15,00 members to strengthen the voice of back country recreational users and help us ensure future generations have the same opportunities you enjoy now.

## By joining you help us
- advocate for the interests of trampers, climbers, skiers, hunters and walkers.
- promote and retain free public access to and over our parks, protected lands and the coast.
- fight for full public ownership and control of the public conservation estate.
- support and enlarge national parks, reserves and the public conservation estate
- protect natural heritage values.
- oppose privatisation and tourism pressures.
- promote the wilderness and preservation ethic.

## You benefit directly by
- Keeping up-to-date through FMC's informative quarterly 'Bulletin' and 'FMC News'.
- the FMC Discount Card with significant discounts on maps, books, transport, courses and accommodation.

## Federated Mountain Clubs of New Zealand (Inc)

✁ or photocopy — — — — — — — — — — — — — — — — — —

To **Federated Mountain Clubs of New Zealand (Inc)**
PO Box 1604, Wellington (or Fax 04-233 8244)

Please enrol me as an FMC supporter member. I enclose $30 annual subscription. (This is the 1996 subscription rate. It may rise slightly in future years.

Name  .................................................................................... Date ....... / ....... / ......

Address ...........................................................................................................................

.....................................................................................................................
(Moir South)

The Mountain Radio Service operates on 3261 kHz with the following schedule times: ZKIB Christchurch and ZKIB101 Dunedin, 7:30 pm; ZKFK Invercargill, 8:00 pm. The DoC channel operates on 3336 kHz.

## WEATHER FORECASTS

Weather forecasts for the mountain areas can be heard on National Radio, the DoC morning radio schedule, and the Mountain Radio nightly schedule.

*National Radio* (4YA Dunedin, 810 kHz; 4YZ Invercargill, 720 kHz): Extended range five day forecast, 12:35 pm weekdays, 12:25 pm weekends; Mountain forecast, 1:05 pm weekdays, 1:06 pm weekends; Coastal forecast, 5:05 am.

*Te Anau DoC:* 8:15 am, from late October to mid May.

*Mountain Radio Service*: ZKIB Christchurch, 7:30 pm; ZKFK Invercargill, 8:00 pm.

## INTENTION FORMS AND HUT BOOKS

Parties should fill out an intentions form giving the names of members in the party, routes and escape routes to be taken, and the name of a New Zealand contact person and leave it at the Park Headquarters before leaving civilisation. Even more importantly, *parties must sign back in again at the end of a trip* to avoid launching a costly Search and Rescue operation to look for them.

Similarly, fill in hut books with the party's intentions before leaving so that should there be a misadventure, searchers will have enough information to know where to start searching.

## NEW ZEALAND ENVIRONMENTAL CARE CODE

The New Zealand Environmental Care Code sums up what is really plain common sense and a concern for others. By observing the last two items meticulously, parties should have no trouble in complying with the remainder.

- Protect plants and animals
- Remove rubbish
- Bury toilet waste
- Keep streams and lakes clean
- Take care with fires
- Camp carefully
- Keep to the track
- Consider others
- Respect our cultural heritage
- Enjoy your visit
- *Toitu te whenua* (leave the land undisturbed)

# Experience New Zealand

**An InfoMap is the definitive guide to your wilderness adventure**

**Walking, tramping, skiing, climbing, canoeing, mountain biking – the quality and detail of our maps help to keep you in control of where you're going.**

**Trackmaps** – detailed information on the more popular walking and tramping tracks

**Parkmaps** – 23 InfoMaps focussing on our protected National and Forest Parks

**Topomaps** – ideal for detailed planning and for taking with you on walking or back packing holidays

Other InfoMaps are: **Streetfinder, Holidaymaker, Terrainmaps, Touringmaps, Coast to Coast**

InfoMaps are available from most map retailers and all Department of Survey & Land Information offices, listed in the yellow pages under Land Information

 *InfoMap*

NOCHA5

# Route Finding

## MAPS

All the maps for the areas covered in this guide book are produced by the Department of Survey and Land Information (DOSLI). These maps are available from most Department of Conservation (DoC) offices, good bookshops and DOSLI offices. The following map series are available:

### Terrainmap

At a scale of 1: 250 000 (1 cm to 2.5 km) 262-14 *Te Anau* and 262-16 *Invercargill* are good for general overviews.

### Topomaps

Also known as NZMS 260 Series, these maps have a scale of 1:50 000 (1 cm to 0.5 km) with 20 metre contours. They are scheduled to replace all the NZMS 1 topographical maps by the end of 1997 and are now the standard maps to use in the field, where available.

### NZMS 1 Series

These are the old 1:63,360 (inch to the mile) topographical maps. DOSLI has been withdrawing these maps as the *Topomaps* become available.

### Parkmaps

273-03 *Fiordland* covers Fiordland, the Routeburn and Greenstone Tracks, and east to part way through the Eyre Forest at a scale of 1:250 000 and 273–02 *Mount Aspiring* includes the Routeburn at a scale of 1:150 000. The scales of these maps are insufficient to use in the field in untracked territory.

### Trackmaps

These specialist maps cover the tracks they are named after: 335-01 *Milford* (1:75 000), 335-02 *Routeburn* (1:75 000), 335-03 *Hollyford* (1:75 000), and 335-09 *Kepler* (1:50 000). On the back of these maps is track and other information.

The NZMS 1 and Topomaps topographical maps are extremely valuable for travel in untracked country and they are an essential supplement to, although not a substitute for, this guide book. While the Topomaps are developing a reputation for accuracy, care should still be exercised in interpreting topographical maps as not all of the features are accurate, especially in the steeper areas, and some serious anomalies do exist. It is not wise to plan routes into untracked country relying solely on maps.

Grid references in this guidebook starting with an 'S' refer to the NZMS 1 maps while those starting with an 'A' through to 'F' refer to Topomaps.

## METRICATION

The text has been converted to metric measurements for the most part, but a few exceptions remain. The NZMS 1 maps still shows mountain heights in feet and references to unnamed peaks and contour heights on these maps must therefore still be given in the manner shown, e.g. Peak 5,440 ft.

## "TRUE-LEFT" AND "TRUE-RIGHT"

To avoid confusion, directions in this guide book usually refer to "true-left" and "true-right". "True-left" is the left-hand side of the river when viewed looking down stream. "True-right" is thus the right-hand side of the river, looking down stream. On the few occasions when this term is used for lakes, the rule holds looking towards the outlet.

## "TRACKS", "TRAILS" AND "ROUTES"

The word "track" is confined in this guide book to a properly formed pathway where the ground underfoot has been cleared and the vegetation cut back from the sides. Most tracks are also marked with blazes, metal discs (pre-1970's), permalat markers (1970's–1990's), or orange plastic triangles (1990's). A "trail" is a less distinct, unformed pathway, sometimes blazed or marked with fluorescent spray paint and usually formed by deer or wapiti. Such trails may in time disappear, or revert to rough going. The word "route" is used in a general sense, describing where the better travel lies but leaving it to individual parties to find their own way. Stone cairns are often used to mark the start of trails, river crossings and routes in riverbeds and above the bushline.

## DEER AND WAPITI TRAILS

As deer and wapiti trails often provide the best off-track travel, the ability to follow animal trails is a useful skill for moving easily through un-tracked country. Fluency in finding and following animal trails only comes with experience and practice. To assist those new to off-track travel the observations below are provided as a guide.

On valley floors parties will usually find several trails running more or less parallel to the river. The main trail will be found to follow the river either just on the riverbank or on the edge of a terrace above the river. Before gorges and waterfalls these trails will combine to form a single, well defined trail following the best route through the gorge or around the obstacle. The trail may climb well away from the river to avoid major bluffs and in doing so leave parties wondering if they are inadvertently heading for the tops. With few exceptions it is worth persevering with such trails as the alternatives are generally much worse.

Trails can nearly always be picked up at the ends of clearings, often just inside the bush. Another strategy to pick up a trail is to cut in at right angles from the river, through the bush, until the main trail is reached. Where there are more than a few animals using the trails, well graded ramps up clay banks can usually be found where the trails cross side creeks.

Leading away from the river, good trails can normally be found following up spurs and along ridges. The ease of following such trails is one good reason for making height by climbing spurs. The other good reason is, of course, the ease of navigation on spurs. By comparison animal trails on bush faces will tend to lead from one good deer feeding area to another, often at around the same altitude. When descending from the tops pick up the trails leading down spurs by looking just inside the bushline on the spur itself.

Trails unfortunately tend to disappear in moraine deposits, where they are most needed, as the animals tend to avoid these places, and with good reason. In fern clearings the trail will disperse into many rough, shin scraping trails, all but obscured by the fern leaves. Fortunately, the main trail can always be found at the far end of the ferns. A similar pattern exists in and around swamps.

Deer are considerably stronger than humans and so pepperwood thickets and vines pose no real barrier to them. Here too, strong deer trails are infrequent as the deer individually find their own way through these areas.

In steep country wapiti sometimes have different uphill routes to their downhill routes. For this reason good wapiti trails may suddenly and disconcertingly seem to disappear. To follow a trail in steep country remember that wapiti can easily jump two metres straight down to where the track continues, and so look accordingly.

Roger Lentle[1] notes that wapiti trails in particular do not necessarily run from valley floor to tussock tops. There is some evidence that larger stags remain in the high western areas and do not descend completely to valley floors in winter. Thus there is the possibility that what may start out as a good downward track may not continue to the valley floor. He also points out that contrary to popular belief, wapiti are not infallible mountaineers and frequent discoveries of carcasses at the foot of bluffs are evidence of this. Accordingly, whilst a wapiti trail may offer a reasonable route, parties should always take care when following such trails.

Wapiti tend to change their range as the season changes. Moving from the warmer north facing areas in winter and early spring, progressively through to the colder south facing areas in late summer, they follow the ripening pattern

[1] For a fuller understanding of animal trails, readers are referred to *Red Deer in New Zealand* and *Hunting the Seasons Round*, both by Roger Lentle and Frank Saxton.

of grass growth which forms a large part of their diet. Red deer act similarly, albeit less predictably, than wapiti. These changes in location mean that a set of animal trails may only be used during a particular season. In particular, summer tracks may well be impassable in winter. In winter then, it is worthwhile to examine trails for fresh sign before heading high. On the other hand, following a fresh wapiti trail in winter may still be difficult as wapiti have a prodigious ability to cross soft snow, even up to their bellies. This is not true for humans.

## SOME RULES OF THUMB FOR CHOOSING ROUTES

The following general rules may help when choosing routes:

- Lakes with subterranean outlets invariably have large boulder fields where the outlet could be expected to be. These are very slow to scramble through.
- Wide, flat valley floors in Fiordland tend to be swampy. The best travel is often on the levees forming the river bank.
- It is usually impossible to tell from topographical maps alone how badly bluffed a route is, especially in steep country.
- A line of bluffs of unpredictable severity always marks the end of a hanging valley.
- The words "Pass" and "Saddle" in a place name do not necessarily mean that a route exists or can be followed with ease. For example, Gertrude Saddle is uncrossable and Hunter Pass has a fierce reputation.
- Spurs generally offer the easiest routes for ascending and descending as the trails are stronger there than on faces and there is less likelihood of becoming bluffed.
- Sidles across a face usually take longer than following a ridge or river.
- Expect to climb at a rate of around 300 metres per hour.
- On flat tracks, expect to travel between four and six kilometres per hour.
- Off-track travel may be as slow as 500 metres per hour.

# Bushcraft

Every party must be prepared for the penetrating cold, wet conditions that are commonly encountered in the New Zealand outdoors. It is a sobering thought to reflect that most fatalities in the outdoors can be attributed to either drowning, or exposure. There is strong evidence that many of the former were due to the latter.

The Mountain Safety Council has published manuals on bushcraft, exposure, firearms and hunting, mountaineering and outdoor first aid. These manuals contain information on, amongst other things, equipment, river crossing techniques, first-aid and food that is appropriate for New Zealand conditions. These are recommended reading.

## OFF-TRACK TRAVEL

While Fiordland has a reputation for having very difficult off-track travel, it does not require superhuman effort, or fitness to travel safely through it. More important is an ability to persevere with uncomfortable conditions and to be satisfied with progress that is remarkably slow compared with many other areas.

Fly camp. A fire under a tent fly may sometimes get a little smoky, but at least it stays dry. A tent fly also provides a place out of the rain to open packs and eat lunch in comfort.

By contrast, the Snowdon and Takitimu forests are recommended as excellent areas in which to gain experience in off-track travel.

## CROSSING RIVERS

Techniques for crossing rivers are described in the Mountain Safety Council Bushcraft Manual and need not be repeated here. However, it must be emphasised that rivers may change their course and that channels in their beds may alter. Therefore, always examine a ford carefully before crossing and never plunge in blindly relying on a location described in this guide book. Remember too, that a flooded river will fall as rapidly as it rose after rain ceases so that a delay of a few hours or so can often transform an impassable torrent into a safely fordable stream.

Many Fiordland rivers and streams are remarkably clear and as a result are often much deeper than they appear. What may seem like a knee-deep river is likely to be waist-deep.

## HUTS

Most of the huts mentioned in this guide book are maintained by DoC and with the exception of those on the "Name Tracks", such as the Milford and Routeburn Tracks, are open to all on a first-come first-occupy basis. Homer Hut is owned by the New Zealand Alpine Club and their members have to priority over non-members. In all cases hut fees are payable to DoC, preferably in advance. Please pay the fees, which also go towards maintaining the huts and tracks— they are incredibly expensive to build and maintain.

Hut users should observe back country etiquette. Respect the huts and equipment, thereby maintaining pleasant conditions and shelter for other parties. When leaving, record your visit and intentions in the hut books provided. This not only is of assistance to searchers should you become missing, but DoC uses the statistics to justify maintenance of the huts and tracks. Also ensure that the hut doors and windows are left closed, any billies cleaned and left upside down and any firewood used is replenished. Exercise care with fires and candles in huts and damp down ashes thoroughly before leaving.

While few people relish putting on wet clothes and socks in the morning, even fewer people enjoy having wet socks dripping into their evening meal while it cooks on the fire, or stove underneath. It is considered very poor form to try to dry clothes over a fire, or stove being used for cooking.

## OFF-TRACK CAMPING

All tents in Fiordland need a fly to keep the rain out. A waterproof floor is also a great help as many promising grassy flats on closer inspection comprise of boggy swamps. A "lunch fly" is a very useful addition to party gear for off-track trips as lunchtime stops in wet weather are much more comfortable with a fly overhead. At the end of the day a fire can be lit under one corner, protected from the rain.

*On leaving a campsite you should ensure that there is absolutely no sign left that you were ever there.* The days of leaving fireplaces for subsequent parties have long gone and all fireplace surrounds should be heaved into the river upon leaving. Likewise, the practice of some unthinking parties of leaving bundled up black plastic fly remnants is also unforgivable— nobody wants or needs this sort of rubbish, especially in the bush where parties will be already self sufficient regarding accommodation. It should be unnecessary to remind parties that *all* rubbish should be packed out.

Choose campsites that will withstand the effects of overnight rain. A sound practice is to assume that heavy rain will fall overnight and set up camp accordingly. Sandy areas indicate frequent water flows and so are not good choices for campsites. Likewise, camping in a dried-up streambed runs the risk of having to evacuate the site when the rain is at its heaviest. During very heavy downpours small streams can easily rise over ten centimetres per hour and

Turners Bivvy — one of the more famous bivvy rocks in Fiordland. Providing solid shelter against the elements, rock bivvies are the preferred accommodation for many parties.

over prolonged, usually more than twelve hour, periods of consistently heavy rain surprisingly high riverbanks can become inundated. It is extremely unwise to camp on an island or a potential island.

In alpine areas be aware of avalanche run out zones, especially in valley floors. Unfortunately avalanche catchment zones are usually hidden from the valley floor by the steep sided mountains, so avoid areas that look as if they may be cleared by avalanches.

## FIRELIGHTING

The minimum environmental impact code discourages open fires in frequently used areas and beside tracks. Nonetheless, when travelling off-track fires have their place. A tomahawk, or large sharp knife should be carried in Fiordland as sometimes the only dry kindling to be found is in the centre of large diameter, dead branches. This is especially true in valleys where all the branches are covered in moss and the trees are waterlogged. Even so, it is not uncommon to spend two hours to get a half-decent fire going in Fiordland. In these conditions, plenty of patience, a stack of dry kindling and a candle to start the fire with are invaluable. For any fire, it is imperative that there is a good vapour barrier between the fire and the ground to ensure that the fire does not extinguish itself by "sucking" water out of the surrounding soil as it gets started. A layer of rocks and stones is generally adequate for this purpose.

## COMFORT

Fiordland has a reputation for ferocious sandflies. This is particularly true of the coastal areas. Sandflies are at their worst when bad weather is approaching and during windless, wet days. During hot dry weather and cold frosty weather sandflies seem to go to ground and they do go to sleep when the sun goes down. Take plenty of reputable insect repellent and be prepared to cover up. Mosquitoes are common only in swampy areas, generally later in the summer.

In Fiordland, wet shorts are more common than dry ones and they often lead to chafed upper thighs. The best remedy is to apply a "zinc oxide and castor oil" ointment, commonly used to prevent nappy rash on babies, to sensitive areas. This ointment is available from chemist shops.

No pack is totally waterproof. However, the readily obtainable bright orange heavy duty plastic survival bag/pack liners go a very long way towards dry gear. Check them daily for small holes, which are easily repaired with sticking plaster.

Disposable contact lenses outperform glasses when travelling in wet weather and through wet bush. As pepperwood thickets in shaded valleys can remain wet for days after the rain has gone, contact lenses can quickly pay for themselves.

## LOST!

Should you become lost try and back-track to your last known point and start again. If this is of no use, or impossible to do, stop and have something to eat and drink. At least this will stop any panic and give you time to consider your position carefully and rationally.

If you can still not find your way, remember that Search and Rescue (SAR) teams, probably lifted in by helicopters, will check road ends, huts, tracks, rivers and ridges first, and roughly in that order. The SAR Controller will methodically arrange for each likely area to be searched in turn so it is important to stay in one location. If you do move, ensure that you leave numerous messages and signs indicating your intended movements. You should be found within three to four days after your notified overdue date.

Smoky fires, mirror flashes, waved orange pack liners and shaken tree branches are highly visible to a searching helicopter. Waving arms and stationary pack liners are not easy to spot from the air.

Remember that the early explorers here endured appalling conditions without the benefit of modern gear. Providing you drink plenty of water you should be able to survive for at least four weeks without food.

Overseas visitors should note that an official Search and Rescue does not incur any cost to the party receiving aid.

### SAR NIGHTLY PRAYER

Seek no wisdom, leave no word;
Common sense is too absurd.
Ignore advice, you don't need skill;
Blokes like you are hard to kill.
Take no extra food or gear,
You'll not need it, have no fear.
But, we ask of you before you die:
Please choose a place that's not too high!

# NORTH OF LAKE TE ANAU

# Route Burn Valley

### ROUTEBURN TRACK

The Routeburn Track follows up the Route Burn from the Routeburn shelter to Harris Saddle and then traverses above the Hollyford River to The Divide, on the Milford Road. It is usually walked in three days with overnight stops in Routeburn Falls Hut and Lake Mackenzie Hut. There are also DoC Huts at Routeburn Flats and Lake Howden. Other huts on the track are owned by Routeburn Walk Ltd. who guide on the track. The only camping allowed on the track itself is in the campsites at Routeburn Flats, Lake Mackenzie and down the Greenstone River 20 minutes past Lake Howden. However, camping is permitted further than 500 metres from the track although this is physically impossible between Harris Saddle and The Divide.

From the shelter at the Routeburn road end, the track crosses a swing bridge to the north bank of the river and after half an hour begins to climb steadily up the gorge. Above the gorge and after Forge Flat the track crosses back to the true-right, a short distance below the Routeburn Flats. The Routeburn Flats Hut (20 bunks) lies about 20 minutes up the flats which are soon encountered.

The main track branches a few hundred metres short of the Routeburn Flats Hut and climbs steadily to the Routeburn Falls Hut (30 bunks). The Emily Creek bridge is considered the halfway point between the huts and winter parties should note that avalanches sometimes come down the creek as far as the bridge.

The travel from Routeburn Falls Hut to Lake Mackenzie is above the bushline and is exposed to bad weather. Half an hour above the hut the track skirts around Lake Harris. Keep to the track especially around Harris Saddle (1255 metres) to protect the very fragile cushion plants in the vicinity. There is a shelter and toilet on the saddle and camping is not allowed. A worthwhile side trip from the pass is to climb 260 metres up to Conical Hill.

From Harris Saddle the track sidles along the Hollyford face well above the bushline before making a series of zig-zags down to Lake Mackenzie Hut (53 bunks). From Lake Mackenzie the track continues to sidle, passing through "The Orchard", an open grassy area dotted with ribbonwood trees and subject to occasional avalanches in winter, to Lake Howden Hut. From here the track rises briefly to the Key Summit track turn-off and then heads downhill to the carpark and shelter at The Divide.

Routeburn Track—between Harris Saddle and Lake Howden. (D) Deadmans Track, (E) Emily Pass, (F) Fraser Col, (H) Harris Saddle, (M) Mt Momus, (Ma) Lake Mackenzie Hut, (O) Ocean Peak, (R) Route Burn Valley, (S) Mt Somnus. *Photo: V.C. Browne.*

Parties heading for the Lower Hollyford can leave the track half an hour past Harris Saddle and make a steep descent to Deadmans Bluff, a short distance down valley from Hollyford Camp.

In winter the track beyond Lake Howden is prone to avalanche activity and the track around the Hollyford face is often covered with snowdrifts. From autumn onwards the track above Lake Mackenzie is often very icy.

*Times: Routeburn Shelter and Carpark to Routeburn Flats Hut, 2-3 hrs; Routeburn Flats Hut to Routeburn Falls Hut, 1 ¹/₄ hrs; Routeburn Falls Hut to Harris Saddle, 1-2 hrs; Routeburn Falls Hut to Lake Mackenzie Hut, 4-7 hrs; Lake Mackenzie Hut to Howden Hut, 3-4 hrs; Lake Howden Hut to The Divide, 1-1 ¹/₂ hrs; Harris Saddle to Hollyford Road via Deadmans Track, 3 hrs.*

*For the reverse journey from The Divide to the Routeburn Shelter allow a little over an hour to Lake Howden and thereafter similar times to those above, with a little more for the ascent to the Saddle from Lake Mackenzie and less for the descent to the Routeburn Flats.*

## ROUTE BURN NORTH BRANCH

The route to North Col at the head of the Route Burn North Branch is straightforward if rough in places. Cross the main stream in front of Routeburn Flats Hut and follow up the grassy flats on the west bank of the North Branch. There is a two person rock bivvy on the opposite bank of the North Branch, just inside the bush edge and a little over 500 metres from the Routeburn Track. Towards the end of the flats the track veers away from the river and leads up through a small glade in the bush where the route may seem indistinct for a while.

Once in the bush the track is easily followed and climbs steadily before descending to open flats half an hour from the hut. The track skirts swampy tarns and patches of scrub before entering the bush again to sidle above the river. The track finally emerges onto open flats a little below the couloir leading up to Mt Somnus on the other side of the valley. Here a four person rock bivvy known as Hobbs Bivvy may be found some 100 metres uphill of the track, beside a small stream at E40 303021. The stream may be dry in summer.

The track leads from the head of this last flat through the last of the scrub on the true-left bank and from here on there is open going to the head of the valley. There is a good rock bivvy near the foot of North Col. Parties continuing on to North Col, Lake Nerine and the Rock Burn will need alpine experience and ice axes if there is snow in the couloir.

*Times: Routeburn Flats to Hobbs Bivvy, 2 hrs; Hobbs Bivvy to North Col, 2-3 hrs.*

The Route Burn North Branch and Mt Somnus. Routeburn Flats can be seen towards the bottom of the photograph.

## ROUTEBURN FLATS TO LAKE MACKENZIE VIA EMILY PASS

This route is recommended for experienced parties only as it entails steep scree and snowgrass. The route is not marked and is not obvious in poor visibility.

From the Emily Creek bridge, about half an hour above Routeburn Flats, leave the Routeburn Track and climb up through the bush tongue separating the two streams that combine to form Emily Creek. Keep nearer to the eastern stream and then climb directly up to the bushline as the bush steepens. Above the bushline the route ahead can be seen across the snowgrass basin. The obvious pass to the east of the head leads into Fraser Creek and is commonly mistaken for Emily Pass. Further to the right and north of Mt Emily are two rocky guts leading to two depressions on the ridge, the northernmost of which is Emily Pass.

Cross steep snowgrass on the near side of a small waterfall and then climb up the gut to the pass. The descent on the other side is straightforward and to avoid the last scrubby section stay in the streambed. Follow the eastern shore of Lake Mackenzie to Lake Mackenzie Hut.

In the reverse direction, Emily Pass is the northern depression on the ridge. Descend the gut below the pass until snowgrass slopes lead out to the north. Sidle across these until the descent into the basin below is clear. Once in the basin head north-east to cross the creek draining the basin and continue sidling until about halfway to the next gully before entering the scrub. Descend straight down through the scrub and bush until the Routeburn Track is reached.

*Times: Routeburn Track to Emily Pass, 3 hrs; Emily Pass to Lake Mackenzie Hut, 2 hrs; Lake Mackenzie Hut to Emily Pass, 3 hrs; Emily Pass to Routeburn Track, 2 hrs.*

# Greenstone and Caples Valleys

From Lake Howden a return trip can be made down the Greenstone and back up the Caples over a saddle to Lake McKellar. The same return circuit can be made from Lake Wakatipu, commencing from the road end near the mouth of the Greenstone.

The grassy river flats of the Caples and Greenstone Valleys are leasehold farmland. DoC requests that parties stay on the track which follows the bush edge. Giardia is present in the area so drinking water should be boiled or sterilised.

## HOWDEN HUT TO MID GREENSTONE HUT

From Howden Hut the Greenstone Track follows the western sides of Lakes Howden and McKellar to the 20 bunk McKellar Hut at the top of the main Greenstone flats. Cross the bridge opposite the hut to the east bank of the Greenstone. After travelling through easy tussock flats alternating with bush the track passes through the chasm and the Mid Greenstone Hut (12 bunks) will be found on a terrace close to the bush edge about a kilometre below Steele Creek. There is a bridge over Steele Creek.

*Times: Howden Hut to McKellar Hut, 2 hrs; McKellar Hut to Mid Greenstone Hut, 4-6 hrs.*

## MID GREENSTONE HUT TO LAKE WAKATIPU

Continuing down the Greenstone from Mid Greenstone Hut the track climbs up into the bush at the foot of the flats opposite the Sly Burn just before the valley swings leftwards into a deep gorge. Before the track begins to climb, a swing bridge will be seen leading to the Sly Burn Hut (eight bunks) and the start of the Mavora—Greenstone Walkway.

Slip Flat is reached about an hour later, about halfway down the gorge. There is an emergency bridge up stream if the creek across Slip Flat is in flood. A short distance further on the track branches into two separate routes. The right-hand fork is the original track to Elfin Bay. It crosses an emergency bridge to the south bank of the river and then climbs up past Lake Rere and through a small pass descending to Lake Wakatipu at Elfin Bay.

The left-hand fork leads to the Greenstone carpark and follows down through the Greenstone gorge to the Caples Junction. A swing bridge crosses the Caples River just above the junction and the track soon crosses to the true-right bank of the Greenstone down to a narrow gorge where another bridge crosses back to the true-left bank. The carpark is reached a few minutes further down the track.

***Times:*** *Mid Greenstone Hut to Sly Burn Hut, 1-1 ¹/₂ hrs; Sly Burn Hut to Slip Flat, 1-1 ¹/₂ hrs; Slip Flat to Carpark, 2 ¹/₂-3 ¹/₂ hrs.*

## LAKE WAKATIPU TO UPPER CAPLES HUT VIA CAPLES VALLEY

If coming down the Greenstone cross the swing bridge over the Caples mentioned in the previous section and then follow up the track on the true-left of the Caples to cross a bridge to the twelve bunk Mid Caples Hut. If coming from the Greenstone road end, follow the track to the Caples River where a sign post shows the turn-off.

From the Mid Caples Hut there is easy travel through bush and grassy clearings to the Upper Caples Hut (20 bunks) situated in a clearing where the valley begins to narrow.

***Times:*** *Greenstone road end to Mid Caples Hut, 2-2 ¹/₂ hrs; Mid Caples Hut to Upper Caples Hut, 2-2 ¹/₂ hrs.*

## UPPER CAPLES HUT TO MCKELLAR HUT VIA MCKELLAR SADDLE

From the Upper Caples Hut the track climbs steadily and becomes quite steep as it leaves the beech forest for the subalpine zone. Open tussock tops lead to McKellar Saddle. Here the track is often boggy and care should be taken not to damage the fragile vegetation. There are good views from the saddle.

The track enters bush on the south side of the saddle and drops steeply into the Greenstone Valley to emerge up stream of Lake McKellar. The track crosses the open valley to meet the Greenstone Track halfway between Howden Hut and the Routeburn Track to the north and McKellar Hut to the south.

***Times:*** *Upper Caples Hut to McKellar Hut, 5-6 hrs; Upper Caples Hut to Howden Hut, 5-6 hrs.*

## UPPER CAPLES HUT TO MID GREENSTONE HUT VIA STEELE CREEK

Travel up the Greenstone from Mid Greenstone Hut and cross Steele Creek to sidle up the bush edge on the true-right to a terrace. From here continue up a blazed trail beside the creek. About three hours later the creek forks at the top end of a bouldery clearing and a blazed trail follows the east branch to the scrub. Cairns and snow poles mark the route through the scrub to the saddle. During winter and spring there is avalanche danger near the saddle.

From the saddle follow snow poles to traverse steep, scrubby slopes to the north-east then descend steeply to the bush edge. A good track leads steadily down through the bush to emerge behind the Upper Caples Hut.

***Times:*** *Mid Greenstone Hut to saddle, 6 hrs; Saddle to Upper Caples Hut, 2 hrs*

# Upper Hollyford and Cleddau Valleys

The routes described here are in the same order as encountered on the Milford Road driving to Milford Sound. The area around the Homer Tunnel, known as the Homer Region, is in the Darran Mountains and is one of the most important alpine rock and ice climbing areas in New Zealand. Alpinists and rock climbers are referred to *The Darrans Guide* by Murray Judge and Hugh Widdowson.

The routes in this section range from relatively simple excursions of only a few hours, within the ability of any person of moderate fitness, to those which are full day trips, or longer, to be undertaken only by experienced parties. The most important of the easy routes is that to Key Summit, and other trips in this category would be the Marian Valley (described in the Westwards from the Lower Hollyford section), Homer Saddle, Cleddau Walk, and the Gertrude Saddle. This last is more difficult than the others, but is relatively short and strongly recommended to anyone with a little experience. All the other routes described in this chapter are excursions for a full day or more.

## THE DIVIDE TO KEY SUMMIT AND LAKE HOWDEN

No other spot so easily accessible from the Milford Road reveals a view to compare with that seen from Key Summit. This track is recommended as the best side excursion for any moderately fit passer-by with good weather and a little time to spare. The name Key Summit is derived from the fact that it is the origin of the three main Otago, Southland and Fiordland watersheds.

The track to Lake Howden is followed to its highest point, in the open near bush-level, and a good track then zig-zags steeply up to the right. A plastic pyramid will be found indicating points of interest. The view is extensive, the main features being Mt Christina, with Lake Marian nestling in the valley below and other peaks of the Darran Range rising behind. To one familiar with the area, the outline of the Routeburn Track can be picked out at various points. This track is also the starting point of the routes to Lake Wakatipu, via the Greenstone or Routeburn Tracks, as described in the previous chapters.

*Time:* Carpark to Key Summit, 1 ¹/₂ hrs.

## FALLS CREEK

At the head of this creek stand Mts Ngatimamoe and Pyramid. Leave the carpark at the Falls Creek bridge where there is a good track up the leading spur on the eastern bank of Falls Creek. The track is followed steeply upwards for about half an hour from the road and then bears right to meet the river. From here on the going eases, and the open flats towards the head of the valley will be reached in about two hours. The track emerges onto a large swamp where the valley flattens out. Cross the swamp by keeping to the right and breaking through the last band of bush to the stream bed. To avoid the scrub keep in, or beside the stream bed to reach lateral moraine on the true-right. A three person bivvy rock with a one person bivvy rock adjacent can be found on the upper end of the moraine on the side away from the stream, some 100 metres down stream of the first side creek. From here on open flats can be easily negotiated to the head of the valley.

Another bivvy exists at the head of Falls Creek. Climb through the bluffs at the top of the highest fan below the Ngatimamoe and Pyramid col. Cross diagonally to the right on a large grassy bench until a cave, which forms the bivvy, is seen across a boulder-filled gully.

*Times:* Carpark to first rock bivvy, 3-4 hrs; Rock Bivvy to valley head, $^3/_4$ hr.

## MONKEY CREEK

This is an intriguing short valley with a waterfall 20 minutes from the road. There are climbing routes out to the tops from the head of the valley. The bush gorge at the mouth of the valley is passed by a steep trail up the north bank. From the end of the bush the going is straightforward.

## GERTRUDE SADDLE

This saddle offers some magnificent views of Milford Sound and the peaks of the Darran Range, but is a little more difficult to reach than the other short excursions mentioned in the introduction to this chapter. The route commences from the New Zealand Alpine Club's Homer Hut at the Hollyford Forks, $1^1/_2$ kilometres before the Homer Tunnel, and follows a gravel track for a short distance up the east side of the usually dry stream. Depending on the season, water may be running, in which case it is possible to scramble round the true-right bank for some distance until the creek narrows through a steeper section where the track, having crossed to the true-right, is joined. Often the remains of an old wooden bridge, not far from the hut, can be used to cross the stream if the stream level is not too high.

A cairn where the streambed narrows through the bush indicates the blazed trail up the true-right bank. Once beyond the bush, a well defined track leads

Black Lake—descending from Black Lake in wet weather.
*Photo: Hugh van Noorden.*

up through scrub-covered moraine to the open tussock and beyond where cairns on the true-right mark the route to the head of the valley floor.

In the north-west corner of the valley the stream can be seen as it falls down a steep course. A well defined track leads steeply up the true-right of this cataract then crosses to the true-left some distance up, between two waterfalls. There is a seldom used, slightly longer route of more gentle gradient up the true-left side. Continuing up the scree on the true-left, the upper stream will be seen cascading over bare rock slabs. Carry on up the slabs, climbing up the short steep section just before Black Lake with the help of the wire rope there. In winter and late spring these slabs are usually covered by snow, or ice and may be impassable without ice axes. Another wire rope will be found leading up the smooth rock slabs from the lake outlet on the west side of the lake which in turn leads to the snow, or broken rocks later in the season, at the head of Black Lake. The route to Gertrude Saddle is obvious from here. Avalanches often cross the route from before Black Lake to the saddle in winter and it would be prudent to avoid this excursion if avalanche warnings are posted.

**Time:** *Homer Hut to Gertrude Saddle, 2 hrs.*

43

## GERTRUDE SADDLE TO LAKE ADELAIDE VIA GIFFORD CRACK

A route continues up from Gertrude Saddle to Lake Adelaide and Phils Bivvy via Gifford Crack. This is a serious undertaking and requires alpine experience. Climb the Barrier Knob ridge from the saddle for 200 metres to a large ledge on the left. Follow the ledge left to a short rock step onto a scree slope. Step down and cross some wet slabs, taking care in snow, or icy conditions, and climb up a short gut to the skyline ridge. From here the track descends slightly to the ridge above Adelaide Saddle through a rocky col on the ridge.

A less exciting if more tiring route carries on up the ridge to traverse Barrier Knob. Ice axes will be found necessary. From the top of Barrier Knob descend to Adelaide Saddle by keeping well to the left of the main broken rocky ridge, often looking down onto the alternative route described above. Veering too far to the right will lead parties to become bluffed on the faces above Lake Adelaide. Occasional cairns mark the route down to the saddle.

From the lowest point on Adelaide Saddle, descend steep snowgrass until the lowest tussock ledge leading across to the right is reached. This is just above the rocky bluffs at the head of Lake South America. Traverse across this ledge which leads to an exposed, slabby rock section which may require a rope. Pick a way across this section, which includes a small gut, and descend rock steps that eventually lead to the steep gut that forms Gifford Crack. Descend inside this gut to the scree beneath. The rock on the true-right can also be descended— it is less steep, but more exposed. Follow easily down the scree below the gut and around the true-left of Lake South America to its outlet.

When approaching this route from the reverse direction the gut initially heads left after leaving the scree, before angling up to Adelaide Saddle. Do not leave the left angling gut until the main gut up to the saddle is obvious.

From the outlet of Lake South America turn right and sidle around to the grassy slopes below Mt Sabre to Phils Bivvy which is by far the largest boulder in the vicinity and will sleep over 20 people in complete comfort.

Alternatively, a level traverse from the outlet of Lake South America leads through a number of heavily scrubbed gullies to Gills Bivvy. The large cairn on top of the bivvy may be difficult to distinguish from the surroundings. A more pleasant, but longer route is to continue from the outlet of Lake South America, veering right and climbing an easy snow grass ridge to directly below some rock bluffs. Veer left towards Phils Bivvy continuing below these rock bluffs until the bluffs above the left side of Lake Adelaide are aligned with its outlet. From here descend directly down a tussock spur where Gills Bivvy will be found some 250 metres below on this spur. Gills Bivvy sleeps ten people.

Gertrude Saddle. A View from Students Peak. (B) Barrier peak (G) Gertrude Saddle, (T) Mt Talbot.
*Photo: Ron Webster.*

The route from the head of Lake Adelaide to the Hollyford River via Moraine Creek is described in the Westwards from the Lower Hollyford Section.

**Time:** *Allow a day for the crossing.*

## HOMER SADDLE

The Homer Saddle can be reached by a short scramble from the road and is a worthwhile climb although the view it offers is not as extensive as that obtained from the Gertrude Saddle. The easiest route does not, as one might expect, lie up the scree sidling from the tunnel mouth. Follow the stream from the eastern tunnel portal towards Mt Macpherson to reach a huge flat rock lying beside the stream bed. From here zig-zag straight up to the saddle. The final 100 metres to the pass may seem a little exposed for inexperienced parties, but the climb is straightforward. A warning is given against inexperienced persons continuing beyond the saddle. The route down into the head of the Cleddau is an extremely difficult and unsatisfying climb even for mountaineers. The climb up the ridge to Mt Macpherson and the Grave-Talbot Pass is likewise very steep and exposed and the ridge in the other direction towards Mt Moir soon involves a very exposed traverse.

**Time:** *Homer Tunnel to Homer Saddle, 1 hr.*

## GRAVE-TALBOT PASS

The Grave-Talbot Pass route over to the Esperance River fell into disuse when the Homer Tunnel and Milford Road opened and it has not been maintained since then. It was never regarded as an easy route, and as the wire ropes on the Esperance side have been wiped away by avalanches it is now a very serious proposition.

The route up the exposed ridge from Homer Saddle, known as Talbots Ladder, is marked by the old wire ropes, which are now unsafe and should not be trusted. In about 30 minutes the top of Talbots Ladder will be reached and round to the left from here, after crossing patches of snow and big boulders, a large snowfield will be seen ahead. Beyond this is a rock ridge with a pronounced 'V' in it. This is known as Lyttle's Dip which leads to the Grave-Talbot Pass. Alternatively, those who are suitably equipped and experienced may prefer to continue up the ridge from Talbots Ladder and bear to the right on to the snowfield leading up to the top of Mt Macpherson, a relatively easy climb which offers spectacular views.

At Lyttle's dip there is a hole in the ridge just big enough for a person to pass through. On the other side, instead of descending the loose rock gully it is much better to use the natural stairway which gently drops away to the right

46

and starts about three metres down from the hole. A level sidle across the next snowfield arrives at the Grave-Talbot Pass, which is the only obvious dip in the ridge in the vicinity. A few old sardine tins can still be found on the pass. Note that the maps D40 and S122 incorrectly place the pass a kilometre further down the ridge, past two extremely difficult rock gendarmes. The pass is actually at D40 119947.

From the pass descend steep, exposed snowgrass slopes, veering to the right until below rock overhangs. A band of lighter rock is now followed to the left. At this point the traditional route slowly climbs to the west on narrow ledges almost back up to the ridge, with the aid of wire ropes. Recent parties have found neither the ropes, or this ledge and have carried on down, probably using Grave and Talbot's original route. Two, or three abseils on this latter route, after dropping to the west and down as far as is practical, arrive at a wide grassy ledge. This ledge is easily followed down valley, keeping to the same height until the gouged slopes of a large stream is reached. This is followed down to some extensive rock slabs and then in turn the De Lambert Falls. These rock slabs are littered with small stones and require concentration to avoid slipping on them. The rest of the route into the Esperance is given below.

**Time:** *Homer Tunnel to Gulliver road bridge, allow a long day.*

Grave-Talbot Pass. Crossing the Grave-Talbot pass is a very serious undertaking and calls for a good head for heights. The incorrectly labelled pass on the maps can be seen further down the ridge past the gendarme.

## MILFORD ROAD TO MCPHERSON HUT SITE VIA GULLIVER AND ESPERANCE RIVERS

Few people realise the magnificent scenery which lies within a short distance from the Gulliver-Cleddau junction. The well marked pack-horse track starts from the Gulliver River bridge and continues up the true-left to the junction of the Esperance River. From here the foot track climbs for a short distance fairly steeply up the true-left of the Esperance before easing to a gradual climb. The track has been recently recut and is well marked to the upper Esperance end of the track apart from a short section in the middle which is easily traversed.

The track crosses a mostly dry tributary of the Esperance which comes in from the true-left of the valley right under the cliff face at bush line. Having crossed the tributary climb up a natural sloping rock shelf heading to the main river which is reached about 20 to 30 metres above a small waterfall in the main river. Follow the river bed up for about a kilometre to the De Lambert Falls. The old McPherson Hut site is on the true-right bank of the Esperance about 100 metres from the falls.

*Times: Road to Hut Site, 4 hrs.*

## MCPHERSON HUT SITE TO GRAVE-TALBOT PASS

From the cleared site of the old McPherson Hut will be seen, to the right of the De Lambert Falls, the ridge on the south side of the valley culminating in the round-topped Mt Macpherson. About the middle of the ridge stands a great crag of rock or gendarme and halfway between this and Macpherson is a fairly deep nick in the ridge, which is the Grave-Talbot Pass. The top of the falls is reached by climbing up a zig-zag track through the bush on the left-hand side of them. The bed of the main creek soon becomes very steep as it rises up behind the falls to its source, which lies between Macpherson to the south and a long western spur of Talbot to the north.

Above the falls a small creek comes in from the right, and this swings back towards the lowest nick in the ridge. The route follows up this creek bed, but at the top goes up a steep gut leading to a slightly higher nick about halfway between the gendarme and the lowest nick. Those who do not attempt the pass will find it well worth while to climb up as far as the top of the ridge for the views obtainable from the top.

About 15 metres below the ridge lies a small tarn, often dried up, and from here the traditional route to the pass follows quite some distance along a ledge to the left, descending slightly, and then climbs about 250 metres to the pass which will be seen directly above, about one hour from the tarn. From the pass a level traverse of the first snowfield brings one to Lyttle's Dip, thence connecting with a second snowfield and the route from the top of Talbots Ladder described above.

## CLEDDAU TRACK

The old foot track down the Cleddau River leaves the side of the road about 80 metres above the Gulliver bridge and crosses the Cleddau by an old swing bridge above the junction. The true-left bank is followed down river for half an hour to the old Public Works Department campsite. The track from here to Milford Sound is very overgrown and difficult to follow. Opposite the Milford Lodge the river is forded back to the true-right bank. This crossing should not be attempted unless the Cleddau is running low.

**Time:** *Cleddau footbridge to Milford Sound, 6 hrs.*

## CLEDDAU, WEST BRANCH

The main Cleddau is crossed at The Chasm and the west branch, which enters a short distance up stream, provides easy going into the cirque where it forks west and north. The head of the west branch is best reached by boulder-hopping up the streambed and climbers will find a route to Mt Ada and other peaks at the top.

## DONNE VALLEY

This valley provides an access route for mountaineers into the central peaks of the Darran Range. From the Donne bridge, on the main road, the track commences about 50 metres up stream on the true-right bank and climbs over a series of bluffs, interspersed with short level sections beside the river, before finally dropping down a very steep bank into a large, dry creekbed. This is followed up and connects with other streambeds which are followed all the way up to the head of the valley.

**Time:** *Road to valley head, at least 6 hrs.*

## TUTOKO VALLEY UP TO LEADER CREEK

At the head of the Tutoko Valley, which enters the Cleddau from the north-east near Milford, is scenery rivalling that of the Upper Hollyford. Indeed, there is nothing in the latter to compare with the grandeur of the Herbert Ice Falls, breaking off the south face of Mt Tutoko into the Age Glacier.

A well-formed track leads from the road to the first open clearings in about two hours. When first coming out into a clearing do not follow the river but skirt the bush edge on the left until a creek is reached which is crossed three

Mt Tutoko. Rising to 2723 metres above sea level, Mt Tutoko is the highest peak in Fiordland. The Age Glacier can be seen spilling into Leader Creek.

times while bearing left until the open clearings are reached. After emerging out on to the open riverbed follow up a series of dry channels to the west of the main river through open flats until opposite Leader Creek entering from the east.

## LEADER CREEK TO TURNERS BIVVY

The best way into Leader Creek is to continue up the Tutoko River past the Leader Creek junction until opposite the second dry creekbed above it. Ford the river here, opposite a cairn of red-painted stones, and follow up this streambed which is known as Limerick Creek[1]. Near the top of this will be found Daves Cave, a cramped but dry bivvy rock, and a few minutes later the Leader Falls are reached. Ford Leader Creek here. From here then head up stream to cross a small stream on the south bank. Here blazes will be found leading steeply up through the bush to more level terrain, where old campsites will be found. The Age Glacier is not far above the campsites.

Two side creeks are crossed and just above the second, nearly opposite the end of the glacier, where there are good campsites among scattered beech trees, a scrubby trail will be found leading up the steep slopes, initially crossing several exposed rock slabs. To get on to this trail a small and often wet cliff must be surmounted. The route takes the only obvious way and is marked with cairns above this bluff. The route veers up to the left, facing the hillside, rather than to the right. The going is steep and quite exposed, but there is plenty of long snowgrass to hang onto.

Some considerable distance higher up, the snowgrass slopes give way to a rock-strewn platform and a deceptively wide tussock ledge which extends about 100 metres out to the right will be found. Turners Bivvy Rock lies around on this ledge opposite the main ridge at D40 152089. (See photograph). There are two other less substantial bivvy rocks lower down the ridge at D40 149094 and D40 150092. A short distance up from the bivvy are rock slabs and a great snow basin which extends up to Mt Madeline.

*Time:* Allow a full day to reach Turners Bivvy from the road.

## LEADER CREEK TO PAWNBROKER BIVVY AND GRAVE COULOIR

Continuing up the main Tutoko Valley on the true-right past Leader Creek, a lightly-blazed trail leads across two bluffs. If possible, cross the river after the second bluff and follow the dry creekbed over to the east side of the valley. This

---

1. Note that Limerick Creek is incorrectly labelled as Leader Creek on map D40. Limerick Creek actually joins the Tutoko River at D40 128073 and Leader Falls are at D40 135087. This map also has some anomalies in the permanent snow shown.

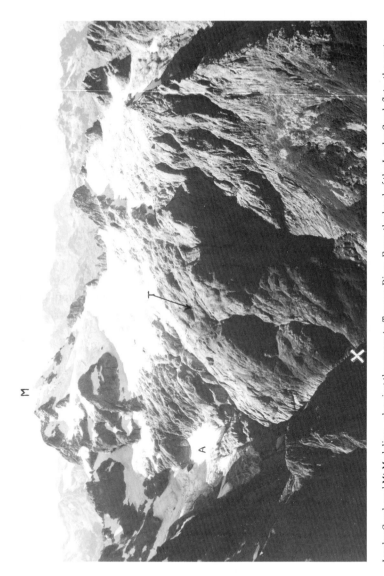

Leader Creek and Mt Madeline—showing the access to Turners Bivvy. From the head of the Leader Creek flats, the route climbs steeply from (X) up the steep bluffs then leftwards round and up the sun-lit slopes, veering back to the right near the top. (A) Age Glacier, (M) Mt Madeline, (T) Turners Bivvy.
*Photo: D.L. Homer, Institute of Geological & Nuclear Sciences.*

provides an open approach to Pawnbroker Bivvy Rock, named for three flax bushes which once grew on it. The bivvy lies on the true-right bank about 100 metres short of the long steep Grave Couloir.

*Time: Leader Creek to Pawnbroker Bivvy, about 3 hrs.*

## NGAPUNATORU PASS VIA GRAVE COULOIR

This is a route to be tackled only by parties with considerable mountaineering experience. From Pawnbroker Bivvy continue up the moraine rubble at the foot of the spectacular Grave Couloir until the base of the clean snow, which leads all the way to the top, is reached. During most seasons with an average snow fall, especially early on in the season, an uninterrupted direct ascent of the couloir is possible. Occasionally crevasses may need to be negotiated and an ice bulge about two-thirds of the way up is passed on its south-west side. If the approaches are cut off, or if crevasses extend the full width of the couloir reasonable rock and scree climbing on the south-west side will permit passage.

From Tutoko Pass, at the head of the couloir, sidle around under Paranui only 30 metres or so below the level of the pass. Then follow around just below the level of the schrund until a prominent rock ledge is reached. Descend this ledge and scramble down a few steps in the ledge. Cross a small snow face and then make a quick dash across the avalanche chute at the base of the Ngapunatoru icefall. From here angle up towards a prominent rock ledge. This ledge has been used by a few parties as a high-level camp although it is unfortunately exposed to the north-west. From here a snow-plod of about 400 metres leads up to Ngapunatoru Pass at about 1970 metres altitude. There are good snow cave sites on the plateau.

For a description of access to Ngapunatoru Pass from the Harrison Valley refer to the Martins Bay to Milford Sound section.

*Time: A fit and experienced party, properly equipped with rope, crampons, ice axe, packs, etc., should be able to reach the plateau from Pawnbrokers Rock in a single day.*

# Westwards from the Lower Hollyford

Between the Marian road junction and the head of Lake McKerrow several routes lead into the Darran Mountains, stemming from the Lower Hollyford road and track already described. These are described in sequence from south to north.

## MARIAN VALLEY

This valley provides an interesting trip from the Hollyford Road and a well formed track will be found all the way to Lake Marian. After crossing the swing bridge a few hundred metres below the Marian road junction, the track leads straight into the Marian Valley on a board walk which leads to some scenic waterfalls. From here the track steepens and climbs steadily until about 150 metres below lake level where a wide boulder-strewn gully is encountered. This is crossed at an up-hill angle, and care should be taken to locate cairns and markers about 40 metres up on the other side. The track is now more level and passes through bush, and groves of fern and ribbonwood at first, and later alpine scrub. The path then drops down to the left-hand corner of the lake. The lake has a subterranean outlet.

Lake Marian. The Marian face of Mt Crosscut is to the middle and left of the photo while the exacting south face of Mt Sabre can be seen in the distance to the right.

With its precipitous northern sides and bush-clad eastern margin the lake has a striking situation, enhanced by the icefields hanging above on the towering slopes of Christina and Crosscut. Beyond the lake there is little bush, and the valley bends round to the west, where the Lyttle Falls will be found. Above these falls lie Lakes Mariana and Marianette, which can be reached by a climb round the lower slopes of Mt Crosscut, but it is a route for experienced parties only. The spire-shaped peak at the head of the valley is Mt Sabre.

*Time: Carpark to Lake Marian, 1 ¹/₂ hrs.*

## HOLLYFORD CAMP TO MT LYTTLE

Opposite Murray Gunn's Hollyford Camp a rough, lightly marked trail leads up through the bush on to the open grass slopes of Mt Lyttle. Ford the Hollyford to pick up the track which starts opposite Cabin 4. The route commences up stream, climbing steadily up through bluffs for 20 minutes to a flat ridge which is followed for 30 minutes. The markers are infrequent but worth looking for. Just past the foot of the main spur to Mt Lyttle the remains of the old track will be found climbing steeply, at first on the true-right of a scoured-out gut, for an hour to a viewpoint on a swampy knob where the rest of the route can be seen ahead. The track carries on straight up the ridge and reaches the bushline beside a very large rock, which serves as useful marker of the re-entry point. The route from here on is obvious. A tussock ledge can be followed along the edge of the bluffs to the snow basin between Mts Lyttle and Gunn, traversing behind a small waterfall at one point.

On the return, false blazes are a problem. Generally choose the blazes leading left until about halfway down, but thereafter avoid the temptation to try to descend the cliffs on the left too soon. Stay high until the main valley floor is seen straight below, then turn left and watch for the track leading down to the base of the spur. This is vital, as the cliffs on either side here are vertical.

*Time: Hollyford Camp to Mt Lyttle, 4-6 hrs.*

## HOLLYFORD TO PHILS BIVVY VIA MORAINE CREEK AND LAKE ADELAIDE

Moraine Creek, which drains Lake Adelaide, is the largest tributary of the Hollyford apart from the Pyke River. It provides climbing access into the central Darran Mountains. In recent years the alpine route from Homer Hut via Gifford Crack has become more popular with climbers than the Moraine Creek track.

The Hollyford is crossed by the swing-bridge at the top of the gorge above the Humboldt Creek junction. The track, which was re-cut in 1993, leads away from the Hollyford across to Moraine Creek in 20 minutes where a walk wire

Moraine Creek—from above Humbolt Falls. Lake Adelaide is out of sight at the head of the valley to the left of Mt Gifford. (G) Mt Gifford. (H) Hut site.
*Photo: B. Campbell.*

gives access to the north bank if the stream is too high to ford. The route up the north bank climbs steadily through heavy bush, crossing two rock gullies. The second of these, two hours from the Hollyford is in the open and offers a good view of Humboldt Falls on the far side of the Hollyford. Rock cairns mark the entrance of the track on the far side, and after another steep pitch the track runs out into a small basin almost hard against the cliffs on the north side of the valley. A few cairns and metal discs lead up to the head of the basin.

From the top of the basin continue up, veering well left through a tangle of fuchsia and ribbonwood with boulders underfoot until more bush is reached. After sidling a small tarn, the track follows deer trails through thinning bush out on to a wide swampy flat. Cross the flats, passing through a gap in the bush to Moraine Creek, which is followed up until a large creekbed comes in on the true-left from the hanging Korako Glacier. Just beyond this, go up a smaller and half-concealed stream which leads on through scrub and boulders to a snowgrass hillock on its true-right bank. From the top of this hillock, pass through a small dip with trees on either side to grassy slopes which lead up to the foundation remains of the old Moraine Creek Hut, destroyed by avalanche in 1983.

The western side of Lake Adelaide provides the better route to the head of the valley and access to Adelaide Saddle. Commence by following up tussock slopes above the hut site, with the bush covered moraine on the left, until almost against the mountain wall. From here drop down past a small tarn and follow round a trough between the moraine and the mountains. The moraine is more extensive than is first appreciated and very slow to travel through so shortcuts are not recommended. As the lake is approached below The Sentinel, ledges can be picked out at the bottom of the seemingly blank bluffs, very close to the lake edge. They provide easy travel to the outlet of Lake South America.

Cross the outlet of Lake South America to Gills Bivvy or carry on to the tussock slopes below Mt Sabre where half way up from Lake Adelaide Phils Bivvy will be found. Phils Bivvy will sleep 20 people comfortably and is the largest rock by far in the vicinity. Gifford Crack is at the head of the valley from Lake South America. See the Gertrude Saddle to Lake Adelaide via Gifford Crack section for a full description.

The eastern side of the lake provides a shorter route if a trip to the head of the valley and not Adelaide Saddle is intended. The stream behind the hut site leads down to Moraine Creek, which can be crossed below the junction, and deer trails up stream lead off to the west bank of a small creek running down hard against the sheer cliffs of Mt Gifford. This stream is followed up as far as practicable and steep deer trails are then ascended up the bush ridge which contains the stream on its true-left. Once clear of the bush these trails continue up a snowgrass face on to the broad slopes above the lake, about 1½ hours from the hut site. Lake Adelaide has a subterranean outlet through a large amount of bush covered moraine. This moraine should be avoided as it is very slow and unpleasant to cross.

A short excursion of 1½ hours up the small side valley to the right above the hut site leads to the col between Mts Apirana and Revelation. From here a magnificent view of the south faces of Mts Underwood and Patuki is obtained, with the Taoka Icefall breaking off into the Donne Valley far below. The climbing route round to the Korako Glacier commences on the other side of this small valley, directly opposite the col.

When returning to the Hollyford, remember to continue to the end of the swampy flat well to the left of the river before entering the bush.

*Times:* *Hollyford Road to Moraine Creek Hut site, 5 hrs; Moraine Creek Hut site to Phils Bivvy, 4 hrs.*

## CLEFT CREEK

The Hollyford River is a major obstacle for access into this valley. When low there are possible fords above the Hidden Falls junction or ten minutes above the Cleft Creek junction, but these cannot be relied upon owing to the changing nature of the river. Continue down the west bank from the bridge below Moraine Creek fording Chasm Creek on the way. A better course, particularly for parties heading for the valleys further down stream, is to engage the services of a jet-boat.

The route lies up the north bank all the way, close beside the river for the first 30 minutes to the gorge, then climbing up the side of the gorge within ear-shot of the river most of the time. About halfway up the gorge the sparse deer trails pass a high but shallow rock bivvy, but a better bivvy will be found nearby on the far side of an adjacent rock. Above this a steep spur is crossed, straight up and down again, and easy going then leads on through the bush to the lower flats. The top flats will be reached after skirting more bush on the same bank, and an excellent bivvy rock will be found 150 metres off the top flats beside the streambed leading from the ravine south of Mt Milne.

*Time:* *Hollyford Road to top flats, 6 hrs.*

## GLACIER CREEK

See the comments concerning Cleft Creek regarding the initial approach and crossing the Hollyford. Prior to 1950 Glacier Creek provided the standard approach to climb Mt Tutoko. However, the route is for experienced parties only. A spur is climbed and crossed over into a high basin from the top of which one can traverse back down onto the Donne Glacier. The glacier has receded a lot in recent years making the route much more difficult than it was formerly.

## STICK-UP CREEK

This is subject to the same difficulty in crossing the Hollyford as Cleft Creek. Stick-up Creek can likewise be approached down the left bank from Hidden Falls, but access also is by boat from the head of Lake McKerrow. Follow up the south bank all the way up the valley. This valley gives access to the north-west ridge of Mt Tutoko, although the Glacier Creek approach is the better, and also to Ngapunatoru Pass, a high alpine route leading into the head of the Harrison Valley.

*Time: Lake McKerrow to valley head, allow 2 days.*

## O'LEARY PASS TO KAIPO VALLEY

A boat is necessary to cross the head of Lake McKerrow to the mouth of the stream draining from O'Leary Pass, to the west. A ridge to the north of this stream provides reasonable going until, at about 600 metres, a steep bluff is reached. This is surmounted by following up a dry watercourse and after further steep going through tangled undergrowth a level terrace is reached a little below what appears to be the pass. This is actually only the mouth of a hanging valley containing quite a large lake, beyond which a low col provides the true pass over to the Kaipo, almost due east from the Kaipo Slip described in the Martins Bay to Milford Sound section.

# Hollyford Track

The Hollyford Track is the only major Fiordland track that can be walked safely in any season although some sections of the track, especially those on the Demon Trail, can become impassable after heavy rain. The 56 kilometre track, linking the Hollyford Road end to Martins Bay is usually walked over four days. There is access to good hunting and fishing from the track.

Accommodation and supplies may be obtained from Murray Gunn's Hollyford Camp, a worthwhile destination in itself. Guided tours are also conducted in the valley and use private lodges at Lower Pyke and Martins Bay. Jet boats from Lake Alabaster to Martins Bay, and fixed wing aircraft from the Hollyford Strip and Milford Sound to Martins Bay can be chartered. Jet boats can normally navigate from Martins Bay up the Hollyford River as far as the boat landing near Little Homer Saddle, and up the Pyke River to the Olivine Hut.

The track commences at the end of the road, where a footbridge crosses Humboldt Creek, eight kilometres down valley from Hollyford Camp. This point can also be reached on foot from the Routeburn and Greenstone Tracks described previously descending by Deadmans Track from Harris Saddle or by the Pass Burn track from Lake Howden. If travelling the other way, from the Hollyford, Deadmans Track is sign-posted at the lower end of Deadmans Bluff, two kilometres below Hollyford Camp. The Pass Burn track is also sign-posted, 400 metres up the road from Pass Burn, and climbs to Lake Howden. The normal route to Howden is the track from The Divide.

## ROAD END TO ALABASTER HUT

The all-weather track to Hidden Falls is well formed and avoids the flood-prone areas by means of walk-ways round the rock bluffs on the east side of the valley. The 20 bunk Hidden Falls Hut lies five minutes past the swing bridge over Hidden Falls Creek. A four bunk unit adjacent to the main hut can be booked through DoC, Te Anau. The falls themselves can be viewed two minutes up stream from the bridge, following up the south bank. From the hut the track climbs over Little Homer Saddle (143 metres) where there is a view through the forest to Mt Tutoko, and then descends to Homer Creek, a small stream with a misty waterfall over 60 metres high. The Hollyford is met again near the junction of Rainbow Creek, where the jet boat picks up guided parties. The track itself follows the river for some distance and then cuts away to a clearing on the Lower Pyke. Pass the private huts here and the 12 bunk Alabaster Hut is reached 20 minutes further on from the confluence of the Hollyford and Pyke Rivers at the foot of Lake Alabaster. Do not cross the swing bridge by mistake.

Mt Madeline—viewed from the Hollyford Track below Lake Alabaster.

## ALABASTER HUT TO HOKURI HUT

Backtrack to the Lower Pyke swing bridge, which was passed on the inward journey a few minutes north of the Pyke clearing. After crossing this bridge the track follows down the Pyke and then leads off through mixed forest to meet the Hollyford, now a much broader river than it was when seen above the Pyke junction. Shortly before Lake McKerrow, 2$^1$/$_2$ hours from Alabaster, the main river swings away to the west side of the valley, but a smaller channel, usually dry, cuts through to the lake on the eastern side. Parties may cross this channel to reach the 12 bunk McKerrow Island Hut on the island near the mouth of the main river, but if the river is flooded, or if rain is threatening it is better to continue down the east bank to the 12 bunk Demon Trail Hut, 1$^1$/$_2$ hours further on. From here there is an impressive view up Stick-up Creek to Mt Tutoko.

The track round the eastern side of Lake McKerrow is aptly named the Demon Trail, although a lot of work has improved it over the years. It is now well defined and climbs up and down over numerous ridges in bush all the way to the Hokuri River. All the streams entering the lake are crossed on three-wire bridges and there are two difficult to locate rock bivvies approximately halfway along the track which provide shelter in an emergency. The 12 bunk Hokuri Hut is near the lake at Gravel Cove.

The Hollyford below the Pyke confluence.

## HOKURI HUT TO MARTINS BAY

In normal conditions the Hokuri can be forded near the mouth, ten minutes from the hut, but if in flood there is a walk wire 15 minutes up stream. From Hokuri onwards is easy going along the lake shore. The site of the surveyed township of Jamestown is reached in half an hour and 45 minutes further on, just before the end of the lake, a sign indicates where the track heads inland. The Hollyford Walk Limited's airstrip in an open clearing is reached in an hour and private huts will be seen westwards on Daveys Clearing beside the river. Continue straight across the clearing and through tall tutu and scrub to Jerusalem Creek. More huts on the riverbank close to the point where the track meets the Hollyford estuary are also privately owned.

To reach the Martins Bay Hut (24 bunk) at Long Reef continue along the coast to the northern end of the bay opposite the mouth of the river. An obvious break occurs in the sandhills and the track passes through this to the hut site where it is possible to camp. There is a seal colony on the reef, 25 minutes further on.

*Times:* *Hollyford Road to Routeburn Track via Deadmans Track, 4 hrs; Hollyford Road to Lake Howden via Pass Burn Track, 2 hrs; Hollyford Road-end to Hidden Falls Hut, 2-3 hrs; Hidden Falls Hut to Lake Alabaster Hut, 3-4 hrs; Lake Alabaster Hut to Demon Trail Hut, 4-5 hrs; Demon Trail Hut to Hokuri Hut via Demon Trail, 5-6 hrs; Hokuri Hut to Martins Bay, 4-5 hrs.*

# Martins Bay to Lake Alabaster via Pyke River

The Martins Bay–Big Bay–Pyke River–Lake Alabaster route can be combined with the Hollyford Track to create a round trip of about ten days. The routes are not well defined in places and the travel is much harder than the Hollyford Track. Parties need to be self-sufficient with tents and cooking equipment. Sections of the track flood regularly, making travel impossible for days at a time. There are several unbridged rivers to cross. Route times are highly variable, depending on party experience and fitness, and weather conditions.

From the end of the track at Long Reef, Martins Bay, follow the coast around to Big Bay passing behind the headland of Penguin Rock then onwards to McKenzie Creek at the southern end of the beach. Follow the beach to Big Bay Hut (nine bunks) which is found behind the sandhills before reaching the Awarua River. There is a sign on top of the sandhills pointing to the hut situated behind two locked private huts in the scrub.

The Awarua can be forded at low tide near the river mouth or the swing bridge five minutes up stream from the hut can be used. On the north bank near the river mouth a bulldozed road leads away from the river before swinging eastwards, gaining height up the Awarua Valley. The bulldozed road ends at the Upper Awarua, which is usually dry. Cross the river bed to find the track heading eastwards towards Paulin Creek. Having reached the normally dry Paulin Creek, follow it down stream to the Pyke River.

Big red marker poles mark either side of the ford across the Pyke. Cross here to the east bank which is then followed down past an airstrip and a small shed. After rain this ford can be impassable. At the start of the track around Lake Wilmot is a dry rock bivvy and there is a good campsite at Larnachs Creek. From here the track continues around Lake Wilmot, where travel is difficult if the lake level is high, to the south-east corner where it goes directly through the bush to the Barrier River and not around the bottom of the lake as shown on S105. The Barrier River is crossed where it forms two branches and from the south branch follow the red and orange marker poles down stream along the track through the bush to the old cattle yards in a grassy flat.

The track diagonally crosses the flats through a series of scrubby glades until the slow moving and deep Diorite River is reached 200 metres above the Pyke. Cross the Diorite and follow the old cattle track, at times along the edge of the Pyke and at times inland to the Olivine River. Where the track is close to the river it is washed away in places. Under normal conditions the Olivine River can be crossed about 400 metres up stream from the Pyke or the flying fox can be used. Once on the other bank, head down stream to the six bunk Olivine Hut. Note that after rain both the Barrier and Diorite Rivers can be impassable.

From the Olivine Hut the cattle track follows the river until a grassy flat is reached. Two solitary cabbage trees stand here festooned with markers. From the cabbage trees follow across the flat into a corridor of bush which cuts across a large loop in the river and then emerges onto the riverbank again where the cattle track ends.

The track now heads through Black Swamp which is a wet and muddy flax strewn area. Head through the swamp towards the hill until a shingle creek bed is reached. This is followed up for 150 metres and then carry on along the base of the hill to reach grassy clearings. Markers continue from here across the clearings to Lake Alabaster. Cross the deep, slow moving Alabaster Creek on the gravel and sand bar at the mouth of the creek to continue along the track to Alabaster Hut (12 bunks). When the lake level is high the Alabaster Creek bar is deep and impassable.

**Times:** *Long Reef to Big Bay Hut, 5 hrs; Big Bay Hut to Pyke Crossing, 3-4 hrs; Pyke Crossing to Olivine Hut, 8-9 hrs; Olivine Hut to Alabaster Hut, 8 hrs. (These times are highly variable).*

# Martins Bay to Milford Sound

The Martins Bay–Kaipo River–Milford Sound traverse provides a good introduction to the more demanding off-track travel in Fiordland. The going is on the whole good and the scenery is spectacular, especially at the head of the Harrison. The trip is sufficiently challenging and remote that beyond the top Kaipo flats it is not suitable for parties without a few seasons' off-track experience.

## MARTINS BAY TO UPPER KAIPO FLATS

The Hollyford is crossed by boat from the huts near the air-strip to a small tidal channel opposite. From here follow the line of the sandhills, or beach to a group of macrocarpa and bluegum trees which mark the site of the old McKenzie homestead passing the McKenzie lagoon on the way.

Southwards, the track crosses the sandhills and the usually dry Jericho, or as it was called by the Maori, Waipawa Creek. It then follows around the coast past the boat landing, mostly on sandy beach until in 1½ hours it reaches the point at the northern end of the Kaipo Bay. This route can be traversed at any tide. The route then turns inland over the sandhills and up the river flat, the river itself turning sharply to enter the sea past the sandhills at the far south end of the bay. There is a well hidden hunter's hut and good campsites on the true-right at the entrance to the valley.

Entering the bush near the river, the track follows up stream for 100 metres, then climbs round the top of a shingle cliff passing a long bend in the river. Continuing up the east bank, the track climbs through mossy beech forest around the gorge. In an hour from the sea-beach the track leads down to the river opposite tussocky flats. Cross the river, with difficulty if it is above normal, and follow up flats and open glades in the bush. The old four bunk Mid Kaipo Hut will be reached in half an hour from the ford, under a clump of beech trees about 100 metres from the river. If the river is too high to cross at the ford carry on up the true-right until a good ford is reached, up stream of an island and just before the top of the mid flats. Keep close to the river in this case to avoid the swamp.

To reach the next hut, known as Upper Kaipo Hut, beside the air-strip on the upper flats, continue up the west bank for half an hour then cross to the east bank to avoid bluffs. After crossing and re-crossing several times the Kaipo Slip is reached in about two hours and the air-strip lies about 20 minutes further on.

***Times:*** *Hollyford to McKenzie homestead, 1 hr; Homestead to Kaipo Bay, 1 ¹/₂ hrs; Kaipo Bay to Mid Kaipo Hut, 1 ¹/₂ hrs; Mid Kaipo Hut to air-strip and Upper Kaipo Hut, 2 ¹/₂ hrs.*

## UPPER KAIPO TO HARRISON SADDLE VIA JOHN O'GROATS

Parties continuing to Milford Sound must now climb to the John O'Groats Saddle. There used to be a lightly-marked track which ascended the Kaipo Slip and then traversed the ridges southwards to the saddle, but this can no longer be followed. The route described below is shorter and more direct.

From Upper Kaipo Hut, follow a good track down towards the main river then along a blazed track on the true-left of the west (Galilee) branch for about ten minutes until a normally dry creek bed is encountered, entering from the south with its source just north of Ongaruanuku.

Follow along deer trails up the true-left of this creek and soon the water bearing channel will be reached. About a quarter of an hour later the river forms into a gorge and the river side steepens up abruptly. Climb away from the river on deer trails until a terrace some 50 metres above the river is reached. Follow along this terrace on good deer trails. After a while the terrace flattens out and the best travel is near the river. Follow up the river till the junction

Looking north across the mouth of Milford Sound.
*Photo: Susan McNeill.*

with the creek coming down from the John O'Groats Saddle is reached and follow it up directly to the saddle. Some difficulty may be experienced in correctly identifying this creek as the maps do not show all the creeks in the vicinity.

The description which follows provides a direct high-level route to reach the Harrison. While it involves a considerable amount of climbing it does avoid the gorge, swamps and featureless flats of the John O'Groats around Lake Unknown. However, a descent to the John O'Groats and Lake Unknown followed by an ascent to the Harrison Saddle via the main stream is perfectly feasible if weather conditions are bad and is described later in this section.

From the saddle climb directly up through the bush, mainly beech and ribbonwood, on to grassland at 980 m altitude. Do not climb too high on these rolling grassland terraces as soon the only disadvantage of this high-level route, namely a 500 metre descent into a hanging valley, is encountered. The initial descent is hindered by a rather abrasive band of sub alpine scrub but some faint deer trails lead through this. Veer well to the left to avoid a large bluff near the valley floor, which can be picked out from the scrub line. The beautiful flats at the bottom provide excellent campsites.

From the flats travel a short distance down stream and follow a deer trail on the ridge on the true-left just above the start of a deep, steep gorge. Ascend this ridge and commence sidling right towards the Harrison Saddle on broad benches below a line of bluffs, continuing across the face until the steep rocky scree slope leading up to the saddle is reached at 750 metres altitude. Do not head up before reaching this scree, which becomes a dry stream further up, as the travel is hindered by vines and loose boulders. Now commence the steep, but pleasant haul up to the Harrison Saddle (1,240 m). A short distance up the scree divides— climb the true-left fork until an obvious place to sidle across to a point just below the saddle is reached. Some large granite boulders lead to the threshold of the heavily glaciated Harrison Valley. There is a small tarn on the Harrison side of the saddle and a large one about 70 metres below it.

The descent to Lake Dot and the shores of Lake Never Never is steep. If dry, the better route is well to the left towards the head of the valley down a long, steep, grassy gut which eventually runs down to scree slopes and a deer trail. There are ideal campsites near the head of the lake.

## HARRISON SADDLE TO MILFORD SOUND

It is impossible to pass around the shores of Lake Never Never to its outlet. To reach the lower Harrison, climb to about 200 metres below the Harrison Saddle and sidle on very easy, wide terraces to the outlet of Lake Pukutahi at 1,125 metres. There is a good campsite 100 metres south-west of the lake outlet on a small saddle. From the head of the lake, Te Hau can be easily climbed for excellent views.

68

Head of Harrison Valley—from above the head of the Kaipo River. (M) Moulin Creek, (N) Lake Never Never, (P) Lake Pukutahi, (Pe) Mt Pembroke, (T) Mt Te Hau.
*Photo: D. L. Homer, Institute of Geological & Nuclear Sciences.*

From the outlet follow down the only feasible and reasonably obvious spur dropping into the Harrison above Moulin Creek. Soon a deep gut with a finger of bush in it will be encountered, heading away to the right into Moulin Creek. Go down the spur and into the bush to shortly afterwards drop steeply down along the true-left edge of the gut. Although it looks unpromising at first, this is the only route and the thick scrub provides plenty of useful holds. Eventually the angle eases and Moulin Creek is reached. Cross the creek and keeping at the same height, angle in a south-westerly direction away from it. Exposed rock slabs, swampy grass and scattered scrub offer interesting and good travel. From here, altitude can be slowly lost until opposite a big waterfall with a large pool at its base on the Harrison floor, which is then aimed for.

On reaching the Harrison cross it and continue down the true-left staying close to the river, boulder-hopping on the bank on some stretches where necessary. After about an hour, just below Selwyn Creek, cross back to the true-right to avoid bluffs. From here on, travel on the true-right is both possible and preferable right down to Harrison Cove. The route is never far from the river and apart from a very short section of gorge near the impressive Wairereata Falls, the going is easy. Pembroke Creek is crossed just above the junction. The huge Grave Bivvy rock about 20 minutes below the junction could provide shelter for 50 people, provided the river is not in high flood. Deer trails close to the river lead to Harrison Cove in two to three hours from here. Usually passing boats will pick up parties from the shore who signal with a fire if a Red Boat, or fishing boat has not been arranged previously.

*Times: Upper Kaipo Hut to top tributary of Kaipo, 7 hrs; Top tributary to bottom of hanging valley, 7 hrs; Hanging valley to Lake Never Never, 6-7 hrs; Lake Never Never (head) to Selwyn Creek, 6 hrs; Selwyn Creek to Wairereata Falls, 2 hrs; Falls to Pembroke Creek, 3/4 hr; Pembroke Creek to Harrison Cove, 3 hrs.*

## LAKE NEVER NEVER TO NGAPUNATORU PASS

It is advisable to study the 1,000 metre haul from the shore of Lake Never Never to the Ngapunatoru Plateau closely from near the Harrison Saddle where the entire route can be seen. Initially ascend to the right of the face on a shoulder of the creek emanating from the foot of the Ngapunatoru Icefall, then veer to the left and commence zig-zagging to avoid small bluffs and ledges. Remain somewhere near the centre until the base of the snow is reached. There is a broad rock ledge about two-thirds of the way up the pass, almost level with the bottom of the icefall below Mt Paranui. This rock ledge has provided an exposed, though reasonable campsite for two parties. From the ledge carry straight on up the middle to the pass at 1,970 metres. There are good sites on the plateau for snow caves. For access to this point from Tutoko Valley via the Grave Couloir see the Tutoko Valley description.

*Time:* *Lake Never Never to Ngapunatoru Pass, 3-4 hrs;*

## UPPER KAIPO VALLEY TO DALE POINT VIA JOHN O'GROATS

The John O'Groats Saddle can be reached either from the Galilee branch of the Kaipo, or by an overgrown route along the undulating bush ridges from the Kaipo Slip. From the saddle at first follow down good deer trails. When the stream enters a gorge about half way down it is probably best to stay well away from it on the true-left side. There are good campsites at Lake Unknown. Follow round the straightforward eastern edge of the lake then continue up the south side of the main and the possibly dry stream entering the top end of the lake to the Harrison Saddle. Parties coming by way of the Kaipo Slip would drop to Lake Unknown from another saddle further north.

The John O'Groats Valley itself provides an alternative, but rough and rarely-used route to Milford Sound, down the north bank and through heavy forest in the lower reaches to the mouth, then due south down the coast to Dale Point, at the entrance of the Sound. A party would have to make prior arrangements to be picked up.

The coastal route from the Kaipo to Dale Point involves a day of tough scrambling along the scrub-covered sea-cliffs, with climbs over the higher bush ridges. The route from Wolf River to Dale Point is reasonable going with some rock hopping in places.

*Time:* *Upper Kaipo to Dale Point, allow 2 days.*

Milford Sound and environs. (A) Age Glacier, (B) Barren Peak, (G) Mount Grave, (H) Milford Hotel, (M) Mt Madeline, (P) Mt Paranui, (S) Sandfly Point, (T) Mt Tutoko.
Photo: V. C. Browne.

# The Milford Track

## "The Finest Walk in the World"

George Moir's original description of the Milford Track in the first, 1925, edition of this guide book became the established authority for all track walkers, not only as a route guide, but also as a definitive reference work for information on history, exploration, place-names and other general information on this region.

All independent parties wishing to walk the track during the summer months must make prior bookings with DoC, Te Anau, and must walk the track fully self-supporting, carrying their own equipment and food, and staying in the DoC huts at Clinton Forks, Lake Mintaro and Dumpling. Camping is necessarily prohibited to prevent uncontrolled parties and over-use of the track. Bookings open around the start of July for the coming summer season.

The track season generally runs from late October to mid April, but can be closed from time to time as a result of exceptional storms and rainfalls. The track is subject to avalanches in winter and spring and advice from DoC staff regarding any avalanche hazard must be heeded. Cancellation of bookings because of weather conditions, with consequent expense and inconvenience, are hazards which all walkers must be prepared to accept.

The track is also open during winter, but the cooking facilities and running water at the huts are not provided. There is no requirement to book the track during the off season and no timetable to keep to. The Pompolona, Avalanche Creek, Roaring Burn and Moraine Creek bridges are removed for the winter. There are 56 avalanche paths that cross the track, any of which may be active. The majority of these paths lie between Six Mile and Mintaro Hill, with others in the vicinity of the Jervois Glacier. Do not attempt to cross these areas if avalanches can be heard, or heavy rain and snow are falling. The emergency avalanche track between Mackinnon Pass Hut and Quintin Huts on the west side of Mackinnon Pass should be used to reduce the avalanche exposure time from around four hours for the track to half an hour. As there is no regular transport at either end of the track during the off season, this must be arranged before starting the track. A number of concessionaires provide charter services, including sea-kayaking from Sandfly Point.

The track is walked from south to north, in order to preserve the wilderness nature of the walk, commencing by boat from Te Anau Downs to Glade House, and ending by boat again from Sandfly Point to Milford. As it is impossible to get from Sandfly Point to Milford without a boat it is not worth freeloading the track. Written permission will be granted by DoC to *bona fide* parties wishing

The Milford Track in winter. Approaching Mackinnon Pass from the north.
*Photo: Hugh van Noorden.*

to use the track for access to the side valleys and mountains. Take the letter with you to explain yourselves to track staff. Note that the side trips from the track are described in the Clinton and Joes River, and Westwards from the Arthur Valley sections.

## GLADE HOUSE WHARF TO MINTARO HUT

During the season, the launch leaves from Te Anau Downs at 2pm to arrive at Glade House wharf at the head of the lake at 4pm. This allows sufficient time to reach Clinton Forks Hut from the wharf in time to cook a late-ish dinner. It is suggested that to give parties time to enjoy the walk this meal should be planned to be quick to prepare. The track to Clinton Forks Hut gains little height and passes through attractive beech forest along the banks of the deep Clinton River. The first night must be spent at Clinton Forks.

From Clinton Forks the track climbs gently through a gorge to the upper flats of the Clinton. The Pompolona Huts are passed beyond the flats and the hut at Lake Mintaro, the source of the Clinton River, is reached about an hour further on. Parties with energy to spare should consider climbing up to the pass to admire the view if the weather is fine as bad weather, with poor visibility the following day, is always a possibility.

The Milford Track. It is claimed that to walk the Milford Track properly it should rain on the first day to make the waterfalls flow and then come fine in order to see from where the waterfalls came. Here trampers descend from Mackinnon Pass to Pompolona through sub-alpine scrub.

## MINTARO HUT TO SANDFLY POINT VIA MACKINNON PASS

From Mintaro Hut the track continues up valley to cross the head of the Clinton and then climbs a well graded zig-zag to the pass (1073 metres). From here, on a clear day, magnificent views are obtained northwards into the Arthur Valley and its tributaries, southwards back into the Clinton, and round the towering peaks on all sides— Castle Mount, Mts. Hart, Pillans, Elliott, Balloon and other more distant summits. Mackinnon's monument stands at the left end of the pass, and the track climbs a little further to the right before reaching the Mackinnon Pass Shelter Hut, past Lake Ella, and then zig-zags steeply down over rocky terrain into Roaring Creek which is crossed and followed down to Quintin. Most parties will wish to cross back here and follow up the two kilometre side track to view the foot of the Sutherland Falls, or even traverse around the back of the falls themselves. It is worth taking wet weather gear to view the falls as the spray is cold, even on a hot day. Down the Arthur Valley from Quintin, Dumpling Hut will be reached, opposite the mouth of Green Valley, in about an hour from Quintin Hut.

The final day's walk from Dumpling to the Sound takes about 5 1/2 hours, so it is wise to make an early start to ensure catching the boat from Sandfly Point. Too many parties make the mistake of keeping to the track and only looking ahead on this stretch. Take time to walk out onto the riverbed to look back up river to some very picturesque views. The Arthur River is crossed by a swing bridge at Boatshed (see cover photograph), and the track leads over to Mackay Falls and Bell Rock before heading north again to Lake Ada. Make a point of climbing into Bell Rock.

The western shore is followed to Doughboy, at the foot of the lake, passing Giant's Gate Falls on the way, which is a good lunch stop with shelter and toilets. The track then follows the lower portion of the Arthur River down to the sound. From here the launch leaves daily for Milford Sound during the season at 2pm. The trip takes 20 minutes and connects with buses to Te Anau.

*Times: Day 1- Glade Wharf to Clinton Forks Hut, 2 hrs; Day 2- Clinton Forks Hut to Lake Mintaro Hut, 4 hrs; Day 3- Lake Mintaro Hut to Quintin Hut, 6 hrs; Quintin Hut to Sutherland Falls, 1 1/2 hrs return; Quintin Hut to Dumpling Hut, 1 hr; Day 4- Dumpling Hut to Sandfly Point, 5 1/2 hrs.*

# Clinton and Joes Rivers

The West Branch of the Clinton River is described in the Milford Track section. The exception to this is the description below for the ascent of Mt Hart from Mackinnon Pass.

## NEALE BURN

The Neale Burn is the biggest tributary of the Clinton, having its source under Mt Belle, which rises south of the Homer Tunnel.

Instead of crossing the swing bridge near Glade House, follow the true-left bank of the Clinton close to the river for two hours through pepperwood thickets until a branch of the Neale Burn is reached. The river forks into two branches which flow into the Clinton about a kilometre apart. Cross this first fork and follow up the far side, gradually moving away from the stream, until the second fork is reached and also crossed. If these streams are above normal fallen tree trunks can generally be found to shin across. The faster up stream branch can also be forded some 150 metres up stream from the confluence with the Clinton when the Neale Burn is high. A deer trail should be found leading away from the river up on a terrace which finds a way through the moss covered boulders and holes which seem to comprise the rest of the hillside. This eventually leads back to the river then and Lake Ross. It takes half an hour round the western side to reach the head of Lake Ross.

Cross the river above the lake to avoid bouldery swamps and backwaters and after two hours of easy travelling up the east bank a tributary coming down from Lake Erskine is reached. Just below this creek is a large, tree studded clearing, while on the other side of the river a large unnamed creek comes in from the west. Erskine Creek is crossed and in an hour or more another clearing is reached which gives an impressive view of Mt Park.

If the river is normal, it is better to cross it just above this clearing and continue up the west side. After 1 ½ hours one arrives at a point opposite a small clearing on the eastern side of the river. Cross the river above this clearing and then, after a short distance, re-cross to the west side. In approximately three hours from Erskine Creek another short tributary comes in from the west. This is also crossed and a deer trail is followed for 15 minutes before crossing back to the true-left or eastern side of the river. Much of the valley is now covered in ribbonwood and subalpine scrub, and directly ahead Students Peak rises sheer from the lonely waters of Lake Thompson.

After travelling for half an hour on the east side of the river recross to the west side where the best travelling will be found well back from the river. Lake

Thompson is reached in about 45 minutes. It is possible to scramble round the last stage of the lake and in one and a-quarter hours the head of the valley is reached.

**Times:** *Glade House to Neale Burn confluence, 2 hrs; Confluence to Lake Ross, 2 hrs; Lake Ross to Lake Erskine tributary, 2 hrs; Lake Erskine tributary to Lake Thompson, 5 hrs.*

## NORTH BRANCH OF CLINTON RIVER

After following the Milford Track both branches of the Clinton are forded at Kakapo Point. The main branch of the Clinton River is generally deep and may be difficult to cross. However, there is a good ford below the junction and at the time of printing a log jam could be used to cross. Head up open grassy flats until the bush closes in. Good deer trails are followed where the river steepens which lead up the true-left side of the North Clinton through a gorge. After three to four hours Lily Creek comes in from the right or eastern side. The head of this creek, where there is a bivvy rock, can be reached in a further 5 ½ hours by following for the most part the creekbed itself. Do not bother going up the side of the valley looking for better routes. The last 2 ½ hours is slow travel through subalpine scrub. From here an hour's climb to the east gives access to the head of an unnamed creek, the largest western tributary of the Neale Burn. At the very head of Lily Creek is a saddle overlooking Surprise Creek, a tributary of Joes River: head up an obvious rocky gut starting at about S122 876945 to meet the ridge at S122 872944, 2 ½ hours later. The gut consists of crumbly rock leading out onto the good, if steep, snowgrass tops. Follow down the ridge on enjoyable big blocky boulders to Marshall Pass. The routes down from Marshall Pass are described later.

Half an hour's travelling up the North Clinton past Lily Creek is Epidote Cataract, also coming in from the east. The route up the North Clinton from Epidote Cataract is rough going. Cross to the west bank up stream from a rock slide a short distance above Epidote Cataract and a light trail leads to open flats in about 1 ½ hours from which an impressive view of Mt Elliott is obtained. Continue up the west side all the way to the head of the valley. Near the head, just beyond a small lake, lies a saddle which could probably be reached by an experienced rock climber and should give access to a western tributary of Joes River.

**Times:** *Clinton Forks to Lily Creek, 3-4 hrs; Lily Creek to Epidote Cataract, ½ hr; Epidote Cataract to head of North Clinton, 6-8 hrs; North Clinton to head of Lily Creek, 5-5 ½ hrs; North Clinton to head of Lake Iceberg via Epidote Cataract, 4 ½ -5 hrs.*

## EPIDOTE CATARACT TO MARSHALL PASS

This tributary is a double hanging valley and has its source in Iceberg Lake. The first hanging valley can be reached up either side of the creek although the south side is probably easier. From here the best travelling is found on the south side of the basin and a short distance ahead Flower Falls comes down from Iceberg Lake. The only feasible, and obvious, route to the lake is 150 metres up steep snowgrass bluff ledges 200 metres to the south side of the falls. The foot of Marshall Pass, which leads to Joes River, can be easily reached by travelling round the eastern side of the lake. There is a two person rock bivvy half way round Iceberg Lake and there is a good, well sheltered campsite at the head. The top section of Marshall Pass comprises of very steep snowgrass and pineapple scrub.

In reverse, the descent beside Flower Falls is not obvious and the best way to attack the descent is to pace out 200 metres and descend from there. A rope to lower packs is helpful when descending from the pass to Lake Iceberg and again when descending beside Flower Falls. It is easier to cross from the Clinton to Joes River rather than in the reverse direction.

***Times:*** *North Branch of Clinton to Iceberg Lake, 3 $^1/_2$-4 hrs; Iceberg Lake Outlet to Marshall Pass, 1 $^1/_2$ hrs.*

## ASCENT OF MT HART FROM MACKINNON PASS

This side excursion from the crossing of the MacKinnon Pass can be undertaken by any person of average fitness and with some climbing experience. If the trip is intended an early start should be made from Pompolona or Mintaro to allow time for the additional scramble from the pass to the summit. The hut wardens should be informed of the party's intentions. There is a short, steep snowgrass section soon after Mackinnon Pass that is very exposed and must be traversed with care. On no account should the climb be attempted in unfavourable conditions. The view from the summit is, of course, much more extensive than that from the pass and experienced parties can descend easily to Lake Quill, sidling the northern slopes of Mt Hart. For details of a high-level route from here onwards into the head of the Dark River, follow in reverse the description given in the Light and Dark Valleys chapter.

## JOES RIVER TO MARSHALL PASS AND NORTH BRANCH OF CLINTON

Access into Joes River is best made by boat across the head of Lake Ada where a narrow, but deep entrance leads into a large lagoon. If no boat is available on Lake Ada, access may still be made by foot. The Arthur River below the track

Mount Hart and environs. (H) Mount Hart, (C) Castle Mount, (Ca) Castle River, (Cl) Clinton Valley, MacKinnon Pass and surrounds, (M) Mackinnon Pass, (Q) Lake Quill, (R) Roaring Creek, (S) Sutherland Falls. *Photo: V.C. Browne.*

crossing flows wide and deep with one possible exception—a shallow ripple directly opposite Joes Valley some 40 minutes above Giant Gate Falls. In dry weather the boatman frequently had to haul his dinghy up this stretch which provides an excellent ford. A 15 minute scramble through swampy bush and tree nettles will bring one to Joes River.

There are light deer trails up both banks of the river, but the better route is probably on the true-left. In an hour a small island-like clearing on the south bank studded with toi-toi offers a view of the valley ahead. There are no gorges in the lower reaches and in 3 $\frac{1}{2}$ hours from Lake Ada more extensive clearings will be encountered. The valley now swings gradually to the right (or south) and the valley of the Talbot River branch can be seen entering from the left. There are some excellent fords and good campsites here and immediately down stream.

A side trip up the Talbot River is very slow going with the better travel close to the riverbed. There are no views until at the head of the valley which is too far away for a comfortable day trip from Joes River.

The confluence of the Talbot River is passed at the topmost end of clearings, and the main valley then rises into a moderate gorge which is climbed on the western bank for 1 $\frac{1}{2}$ hours until the Surprise Creek junction is reached. More level travelling is encountered now through bush and occasionally along stony river shores. The river breaks around several small islands but one can cross and pick the best route. Another good clearing, offering extensive views of Surprise Creek and up valley, is found at the head of these islands and offers good campsites.

A side trip up Surprise Creek offers few deer trails. After the first half hour the going reverts to crown fern and the best travel is in the creekbed. Open going will be reached in about three hours from the Joes River junction where the first views are to be had. Like the Talbot River, to get to the open requires a slog.

Continuing up Joes River there is good travelling on either side of the stream. Two unnamed branches come in from the west at short intervals just as the main valley swings to the left, or south-east. A rewarding side trip is to the lake at the head of the first branch at S121 823988. There is easy going on the true-right close to the creek all the way to the lake 1 $\frac{1}{2}$ hours later.

After a climb through a short gorge it is better to travel on the true-right, level going leads on through some small clearings and where a view of Marshall Pass is obtained ahead. The valley rises again, through a moderate gorge swinging gradually to the south until, amongst a wealth of rocks and ribbonwood, the final branch joins from the west, almost at bush-level. The pass can be seen above and the river swings back to the left below a steepish rock face which rises almost to the pass. A convenient bush spur to the left gives good access to climb above this rock face, down which the river cascades, and the pass will be reached by traversing diagonally to the right across delightful and extensive rock slabs and snowgrass faces above the rock face. It may be more convenient to get high up into the bush via an avalanche swept area. When going up to the pass stay in the middle of the slabs below the pass but in the reverse direction stay on the western edge of the slabs where the rock meets the scrub for as long as possible.

The remainder of the route, down Epidote Cataract and the North Clinton, is described earlier, approached from the Clinton. Glade House can be reached in a day, about eight hours to Kakapo Point, making the full journey from Lake Ada a tough three day trip, or a good four day trip.

# Westwards from the Arthur Valley

A series of streams, approximately of equal length and running in the same north-west to south-east direction, form the western tributaries of the Arthur Valley. The striking features of these side valleys are the extremely precipitous canyon walls and the headwaters that end in narrow cirques surrounded by high, jagged mountains.

## STAIRCASE CREEK

From Quintin Huts follow the Sutherland Falls track to where the valley levels after a climb. A branch track on the right leads to a swing bridge over the main creek. Climb about 100 metres beyond the bridge to a large rock on the left of the track where another track will be seen leading up valley to Disappearing Lake. From this swampy lagoon take a gradual course to the main creek. Cross Staircase Creek and follow the true-right bank to where a large bouldery watercourse descends from the slopes of Mt Mackenzie. This watercourse is climbed to a point about halfway up where the stream splits, one half dribbling over a smooth rock on the right. Climb out of the main watercourse and follow the upper branch to the top. Again, climb out of the channel and descend slightly across open rock and fern to the fringe of ribbonwood and fuchsia forest where deer trails sidle across to beech forest and ribbonwood clearings above the Staircase Creek rapids. It may be preferable to climb the rapids directly, especially if the river is low even though the rocks are slippery for the bush on either side is unpleasant to negotiate.

Above the clearings follow close to the north bank for about half an hour then cross and remain on the true-right side to the head of the valley. Bushline is reached beyond a sharp turn in the valley not far above an attractive waterfall on the main stream. Keep above the bush that extends along the creek and sidle across to moraine and a lake at the head of the valley. The pass to the Light River lies to the north-west of the lake and is easily approached via snowgrass bluffs. For the descent to the Light Valley, refer to the next chapter.

*Time: Quintin to Staircase Flats, 2-3 hrs; Flats to Valley head, 2-3 hrs.*

## GREEN VALLEY

This is a classic hanging valley with an extensive ribbonwood parkland area about 300 metres above the Arthur River. An excellent view of the valley is obtainable from the Mackinnon Pass. Easiest access into the basin is apparently

Staircase Creek. A tussock clearing gives respite from sub-alpine scrub for a tramper.

via the streambed when the creek is low. However, there is a slow route up the steep bush slope north of Dumpling Hill. The prominent spur rising between the forks at the head of the basin gives access to Lady of the Snows, the highest and most attractive mountain in the area.

## DIAMOND CREEK

In normal conditions the Arthur River can be crossed about a kilometre up the Milford Track from Boatshed, just above the confluence of Diamond Creek. It is also possible to reach Diamond Creek from Mackay Creek following the north side of the Arthur River.

A light deer trail leads up the true-right of Diamond Creek to an open scrubby fan near the turn of the valley. The track is easy to lose and is not always close to the river bank. Cross the creek twice at the turn in the valley and then keep close to the streambed until the head of the valley where a series of waterfalls cascade down steep rock slabs. The pass, high above to the right, is by no means easy to reach and should be tackled only by parties with mountaineering experience. Climb the waterfalls to the top which are deceptively arduous then turn north up a very steep, bluffed slope to the saddle.

*Time: Boatshed to head of valley, 5 hrs; Head of valley to pass, 3 hrs.*

## DIAMOND CREEK TO POISON BAY

A difficult alpine route has been traversed to Poison Bay from the Diamond Creek pass via the outlet of Lake Moreton and Peak 5,130 ft . It is likely that an easier and more direct route exists by way of the sharp-pointed Peak 5,440 ft to the west and terraces below the ridge linking Peak 5,130 ft. Such a journey should be undertaken only by a strong, well-equipped party experienced in mountain travel.

To descend to Lake Moreton traverse the pass to the east and climb about 150 metres towards Peak 5,400 ft then sidle across easy snowgrass slopes to a small col between the north side of the lake and the Transit Basin. Climb a knob and descend the spur to the flat, swampy land between the lake outlet and an impressive waterfall that crashes down into the Transit Cirque. The final bluffs, about 30 metres high, may require the use of a rope. Near the lake outlet is a huge boulder that is split horizontally making a fine shelter in most weathers.

There is no record of any successful party reaching the Transit River from the vicinity of Lake Moreton and considering the vertical nature of the Transit Cirque a practicable route may not exist.

## MACKAY FALLS CREEK

Unlike the previous Arthur tributaries described, the Mackay and Poseidon Valleys are virtually devoid of deer, and the forest, which comprises beech stands and ribbonwood and fuchsia thickets, is often difficult to penetrate. Thus the easiest means of access to the headwaters of these tributaries is boulder-hopping when the creeks are normal or low.

A slip on the true-right provides a route into the hanging the basin of Mackay Falls Creek. Climb to the top of the falls and descend gradually through beech forest to the creekbed which should be followed closely until the next major step in the valley. Here climb the rapids on the true-right, through some dense vegetation, until a large lake is reached in the basin above. The east shore of the lake is impassable due to impressive rock walls descending vertically into the lake. On the west side tangled vegetation grows to the water's edge, but with wading it is possible to get around to where a steep scrubby ridge appears to block the way. Parties wishing to reach the head of the Mackay may be forced to swim with packs on a raft.

A comparatively low, scrubby saddle links the head of the Mackay with the Transit River. Although the Transit side of the saddle has been scaled there are no records of anyone having completed the traverse.

*Time: Boatshed Hut to Mackay Valley lake, 4 hrs.*

## POSEIDON CREEK TO TRANSIT RIVER

Poseidon Creek enters the Arthur Valley a little distance above head of Lake Ada. Although access is easier along the streambed in most places, it is possible to follow the true-right bank to the head of the valley. In three to four hours a small lake is reached. Pass this on the west side then cross open scrubby swampland and river flats to the rapids. Keep to the streambed as much as possible until waterfalls descending from the cirque basin are reached. The sheer and overhanging face of Terror Peak now overlooks the valley. This is surely one of the most impressive rock walls in the Southern Alps.

The cirque is gained by climbing steep grass and scrub-covered slabs on the true-right. An excellent campsite, close to running water, is located within a small belt of beech forest at the top of the waterfalls. The pass, which has been crossed to the Transit Valley, lies immediately above to the west.

From the cirque a high-level route leads to the Transit Valley and would take a full day to accomplish. The climb begins up a small creek running down rock slabs at the forest edge. Continue climbing steeply above scrubline until feasible to sidle up between snowgrass ledges in a north-west direction towards the pass. Immediately to the west of the pass is a basin shaped like an amphitheatre enclosing a small, attractive tarn known as Lake Liz. To reach this lake descend scree close to the wall of Peak 5,360 ft until on a level with the lake outlet. Do not try to reach the lake directly as bluffs will be encountered. It is also possible to reach the tarn from the northern end of the saddle. Cross the subterranean outlet of the lake towards the northern end of the basin then work down very steep rock slabs and snowgrass to the scrub. Keep high, and traverse to a prominent beech forest ridge that gives access to valley floor.

*Time: Footbridge on Milford Track (Poseidon Junction) to Poseidon Cirque, 8 hrs.*

# Light and Dark Valleys

### LIGHT RIVER FROM STAIRCASE CREEK

From the Staircase Creek Saddle described in the Westwards from the Milford Track section, descend into the Light Valley by sidling left on benches at the level of the saddle until the first prominent ridge is reached. Descend the ridge to the valley floor and easy travelling in the riverbed leads to the confluence of two streams. Alternatively there is a more direct route down the obvious gut from the saddle, but this is steep and requires considerable care. Directly opposite the confluence will be seen a steep fault gut which can give access to the Poison River and thence to Poison Bay. A major cascade below this confluence is descended on the true-left, and a crossing at the bottom to the true-right will yield easy travel through open bush and clearings to a minor gorge. A small tributary enters from the left just above this gorge. Descend the gorge by boulder-hopping in the riverbed.

A tributary draining Lake Dale enters from a large waterfall on the true-left below the gorge. Lake Dale lies to the north of a large rocky knoll separating the main and east branches of the Light and a route can be traversed from the

Sutherland Sound—looking up the Light Valley.

88

main branch to the East Branch through a low saddle at the head of the valley containing Lake Dale and is described below.

Continue down the main branch to a large waterfall. From the top of the waterfall the East Branch is visible directly below and the Dark River is the next major valley on the left. Descent of the waterfall to the East Branch confluence is by difficult scrambling on the true-left above bluffs. Sutherland Sound is reached by easy travelling on the true-left. There are campsites just before the sound.

*Time: Staircase Creek Saddle to Sutherland Sound, 8 hrs; Confluence of East Branch and Main Branch of Light River to Sutherland Sound, 1 hr.*

## EAST BRANCH OF LIGHT RIVER FROM STAIRCASE CREEK

Possibly the easiest route from Staircase Creek Saddle into the Light River is via Lake Dale. Climb the steepish ridge to the left of the saddle and follow it along past a small peak (Peak 4,725 ft) as far as a rocky out-crop. From here descend an obvious spur down easy grass slopes then reasonably steep bush to Lake Dale. Sidle westwards through thick bush on the northern shore staying about 50 metres above the lake to avoid swamps and then drop down to the outlet. A waterfall 15 metres from the outlet drops 60 metres down to the main branch of the Light River. If the lake level is high the outlet can be uncrossable unless the expedient of bridging the narrow stream with a tree trunk is used. The eastern shore is impassable owing to steep bluffs.

From the outlet of Lake Dale continue round the western and southern shores. A short climb of about 30 metres then leads to a low saddle. From here sidle left, losing height slowly, until a tributary stream is reached. Follow a light deer trail down the eastern bank to the East Branch.

*Time: Staircase Creek Saddle to outlet of Lake Dale, 3 $^1/_2$- 4 hrs; Outlet of Lake Dale to East Branch of Light River, 3 $^1/_2$-4 hrs.*

## EAST BRANCH OF LIGHT RIVER

The East Branch of the Light River offers easy travelling from Sutherland Sound to the head. The ascent of the Dark-Light Saddle is very steep and obvious although one party reports difficulty in navigating through the jungle at the bottom of the climb. It is possible to camp on the saddle. For the descent route into the Dark River see the ascent description given below and refer to the photograph.

*Times: Sutherland Sound to head of East Branch, 7 hrs; Head of valley to Dark-Light Saddle, 3-5 hrs.*

## LIGHT RIVER TO POISON BAY

It is quite straightforward to cross from the Light River to Poison Bay via an obvious saddle in the ridge at the head of the Light, at about scrubline. While the access to the saddle from the Light is easy the descent on the other side is steeper with a few small bluffs in the creek leading straight down from the saddle. Follow the Poison River all the way to the sea in, or near to the river itself. Lower down there are swamps away from the river. At low tide the river is crossable to the main beach at the bar. There is a campsite on the true-left.

## HEAD OF LAKE GRAVE TO SUTHERLAND SOUND VIA DARK RIVER

The route round Lake Grave from its southern end lies by the western shore. From all accounts travel is unpleasant and a full day should be allowed. From the bluffs at the western end of the beach climb for about 300 metres through the bush, and then sidle at this level until the comparatively flat ground at the outlet of the lake is glimpsed ahead. A careful descent is made from here and the lakeshore followed to the outlet. Cross here to the east side and continue past a small lake 15 minutes down the river, boulder-hopping, until the gorge becomes too steep to negotiate. From here climb out to the true-right through bush until an easy spur is reached and then follow deer trails down to the beach at the head of the Sutherland Sound.

*Time:* *Head of Lake Grave to outlet, 10 hrs; Outlet to Sutherland Sound, 2 $^1/_2$ hrs.*

## LAKE GRAVE TO HEAD OF DARK RIVER

An excellent campsite exists at the southernmost tip of Lake Grave, some 50 metres back off the shoreline where a dinghy is usually kept. Immediately behind this campsite a blazed trail heads up stream, close to the foot of the hill on the south side of the Dark River. The first clearing between Lake Grave and Swan Mere is reached in about one hour. The blazes then disappear and travel becomes more difficult, but remain close to the foot of the hill, still on the south side of the valley. After skirting the second, scrubby swamp clearing travel becomes difficult because of moraine boulders. Remain high until about halfway around Swan Mere then head directly down to Swan Mere and travel round the water's edge to the dry water course at the head of the lake.

Follow the dry riverbed up from Swan Mere and a second campsite is found just before this joins the main river again. This campsite may be subject to flooding by Swan Mere backing up during heavy rain. Some 200 metres up stream from here, at the foot of the gorge, a good river crossing is found. Leading off from this a very well-defined deer trail winds its way, close to the river, up the north bank of the Dark River to the forks of the north branch of the Dark River and Starvation Creek. From here the trail climbs steeply up the north bank of the main river as it passes through yet another gorge. At the head of this gorge a good river crossing is found and from here on the trail leads up the south bank into the head basin. Should the river be in flood, a log crossing exists midway through the gorge, but this can be difficult to locate.

An excellent campsite is found on the southern edge of the large slip within the forks, about midway up its length, which gives very good access to both Starvation Creek and the north branch of the Dark River. Access from this campsite into Starvation Creek is by way of a well defined deer trail leading up the true-right bank into the head basin. For the route over Hunter Pass from the Worsley Valley see the next chapter.

*Times: Head of Lake Grave to head of Swan Mere, 3 hrs; Head of Swan Mere to Starvation Creek, 1 3/4 hrs; Starvation Creek to head basin, 2 1/2 hrs.*

## DARK VALLEY TO LIGHT VALLEY VIA DARK-LIGHT SADDLE

From 15 minutes below the head cirque of the Dark ascend the steep cataract, remaining in the bed of the watercourse. The true-right offers the better going initially, but do not be tempted to climb out of the cataract onto the promising slopes on this side as these become hopelessly bluffed. If the stream is at normal levels good progress can be made and an obvious route from the top of the cataract leads through fern, *Dracophyllum* and steep snowgrass to the saddle. It is possible to traverse the ridge above the nameless lake at the head of the Dark to reach the tops overlooking Lake Quill, connecting there with the Dark River-Mackinnon Pass route described below.

The descent into the East Branch of the Light Valley from the Dark-Light Saddle is extremely difficult and no precise route description is offered as parties have provided differing and complicated accounts. The best strategy seems to be to drop down leftwards through dense scrub across to a rib, reached just below bushline, then descend the rib to the valley floor. The direct ascent upward from the Light Valley described earlier is a much easier proposition than the descent down unseen and unknown cliffs and bluffs.

*Time: Saddle to Head of Light River, 2 1/2 - 4 hrs*

## DARK RIVER TO MACKINNON PASS

The head of the Dark River north branch ends abruptly at a semi-circular rock-swept clearing 15 minutes up stream of the steep cataract leading up to Dark-Light Saddle.

Dark-Light Saddle. The head of the Dark River is in the foreground and the East Branch of the Light River beyond.
*Photo: Alister McDonald.*

From this clearing climb steep scrub and snowgrass slopes to the top of a tongue of beech forest on the left. From here continue to climb up steep snowgrass to a saddle overlooking the large unnamed lake at the head of the Dark River. Proceed to climb about 300 metres up the ridge towards Barrier Peak then sidle across to the Main Divide ridge above Castle Canyon. This ridge is easily followed to the tops overlooking Lake Quill. From above Lake Quill an alpine route of moderate difficulty leads via the Nicholas Peaks and Mt Hart to the Mackinnon Pass. After descending from a high point at the intersection of the ridges south of Lake Quill sidle across snowfields above the Castle River cirque and rejoin the ridge up a low rock wall beyond a craggy buttress. The ridge itself has been negotiated, but the buttress is very exposed for a short section and most parties will require a rope.

Having regained the ridge an easy sidle across scree leads to a half-moon shaped saddle between two impressive rock steeples, the Nicholas Peaks, towering above the Clinton Cirque. Drop 15 metres or so on the Clinton side of the saddle and then sidle the snow slopes just below the bluffs coming off Peak 5,940 ft and regain the main ridge coming off this peak just before a steep ridge dropping towards the Clinton Cirque. Getting onto the snow slopes may be extremely difficult late in the season. With the difficult part of the route now accomplished follow the main ridge in a northerly direction to about 150 metres below the summit of Aiguille Rouge. This peak and Mt Hart are bypassed by sidling around the northern flanks and then the ridge descending from Mt Hart is followed to the Mackinnon Pass.

**Time:** *Head of Dark River to Mackinnon Pass, 9-10 hrs.*

## DARK RIVER TO WORSLEY AND WILD NATIVES RIVERS

The main and easiest route to the Worsley River lies by way of the next tributary past Robb Creek up to the southern ridge of the valley and thence along to the saddle into the north branch of the Worsley. Refer to the Worsley and Wild Natives Rivers section for route descriptions.

# WEST OF LAKE TE ANAU —THE WAPITI AREAS

## Worsley and Wild Natives Valleys

### HOLDAWAY MEMORIAL HUT TO WORSLEY FORKS

From the Holdaway Memorial Hut at the head of Worsley Arm, which will sleep 20 people, the track leads off in a south-westerly direction before emerging from the bush near the river about half an hour up stream of the hut. From here the route follows deer trails, but easier going can be found on the edge of the river if low. The track on the north bank has been eroded into the river. A little disconcerting is the number of large logs and driftwood that is found deep in the bush up to three metres above the river. For those wishing to cross to the south bank there are a number of fords if the river is low, but the main route up valley continues on the north bank all the way to the Castle-Worsley junction. There is a good campsite on the east bank of the Castle near the confluence. There is also a reasonable two person bivvy rock 150 metres up stream of the junction on the true-right of the Castle River at S130 785800, 6 metres above the river level.

After crossing the Castle River just above the junction the route continues up the north bank of the Worsley giving easy travelling through beech forest and ribbonwood. If the river is low it is advisable to cross and re-cross to avoid two small bluffs on the north bank, but if it is high these bluffs can be climbed. The Worsley should be crossed at Prospect Creek as the better route through the Worsley Gorge lies on the south side from here on.

The route starts to rise and soon climbs steadily up a steep ridge until leading out on to the first of two steep rock water-courses. These are both crossed high above the river, which can be heard roaring far below in its narrow gorge, and good views are obtained of the high, steep walls of the Prospect Valley. The route then sidles for some time before descending through ribbonwood and black fern to river level once again. Following the river, the track winds through beech forest before emerging out on the top flats, known as the Bog Clearings, at the far end of which are good campsites. From the top of the flats the track enters the bush once more and leads to the forks of the river in ten to fifteen minutes.

The upper Worsley River.
*Photo: DOSLI.*

**Times:** *Holdaway Memorial Hut to Castle River, 2-3 hrs; Castle River to Terminus Creek, 2 hrs; Terminus Creek to Prospect Creek, 1 ¹/₂ hrs; Prospect Creek to Bog Clearings, 2 ¹/₂ hrs; Bog Clearings to Worsley Forks, ¹/₄ hr.*

## WORSLEY FORKS TO GLAISNOCK RIVER VIA WORSLEY PASS AND HEAD OF WILD NATIVES RIVER

From the Worsley Forks the Worsley Pass is reached by following up the West Branch on its north side. After an initial steep climb followed by awkward travel over broken rocks the upper bush edge is gained, 2 ¹/₂ hours from the forks.

95

Carry on for 45 minutes and turn before the head of the valley to climb up to the saddle, on the west side. The saddle gives access to the upper Bernard Burn which is the northern tributary of the Wild Natives River, which in turn drains into Bligh Sound. Lake Bernard is three hours of rough going away with little in the way of deer trails. Just 15 minutes below the pass on the south west face lies a huge boulder, surrounded by a large field of smaller broken rocks, known as the Worsley Rock Bivvy. The bivvy provides good shelter for two or three people under its western edge.

It is possible to cross to the Glaisnock Valley via the head of the Wild Natives River and Taheke Creek. To do this continue down for approximately $3/4$ hour from the saddle to take the first ridge in the bush on the south side that provides a route up to a fault in the main ridge of the Bernard Burn and the Wild Natives River. It is a climb of 400 metres and takes an hour. The descent over snowgrass slopes into the upper Wild Natives Valley is steep, but is not difficult. Travel south-west, keeping in close to the bluffs on the left. Taheke Saddle can be viewed across the valley as a long, flat, treeless area and it can be reached in two hours from the ridge top. Very soon after leaving the saddle spectacular views down the upper Taheke Valley can be seen.

Travel around the two lakes on the west side and enter the bush. After about an hour cross to the north east side of the creek. Continue for $1 \ 1/2$ hours on the true-left before crossing back to the true-right side. Continue west some way as the descent into the Glaisnock Valley is made.

**Times:** *Worsley Forks to Worsley Saddle, 2-3 hrs; Worsley Saddle to Taheke Saddle, $3 \ 3/4$ hrs; Taheke Saddle to Glaisnock River, $3 \ 1/2$ hrs; Taheke Creek confluence to Glaisnock Hut, 4 hrs.*

## WORSLEY NORTH BRANCH TO DARK RIVER

The main stream, or North Branch of the Worsley may be followed from the Worsley Forks on either side of the river. From the head of the valley a hanging basin will be seen to the west, at the head of which is a high saddle overlooking the North Branch of the Wild Natives River. There is a good deer trail leading up to this saddle, starting on the north side of the creek draining from the saddle. From the top a route to Sutherland Sound via the Dark River starts by following the ridge to the north of the saddle along a distinct deer trail to a point overlooking the upper of two tributaries leading down to the Dark River. From here follow the ridge between this valley and the Wild Natives and after a short distance the route drops abruptly down into this hanging valley. On reaching the bush the route continues down the stream bed for one hour until the grade becomes too steep and then out to the right into the bush and down a ridge, keeping as close as practicable to the stream until the Dark River is reached, some three hours from the bushline.

96

It is also possible to descend into the Wild Natives River from the saddle at the head of the North Worsley and so down to Bligh Sound. Reasonable snowgrass slopes to the south of the cirque give the best route. Another route out from the Wild Natives River to Robb Saddle is described later in this chapter.

**Times:** *Worsley Forks to head of Worsley North Branch, 2-3 hrs.*

## CASTLE RIVER

From the Castle-Worsley junction deer trail lead up the Castle Valley on the west side of the river and in about an hour emerge on to a clearing from which fine views are obtained of Castle Mount. There is also a more difficult route on the east side of the river. Deer trails give fair travelling with the better going on the true-left bank and emerges onto ribbonwood flats near the head of the valley. The Castle River is the largest tributary of the Worsley and merits a visit if only for its magnificent scenery, which rivals the famous Clinton Canyon.

**Time:** *Worsley River to Castle River head, 4-5 hrs.*

Castle Mount. Castle Mount has never been climbed from Castle River in spite of a determined effort by three members of the Southland Section of the New Zealand Alpine Club at Easter 1956. The mountain is almost impossible to view from the Milford Track, on the northern side.
*Photo: B.J. Smith.*

97

## TERMINUS CREEK

This valley is worth a visit to view its spectacular mountain walls, but access to its head is blocked by two small lakes. The Terminus cirque can be reached from Prospect Creek which is described below.

## PROSPECT CREEK TO DARK VALLEY VIA HUNTER PASS

Prospect Creek provides difficult access by a high pass to Starvation Creek in the Dark Valley. From the junction with the Worsley follow a deer trail climbing steeply on the west bank of Prospect Creek. This track may not be very obvious and remains about 50 metres away from the Prospect rapids. After about 45 minutes the going becomes easier as the route levels out in a hanging valley and Lake Brownlee should be reached after a further 30 minutes. The east shore of the lake provides good going though wading in the lake edge will save climbing over bluffs. There is a reasonably sheltered campsite at the head. Continue climbing through dense ribbonwood and boulders along the stream to a dried-up creek shortly before Lake Sumor. Follow up the creekbed for a few minutes to Lake Sumor (named for the hungry man in W. G. Grave's party who always wanted "some more").

The lake can be easily traversed on the western shore. Another hour of easy going through moraine boulders leads out to the large flat at the base of Hunter Pass. An excellent bivvy rock can be seen approximately 100 metres above the flat on the true-right of the valley, just below the gut leading up to the pass. On the opposite side of the valley a high col, reached by climbing up some very steep snowgrass vegetation, offers a feasible route into the Terminus Creek cirque.

The route to Hunter Pass involves a straightforward climb of some 500 metres from the head of the small unnamed lake at the very head of the valley. Some care is needed on the steeper, slippery parts. Several small tarns are found on the pass and there is a small lake 100 metres or so down on the Dark side. The descent into Starvation Creek is extremely steep which explains why this route has been used by very few parties since Grave's discovery of it.

The writer of this description sidled down towards the south-west of the lake outlet then angled down in the same direction through some exceedingly steep scrub towards a steep slip which allows a reasonable descent to the bush edge. A few deer trails continue almost directly down, but soon peter out when the forest becomes exceptionally steep. Descend through this as best you can. The writer's party had to lower packs with a rope in a few places. Another party descended to Starvation Creek above the bushline, thus avoiding the steep bush sections. Then head for the true-right side of the valley floor which offers reasonable travel. A large, open slip will be encountered in the forest a few hundred metres above the junction of Starvation Creek where an acceptable campsite will be found.

*Times: Worsley River to Lake Brownlee, 1 ¹/₂ hrs; Outlet to head of Lake Brownlee, 1 hr; Lake Brownlee to Lake Sumor, 1 ¹/₂ hrs; Lake Sumor to valley head, 1 hr; Valley head to Hunter Pass, 1 ³/₄ hrs.*

## WILD NATIVES VALLEY AND BERNARD BURN

From the head of Bligh Sound, the south side of the Wild Natives River is followed for 1 ¹/₂ hours until a backwater is seen running in from the right. Through this backwater runs the Pitt River and it may be crossed by wading across a very narrow bar where the Pitt joins the Wild Natives. This bar had eroded in 1990 and it may now be necessary to go around the backwater, adding another ³/₄ hr to the trip. Down stream from this point a large tributary from the north also joins the Wild Natives. In another two hours the junction of the South Wild Natives is reached. There is easy travel up the south branch, firstly on the south side for two hours until crossing to the true-right at the outlet of Kiwi Lake. From here an easy saddle leads to Taheke Creek, a tributary of the Glaisnock.

To proceed up the main valley, now named the Bernard Burn, continue on the south side for some three hours before crossing the river just up stream from a point where a creek, the second from the north, joins the river. From here on the deer trail frequently crosses the river and in another three hours Lake Bernard will be reached, the outlet of which is submerged in bush covered moraine. After climbing round the south side of this lake a tributary will soon be seen coming in from the right. This tributary gives access to the Worsley Valley via Worsley Pass. From this junction the head of the valley will be reached in an hour. About 20 minutes before the saddle is the Worsley Rock Bivvy mentioned above.

Previous editions of this guide book recommended negotiating Lake Bernard on the north side. However, the large slip at the bottom end of the lake on this side is not negotiable unless there are extremely low lake levels.

*Times: Bligh Sound to Pitt River, 1 ¹/₂ hrs; Pitt River to South Wild Natives junction, 2 hrs; Junction to saddle at head of South Wild Natives, easy day; Junction to Kiwi Lake, 2 hrs.*

## BERNARD BURN TO DARK VALLEY VIA ROBB SADDLE

From the second north tributary of the Bernard Burn there is a route into the Dark River via Robb Saddle. The crossing is reasonably straightforward though bluffs below bushline on the west side of the saddle are difficult to negotiate.

The hanging basin of the Bernard Burn second tributary is reached by a well-defined deer trail that climbs the true-right side of the cascades then crosses near the top. The trails become more difficult to follow further up the basin as the route swings around to the east up a steep and bluffed slope. From bushline (south of Peak 4,470 ft) climb about 150 metres then sidle across easy slopes to Robb Saddle. If travelling in the reverse direction look for a small terrace at bushline from where a deer trail indicates a suitable route into the valley below. An alternative route to Robb Saddle, avoiding the bluffs mentioned above, sidles further up into the basin of the Bernard Burn then sidles out to the true-left gaining height all the time, to reach a large stream bed with ferns and ribbonwood. Follow up this to just above bushline then climb snowgrass slopes in an easterly direction and sidle onto the saddle.

The descent into the attractive hanging basin of Robb Creek is direct and simple. Although difficult to find there is a good rock bivvy able to sleep about four people in the scrubby beech forest on the true-right about 60 metres above the stream before it cascades to a lower step in the basin. From the lip of the hanging basin follow deer trails on the true-right through bush and then on to rocky chutes which give access into the Dark Valley.

*Times: Bernard Burn to Robb Saddle, 5-6 hrs (1st route described), 4-5 hrs (2nd route); Saddle to Dark River, 5-6 hrs.*

# Glaisnock Valley and Pitt River

## NEWTON CREEK

The first tributary of the Glaisnock is Newton Creek, entering from the north only 100 metres up from the lake. To enter this valley from a base in the Glaisnock Hut a party will need a boat, or alternatively allow two hours' travelling time to the first Glaisnock crossing and another two hours' return unless the river is very low. To avoid this extra travelling it would be preferable to tent on the north bank of the Glaisnock. The route into Newton Creek commences up either bank, veering out on the north-west side of the valley after some three hours to pass a gorge and waterfall. A spur running down to the creek beyond bush-level is crossed by climbing still higher and from here a good view is obtained of the valley. It is possible to cross into Nitz Creek and also into Narrows Creek to the east.

*Time: Lake Te Anau to head of Newton Creek, 6-8 hrs.*

## GLAISNOCK HUT TO THE FORKS

The Glaisnock Valley climbs gently from the top of the North Arm of Lake Te Anau to The Forks, which is the confluence of Midnight Creek (the left fork) and the Right Fork which is the main tributary of the Glaisnock. The track can still be followed in most places although it has not been maintained for many years.

To travel up the main valley follow the track from the Glaisnock Hut (12 bunks) over to the river and then follow up the south bank to the Henderson Burn. There is also another, rough, track on the north bank of the Glaisnock from the lake as far as the Henderson Burn junction, but from here on the main route up valley is on the south bank so parties on the north should cross over either by the ford at the junction if the river is low or by the Glaisnock Falls bridge another ten minutes up stream.

From the Henderson Burn, the Glaisnock River deviates around several small islands winding this way and that, climbing gradually all the way. The sandy tracks on the south side provide the best travelling and, a further hour from the Henderson Burn, Nitz Creek will be seen joining the Glaisnock from the north. Continuing up the south bank of the Glaisnock past Nitz Creek, Kakapo Creek is the next valley encountered, half and hour later, joining the main valley from the north. Taheke Creek, previously called Waterfall Creek, joins the Glaisnock from the north also, another hour above the Kakapo Creek junction.

101

After the Taheke Creek junction the Glaisnock rises sharply for a short distance and then begins to straighten and level out somewhat. The track crosses to the north bank of the river by way of a large semi-submerged log across a placid stretch in the river 45 minutes from Taheke Creek. This is called the Log Crossing and is clearly marked by blazes on the south side of the river. Alternatively, if the river is too high, another track continues up the south bank, but it is preferable to cross if possible.

The travelling on the north bank is through some swampy ground interspersed heavily with ribbonwood and fern. The track follows close to the river all the

Glaisnock area. A view N.N.E. from above Lake Roxburgh (in foreground), across the mouth of the Glaisnock (bottom right), up Newton Creek (right) and Nitz Creek (left).
*Photo: DOSLI.*

way and in two hours from the Log Crossing the Glaisnock Rocky Bivvy will be reached. This shelter is situated on the opposite, south, bank and will be seen amongst tall ferns some 25 metres up from the river, identifiable by smoke stains curving around the protruding rock and also by numerous tree stumps nearby. If the river cannot be crossed here, the two branches can be forded above. The Glaisnock Rock Bivvy can sleep three comfortably and beside it is a flat campsite.

The Forks are reached in a quarter of an hour further on and here the valley branches north and south. The fork to the south, known as Midnight Creek, leads to the Edith Saddle while the north fork ends in a cirque. There is a steep climb leading on to Oilskin Pass halfway up the north fork, but this route is infrequently used as a crossing to the Pitt Valley. There is a good campsite at The Forks.

***Times:*** *Glaisnock Hut to Glaisnock Rock Bivvy, 7-8 hrs; Glaisnock Hut to Henderson Burn, 2 hrs; Henderson Burn to Nitz Creek, 1 hr; Nitz Creek to Kakapo Creek, $^1/_2$ hr; Kakapo Creek to Taheke Creek, 1 hr; Taheke Creek to Log Crossing, $^3/_4$ hr; Log Crossing to Glaisnock Rock Bivvy, 2 hrs; Glaisnock Rock Bivvy to The Forks, $^1/_4$ hr.*

Glaisnock Falls. The entire flow of the Glaisnock River enters a narrow channel only a metre or so wide for a short distance above the Henderson Burn.
*Photo: Susan McNeill.*

## HENDERSON BURN TO WAPITI RIVER

The track into the Henderson Burn is on the true-right bank and follows up an easy valley, crossing where desirable in the upper reaches. There is a crossing into Wapiti River by way of an easy saddle in the head. Climb up the most southern of two saddles at the head of the Henderson Burn through a belt of scrub. The final drop into the Wapiti River through the bush on the true-right of the stream is steep with a number of dead ends where large slips have occurred in the past.

*Time:* *Glaisnock to head of Henderson Burn, 6-8 hrs.*

## NITZ CREEK

Access to Nitz Creek can be gained by fording the Glaisnock at the confluence, or by keeping to the north bank of the Glaisnock all the way from the Glaisnock Falls bridge. From the mouth of Nitz Creek climb the spur on the true-left for about 150 metres then drop to a small saddle. Steep slopes can now be traversed into the Nitz Gorge. Cross to the true-right where deer trails can be picked up leading through the upper part of the gorge to easier going. A good campsite will be found just past a slip face on the west bank at a point where the river splits forming several bush covered islands. From here it is a short distance to several large clearings.

*Time:* *Glaisnock to head of Nitz Creek, about 8 hrs.*

## KAKAPO CREEK

Cross the Glaisnock at a suitable ford below the junction to pick up a wapiti trail on the true-left bank and after climbing for 150 metres cross to the true-right. There is a steep climb for another 150 metres before the valley levels out somewhat and in an hour from the top of the gorge the valley is blocked by enormous bush clad boulders. Two routes lead past this obstacle: one is a steep climb of 150 metres via a deer trail on the west side of the valley, and the other by crossing the valley floor hard to the east side and climbing steadily towards a scrub-covered shingle fan. The first is probably the better route. From here the head of the valley will be reached in an hour and a further hour's steep climb will lead on to a saddle with the south branch of the Wild Natives River. The usual route to this valley, however, lies via Taheke Creek. By traversing to the south of this saddle some 400 metres another saddle will give access down steep bluffs into the head of Taheke Creek.

## TAHEKE CREEK TO WORSLEY RIVER

After crossing over from the south bank of the Glaisnock above the Taheke Creek junction, a good deer trail climbs steeply for 300 metres up the west side of the creek. It then crosses to the true-left bank and after two hours crosses again to climb for a further hour to bush-level. Moraine debris about halfway up the hanging valley bush section comes as a surprise and if anything may be better circumnavigated on the true-right. More open country will now be encountered and two lakes are passed on the west side before Taheke Creek Saddle is reached. Most of the promising campsites in the open flats passed on the way are bogs.

Taheke Creek Saddle leads over into the south branch of the Wild Natives River and thence down to Bligh Sound. From the saddle a steep, but easy route to the head of the Bernard Burn can be seen. Observe three gullies opposite the saddle: the centre gully with the clump of trees about a third of the way up provides the route. Descend from the saddle, cross the valley and climb the gully. At the top is a defined fault line which leads to the ridge overlooking Lake Bernard and the upper Bernard Burn. To the right lies the Worsley Pass and just below this is Worsley Rock Bivvy. This route is described in reverse in the Worsley and Wild Natives Valleys section.

*Times: Glaisnock to bushline, 6 hrs; Bushline to saddle, 1 hr; Saddle to Bligh Sound, 1 day.*

## THE FORKS TO EDITH SADDLE

The track up to the Edith Saddle follows up the true-left side of Midnight Creek, which is forded at The Forks. Various deer trails ultimately merge into one good lead and climb upwards diagonally, crossing a deep gravel chute after about half an hour. More open ground is now encountered and the Edith Saddle appears ahead and is reached in 1 $\frac{1}{2}$ hours from the Glaisnock Rock Bivvy. The saddle is just on bush-level and a campsite situated between two stunted beech trees will be noticed from the crest of the ridge only a few metres down the south side. This camp gives good access to the headwaters of the Edith River and a deer trail leads directly down from below the saddle into the Edith River itself. This river flows into Lake Alice and thence into George Sound. Stalkers usually enter the Edith Valley from the head by this route. Alternatively, parties may land on Lake Alice by float-plane, or enter from Wapiti River or George Sound on foot.

*Time: Glaisnock Rock Bivvy to Edith Saddle, 1 $\frac{1}{2}$ hrs.*

## EDITH SADDLE TO LAKE BEDDOES VIA EDITH–PITT SADDLE

The route over into the Pitt watershed climbs northwards from the Edith Saddle for 1 $\frac{1}{2}$ hours to the Edith-Pitt Saddle, some 300 metres higher, and thence down to the Pitt River and Lake Beddoes. The route from the Edith Saddle over into the Pitt follows a good deer trail up the ridge from the Edith Saddle for only ten minutes and then sidles to the left around the south shoulder of a peak rising between the two saddles. The ridge of this peak between the two saddles is not traversed to get into the Pitt Valley. The route is a natural one and if one climbs too high, or too low, bluffs will be encountered which will force a party back up again onto the proper route.

From the Edith-Pitt Saddle, Lake Oilskin, which lies on Oilskin Pass, will be noticed some 150 metres below to the north. The route drops from the saddle to the west of this lake by way of snowgrass slopes and obvious rock ledges until a view of the upper Pitt Valley is obtained. A deer trail then leads from Lake Oilskin down into the head of the Pitt and enters the bush on the left of the creek. Just prior to entering the bush a large outstanding rock will be noticed on the left. This is called the Pitt Bivvy Rock and will sleep three, but is not considered a particularly safe refuge from all weathers. There is a steep drop through bush for a short distance after which more level going allows for good campsites. The track down to Lake Beddoes follows a good deer trail, crossing a branch which enters by way of a waterfall from the South Pitt Basin, and continues down the true-left bank of the Pitt River. A small bluff running into the river compels a crossing to the true-right bank and Lake Beddoes is reached a quarter of an hour after recrossing.

*Times: Edith Saddle to Edith–Pitt Saddle, 1 $^1/_2$ hrs; Edith–Pitt Saddle to bush-level, 1 $^1/_2$ hrs; Bush-level to Lake Beddoes 1 $^1/_2$ hrs.*

## PITT RIVER AND LAKE BEDDOES

There is no easy route from Lake Beddoes into neighbouring valleys as the slopes rising around the lake are steep and interspersed with bluffs. The ridge to the south of the lake divides the Pitt from the George Valley, access into which lies up a long slip part way along the south shore of the lake. After sidling to the right from the top of this slip and climbing still further above bush-level a low saddle will be noticed which leads by way of a tributary into the George River. This slip also gives access on to the tops to the south of Lake Beddoes, which can be traversed from Overhead Cone to Oilskin Pass.

To the north of Lake Beddoes lies a ridge dividing the Pitt Valley from the Wild Natives River. This ridge can be traversed from Oilskin Pass over a peak in the head of the North Fork of the Glaisnock and thence westwards along to Tarnagan Point where a difficult descent can be made through steep, bluffed bush to Lake Beddoes, the round trip taking about a day. There is a deer trail from the northern slopes of the Tarnagan Point down a spur into the Wild Natives River.

Lake Beddoes is drained by way of a 400 metre cataract, joining the Wild Natives River two hours up from Bligh Sound. The lake has a very narrow outlet through a rock cleft and consequently rises quickly with heavy rainfall.

## OILSKIN PASS TO BLIGH SOUND VIA OVERHEAD CONE

In fine weather Bligh Sound can be reached by traversing the ridge all the way from Oilskin Pass to Overhead Cone, keeping on, or close to the ridge for the whole distance. The descent to the sound commences from a prominent 'V' in the ridge about 300 metres east from Overhead Cone then down the true-right of a stream to a flat basin, then across to a ridge which is followed all the way down to the sound, time six hours. There is a steep bluff about two-thirds of the way down. Keep veering left to avoid precipitous bluffs then drop into the streambed about 60 metres above the sound, which is reached about 500 metres from its head.

*Time: Oilskin Pass to Bligh Sound, 9hrs.*

# Stuart Mountains and North of Middle Fiord

In this section are grouped the miscellaneous streams, other than the Worsley and Glaisnock, flowing into Te Anau between the Worsley Arm and the Middle Fiord.

## BILLY BURN

From the mouth of the Billy Burn the north bank is followed for 20 minutes until the gorge is reached. A deer trail climbs away from the stream for 1 ½ hours over a 250 metre bluff and a ten minute gradual descent leads back down to the stream where a small clearing will be seen on the opposite side. After crossing to this clearing, cross back again five minutes later to the north bank and continue for another two hours, climbing at first, then sidling until a *hebe* and tussock clearing is reached. At this point a tributary from the south joins the Billy Burn. An earlier tributary, also from the south, joins the Billy Burn about 1 ½ hours down valley. In another two hours of crossing and recrossing the main stream and passing through several clearings the head of the valley is reached. Both Narrows Creek and Saints Creek in the Worsley Valley can be reached by sidling and climbing on the north side towards the head of the valley.

*Time: Lake Te Anau to head of Billy Burn, 6 hrs.*

## NARROWS CREEK

The track into Narrows Creek, formerly called Cow Valley, on the north side of the North Fiord begins from a bay on the north-west side of the bush flat to the west of the mouth of Narrows Creek. After ten minutes on a blazed track the creek will be reached where it comes out of a gorge. The track climbs steeply for 350 metres on the north-west side of the valley before it levels out and then continues mainly on the same side. This valley is very easy to traverse to the open country at the head.

*Time: Lake Te Anau to head of Narrows Creek, 4-5 hrs.*

## LUGAR BURN

The Lugar Burn flows into Te Anau near The Narrows, on the south side of the North Fiord. A good base will be found near the mouth of the river on the west side.

North Fiord, Lake Te Anau. (C) Narrows Creek, (G) Glaisnock Valley, (K) Kakapo Creek, (L) Lugar Burn, (LV) Long Valley, (McD) Mt McDougall, (N) The Narrows

*Photo: DOSLI.*

Access to the headwaters of the McDougall Branch commences by crossing the river at the first reasonable ford up from the mouth to the true-right to pick up deer trails. After a time the trail climbs away from the river to bypass the gorge. Before the trail descends to the forks an open patch of bush will be encountered. This is the start of the route which leads to a saddle with the Mid Burn. The route to the Austral and McDougall Branches descends into the stream at a good crossing point and in a few minutes the stream is forded back again. Between the two crossings there is a leaning rock which makes a good shelter in bad weather, or a point where food could be cached. Another campsite will be found at the forks, complete with chimney and fireplace.

McDougall Branch is the branch coming in from the north-west and the west branch, Austral Creek, should be crossed and the McDougall Branch followed up its south-west or true-right bank. Try and follow the remains of the track closely to find blazes marking a sharp descent into the stream, which is crossed through some big boulders half an hour later. The route can be picked up on the other side and climbs rather high through fern, then sidles for a time before descending once again into the stream. If the blazes marking the crossing cannot be found, carry on up the true-right until the valley sides steepen and progress becomes slow. Pick a crossing to the other bank to find easy travel on terraces above the river.

From here well defined deer tracks can be followed to the head of the valley. Park-like clearings near the head provide good campsites. Above the flats the bush closes in again and is mossy underfoot and slow going.

The tops are accessible from the clearings in several directions. The top of the head of the valley gives access to Wapiti River and through a cleft to the south it is straightforward to follow deer trails into Canyon Creek, which runs into Wapiti River just behind the Hankinson Hut. This route is described in the Wapiti and Edith Rivers section and starts up the true-right of the side creek coming down from the pass, 15 minutes up stream of the top flats.

*Times:* *Lake Te Anau to Austral-McDougal Branch, 2-3 hrs; Lake to flats near head of valley, 6-9 hrs; Top flats to Hankinson Hut, 1 day.*

## MID BURN AND LOCH BURN

To reach the Mid Burn from the mouth of the Lugar Burn follow up the Lugar Burn as described above to the Mid Burn turn-off. From here the route goes almost straight up through the bluffs on a well defined deer trail. Once through the bluffs the route bears off to the left, towards the lake, for about 400 metres then goes almost straight up again through a steep gully.

At the head of this gully a bush saddle connects with the head of Tertiary Creek. A clearing at the head of Tertiary Creek should be used as a campsite and a short, easy climb to the south-west takes one into the Mid Burn. Mid Burn country is very easy by Fiordland standards and here will be found a great area of good tops. From the head basin of the Mid Burn a low saddle to the west leads over into the Loch Burn, which drains into the Middle Fiord of Te Anau.


The brook and road
Were fellow-travellers in this gloomy strait,
And with them did we journey several hours
At a slow pace. The immeasurable height
Of woods decaying, never to be decayed,
The stationary blasts of waterfalls,
And in the narrow rent at every turn
Winds thwarting winds, bewildered and forlorn,
The torrents shooting from the clear blue sky,
The rocks that muttered close upon our ears,
Black drizzling crags that spake by the way-side
As if a voice were in them, the sick sight
And giddy prospect of the raving stream,
The unfettered clouds and region of the Heavens,
Tumult and peace, the darkness and the light—
Were all like workings of one mind, the features
Of the same face, blossoms upon one tree;
Characters of the great Apocalypse,
The types and symbols of Eternity,
Of first, and last, and midst, and without end.

–*The Prelude: Book Sixth*, WILLIAM WORDSWORTH

# George Sound Track

This track is not as popular as the other "tourist tracks" in Fiordland owing to its remoteness. Nonetheless, it offers spectacular scenery and is rich in history.

## LAKE TE ANAU TO LAKE HANKINSON

From the head of the North-west Arm of Lake Te Anau, a well-defined track runs through the bush from the west end of the beach for about 500 metres to Lake Hankinson where two dinghies are provided to negotiate this five kilometres stretch of water. The dinghies are available on a first-come, first-served basis. Proper respect for the dinghies is essential and, in particular, attention should always be given to tying them up WELL CLEAR of the water after use. Life jackets should be worn by each member of the party as the lake can become rough. A small outboard motor on the dinghy is a very useful time and struggle saver. There is no track round the lake. Currently a motor boat on the lake can be chartered as an alternative.

At the head of Lake Hankinson the boat should be tied up on the beach about 100 metres east of the river where the short track to the hut is marked. In wet weather both the lake and the river may rise a metre, or more overnight, which should be borne in mind when mooring the boat. During severe floods in 1984 the hut itself had water through it. Hankinson Hut contains platform bunks and can accommodate a party of 20 if necessary.

## HANKINSON HUT TO LAKE THOMSON

To continue to Lake Thomson, cross the river on a three-wire bridge about 300 metres above the hut or, if conditions permit, by wading the nearby rapids. The marked track is well defined and follows the river for about three kilometres and then crosses back to the north bank by a three-wire bridge just below the subterranean outlet from Lake Thomson. Carry on up the true-right, instead of crossing, to reach the Lake Thomson boatshed where there is a battered but serviceable dinghy.

From the bridge a well marked track leads round the north side of the lake and onwards to the Thomson Hut. The section of track just above the lake outlet wends through boulders and can be treacherous in wet weather. What appears to be a promising shortcut out onto the flats above the lake is both muddy and unpleasant. A kilometre above the lake the river passes through a narrow gorge where a swing bridge gives a fine view of the waterfall in the Wapiti River crashing into the gorge to pass 10 metres or more below the bridge. The eight bunk Thomson Hut is situated about 80 metres east of the bridge behind trees at the top of the bare rock slope and is not difficult to locate.

## THOMSON HUT TO HENRY SADDLE

A day of ten hours, perhaps more, should be allowed for the journey from Thomson Hut to George Sound Hut and torches may well be needed for the final stage. From the bridge the marked and well defined track leads along the almost flat spur between the Wapiti River and the Rugged Burn and after 1 $\frac{1}{2}$ kilometres a steep climb of about 100 metres is encountered with a waterfall, on the left, indicating that the track is now following up the north bank of the Rugged Burn. After this climb the track is still well defined and is mainly flat to Deadwood Lagoon, although there are some short climbs and some of the level stretches are very wet. Three red markers on a tree, shortly after the last of the climbs, indicate the point to turn hard right up a ridge if one is interested in visiting the site of an old (1896) open-cast mica mine. This track is described below.

Continuing towards Henry Saddle from these markers, there are no climbs until after Deadwood Lagoon and the track is very muddy. Cross the stream at the top of Deadwood Lagoon and continue over the peaty swamp in much the same direction as before, but moving gradually away from the Rugged Burn. There is a natural line to take and blazes will be found where blazes are possible.

Henry Saddle looking west. The tent is on one of the few sites on the pass that are both dry and flat. The steep descent to Katherine Stream starts beyond the tarn.

Henry Saddle and the Rugged Burn. (G) George Sound, (H) Henry Saddle, (R) Rugged Burn, (T) Lake Thomson, (W) Lake Wade.
*Photo: DOSLI.*

Within about 200 metres the boggy track becomes unmistakable and shortly begins the steepish climb to Henry Saddle.

When nearing the saddle the track breaks from the bush occasionally but there should be no difficulty in locating it again after the brief clearings. In a flat clearing before the last patch of bush beside a small cataract is a group of rocks known by the pretentious title of "Hotel Henry". As it offers only meagre, damp shelter it is not recommended. Although this area is well marked it is advisable to note the points of leaving the bush and re-entry for the return journey.

There are two tarns on Henry Saddle but the only non-boggy campsite, just before the first tarn, is poor. The tarns are passed on the north side and shortly small stone cairns will be found. It is advisable to study the lie of the land for a return trip before leaving the saddle. Because of the precipitous terrain a little further down, it would be unwise to attempt to continue beyond the saddle in fog. Look for the track about 50 metres up to the right from the outlet of the tarn.

## HENRY SADDLE TO LAKE KATHERINE

Looking down from the Henry Saddle, a narrow cleft to the left may be seen where scrub and bush meet and the sudden drop to the valley begins. This point is reached by following cairns and markers on the ridge which leads down and swings left across the top of the sudden drop as it nears the cleft. When near the cleft, scrub is encountered. The track crosses a stream in the cleft and begins to descend under the overhanging rock which is the prominent part of the cleft. From here to the valley floor the marked track is followed as it winds under bluffs and down steep faces.

As the track flattens out into the valley floor it meets the main stream and follows it down on the true-left. A track sign here marks the turn-off for the return trip. The stream has a gravel bed and it is easier to walk there than struggle along its rather swampy banks. Markers lead to the true-right bank just before the stream begins to drop away again. The track now leads round to sidle down a spur until it once more reaches a flat section. Eventually it swings hard left after crossing a small side stream which flows from left to right. The river now turns away to the left a little and cascades steeply. In leading down the slope, which is now encountered, the track twists past an overhanging rock which would serve as shelter if required. As the track levels out it meets the main stream again and there is a good view of the cascade from the riverbed.

## LAKE KATHERINE

Lake Katherine is not far distant. Cross the river at the sign, 50 metres down, or if the river is high on one of the fallen trees which span it further down stream. There is quite a large swampy area at the top of Lake Katherine. To avoid this the track heads across the valley to its far edge before heading towards the lake. It then skirts the southern shore, generally about five metres above it. Under normal conditions it will be necessary to wade the lake in one place. The white-topped rock against the bush edge at the bottom end of the bay should be the next objective.

## LAKE KATHERINE TO GEORGE SOUND

A few metres past this rock a stone cairn marks the entrance to the bush, and a nearby rata carries a track sign. The well-defined, marked track from Lake Katherine to the sound is a straightforward 1-1 $\frac{1}{2}$ hour journey in daylight. Near the sound there is a three-wire bridge spanning the river, but it is often possible to cross the river without using it.

The George Sound Hut will be found ten minutes after the crossing, close to the beach where it has been moved to after the Katherine Stream spread its banks. It has platform bunks and can accommodate ten people. There is a dinghy at the sound and good fishing can also be had off the rocks at various places. Mussels may be gathered at low tide. A fine waterfall cascades into the sound from Lake Alice and with care this may be reached on foot by picking up the marked route at the north-east end of the bay. Further notes are given in the Wapiti River and Edith River section.

*Times: North Arm of Lake Te Anau to Hankinson Hut, 2 $\frac{1}{2}$-3 $\frac{1}{2}$ hrs; Hankinson Hut to Lake Thomson, 1 hr; Lake Thomson outlet to Thomson Hut, 1 $\frac{1}{2}$ hrs; Thomson Hut to Henry Saddle, 4 $\frac{1}{2}$ hrs; Henry Saddle to George Sound Hut, 4 $\frac{1}{2}$ -5 $\frac{1}{2}$ hrs.*

## THOMSON RIDGE

On a fine day grand views are obtained from the shoulder of the hill behind Thomson Hut. Starting from behind the toilet, the track is generally well-marked and clearly defined. Windthrow has now obliterated some parts of the track and some care is needed in these places to find the track again. As the track climbs it leads first slightly left and then swings right and is steep at times. After 1 $\frac{1}{2}$- 2 hour's climb, the track leads out of the bush on to tussock. From here, climb about 60 metres to some tarns then sidle generally horizontally right, under a shoulder, until Lake Hankinson comes into view. Continue a short distance to lose a little height and Hankinson Hut will be visible below. Allow 2 $\frac{1}{2}$ hours to this viewpoint from Thomson Hut with light packs. Care should be taken when leaving the bush to note where the track enters for the return journey.

*Time: Thomson Hut to Thomson Ridge viewpoint, 2 $\frac{1}{2}$ hrs each way.*

## MT ELWOOD MICA MINE

The track leaves from the three markers on the Rugged Burn track to Henry Saddle described above. The track up the ridge is lightly marked to bushline. It emerges on a knoll, with a dip 100 metres ahead. Pass through the dip and ascend to the tussock beyond making generally for the right-hand skyline spur whilst climbing. There are no markers now. When nearing what has, until now, appeared to be the top of the hill, it will be logical to level out and sidle under on the eastern side. A short and more gradual climb soon mounts the main top spur leading to the open cast mine which is 100 metres short of the top ridge, which runs at right angles to the spur, and five to six metres down the eastern side. There is still mica here although of no commercial value. The view from the top of the main ridge into Rum Gully is sudden and surprising. The many views in various directions make the climb worthwhile in itself.

**Time:** *Thomson Hut to Mt Elwood Mica Mine, 3 $^1/_2$-4 hrs (2 $^1/_2$-3 $^1/_2$ hrs in reverse).*

## HENRY SADDLE TO GEORGE SOUND VIA MARGUERITE PEAKS

A good-weather route to George Sound for experienced parties traverses the Marguerite Peaks and Saddle Hill. The route from Henry Saddle is good apart from two steep gullies. These are worked across using the topographical map to assist navigation. They may be easier to travel in the reverse direction. Follow down Overlander Stream from Saddle Hill, which initially proves to be good going, but deteriorates further down. In bluffs about 120 metres above the sound it is best to traverse eastwards for about 300 metres into a gully which runs parallel to Overlander Stream. Descend the gully to the sound.

**Time:** *Henry Saddle to George Sound, allow a long day.*

## GEORGE SOUND HUT TO LAKE ALICE

After walking around the shore from the George Sound Hut to the north-east end of the bay, look for a red marker where the stony beach finishes soon after Nita Creek is crossed, about 15 minutes from the hut. The route around to Lake Alice is now overgrown and the blazes are difficult to find. It rises to about 30 metres above water. In about ten minutes a slip is encountered and crossed and the route then leads around into a ravine which it crosses on a shelf. The climb out begins immediately. Now the route is generally straight up the ravine shoulder to the top. Here markers lead off to the left and maintain roughly horizontal travel to a bare rock section where Lake Alice sometimes overflows.

Cross to enter the bush again near the top of the rock section and follow the overflow channel to where more open lake is met. Note that markers which turn left soon after the rock section indicate the route to the top of the falls. The first view of the lake reveals only an insignificant and sheltered fraction of its whole length. There is no longer a boat on the lake.

*Time:* *George Sound Hut to Edith Falls, allow 1hr.*

# Wapiti and Edith Rivers

Travel up the Wapiti River to Thomson Hut is on the George Sound Track and is described in the George Sound Track Section. Route descriptions for the Rugged Burn to Henry Saddle and Mt Elwood are also included in that section.

## UPPER WAPITI RIVER AND LAKE SUTHERLAND

The upper Wapiti River provides an excellent side trip from the George Sound Track and is also a satisfactory means of access into the Edith Valley.

Both banks initially afford easy travelling. The true-left bank of the river can be followed from the Thomson Hut for about half an hour until a series of bluffs forces an easy crossing. Alternatively this crossing can be avoided by commencing on the true-right bank and following the main George Sound Track. About ten minutes past the bridge over the Wapiti River and about 100 metres before the distinct dog-leg bend in the track, leave the track. Initially the route lies some distance from the river on easy going flats, but it converges with the river after quarter of an hour. From here onwards continue close to the bank. Rum Gully Creek, entering from the west, is crossed about an hour after rejoining the river and the impressive two kilometre long Lake Sutherland is reached an hour or so later. The west shore provides the better route to the head of the lake. There is a well used lakeside campsite ten minutes northward from the lake outlet.

To continue up the main valley of the Wapiti, continue around the head of the lake and follow the now much smaller stream at the head, on the true-right bank. The going becomes more difficult, through large moraine boulders and dense ribbonwood, but the head of the valley can be reached in about 1 $\frac{1}{2}$ hours from the lake. A high route along the ridge to Edith Saddle is possible in fine weather from its western head. The eastern head yields a high saddle to the Henderson Burn and Glaisnock River.

**Times:** *Thomson Hut to Rum Gully Creek, 1 $\frac{3}{4}$ hrs; Rum Gully Creek to Lake Sutherland, 1 hr; Head of Lake Sutherland to valley head, 1 $\frac{1}{2}$ hrs; Western valley head to ridge crest, 2 hrs; Ridge crest to Edith Saddle, 2 $\frac{1}{2}$ hrs.*

## WAPITI RIVER TO EDITH VALLEY VIA MASSACRE GULLY AND WAPITI-EDITH SADDLE

The stream entering the head of Lake Sutherland from the west, known as Massacre Gully, gives good access to the Edith Valley over a low open saddle. Prominent deer trails lead through easy bush on the true-left of this stream until the valley turns abruptly to the north-east. Ford the stream here and climb

Stuart Mountains. (C) Canyon Creek, (H) Lake Hankinson, (L) Lugar Burn, (S) Lake Sutherland, (W) Wapiti River. *Photo: V.C. Browne.*

steeply through bush and clearings, avoiding the leatherwood as much as possible, to the pass.

Do not attempt a direct descent down a scrubby gut into the Edith tributary, but climb and sidle northwards first. The valley below is slightly mossy underfoot and the best going seems to be in the creekbed itself, or a little distance away from it. In about two hours from the pass the mouth of "Impassable Gorge" is gained. Stay in the streambed initially until it becomes a steep cataract. An obvious, narrow and diagonal crack on the true-right then provides an escape on to steep-sloping benches above the gorge. Continue a steep descent on a series of these benches, always keeping the stream within hearing distance. The main floor of the Edith Valley can be reached in about an hour from the gorge and it then takes about 2-2 ½ hours of easy travel down to the head of Lake Alice, or three to four hours up stream to the spacious bivvy rock at the head of the valley described in the Edith Valley Section.

## RUM GULLY

Rum Gully can be traversed to the head and return quite comfortably in half a day from the Wapiti River. Moraine deposits cover the floor of this valley, but no difficulty will be encountered in picking out a good deer trail. At the head of Rum Gully there is a large tarn which dries up at times. From the south-west saddle at the head of the valley a crossing can be made to the Edith Valley down a tributary which is not generally noticed from the Edith itself. This involves a bush scramble of about three hours down from the saddle, first on the east side of the tributary and then on the left side, down water chutes near the bottom, emerging about half an hour above Lake Alice.

*Times: Wapiti River to head of Rum Gully and back, ¹/₂ day; Saddle at head of Rum Gully to Edith River, 3 hrs.*

## BARRIER VALLEY AND LAKE CLARKE

Beach the Lake Thomson dinghy on the true-left of the waterfall of the stream coming out of the Barrier Valley, about midway down the lake. A short steep climb of about 40 metres for ten minutes through thick regeneration on old slips leads to gentler slopes and emerges about an hour later onto a pleasant meandering streambed. An hour later another step in the valley is climbed and finally a rocky moraine bank is crossed revealing the idyllic Lake Clarke. The eastern side of the lake provides the only access to the Barrier Peaks at the head of the valley.

*Time: Lake Thomson to Lake Clarke, 2-2 ¹/₂ hrs.*

121

## CANYON CREEK TO LUGAR BURN

Canyon Creek flows into the Wapiti River ten minutes up stream of Hankinson Hut and consists of three hanging valleys. Apart from where the creek drops the last 300 metres, or so, into the Wapiti River through a steep, narrow and impassable gorge, the river offers on the whole open and pleasant travel.

Travel up the Wapiti River from Hankinson Hut until Canyon Creek is reached. Follow up the creek until it becomes markedly steeper and then skirt around the bottom of the hillside to the left. About 40 metres from the creekbed, on the true-right, a lone red track marker may be found at the lower end of a fern clearing on the hillside. Climb up through the clearing to find deer trails which are then followed to a terrace 1 to 1 1/2 hours later. Care should be taken not to veer too far to the left. The sound of the creek should be kept in hearing all the way to this flat, although the river itself lies a long way below in the gorge. From here follow a poorly marked trail leading round into Canyon Creek for 40 minutes. Look for a track marker where the track suddenly descends through the bluffs steeply down to the valley floor, just up stream of the gorge.

In reverse, look for red permalat markers soon after leaving a boggy open flat on the true-right, just before the gorge begins. Alternatively, climb up the overgrown shingle fan on the true-right, about 120 metres up stream of where the gorge starts, to find a steep wapiti trail climbing steeply up through the bluffs. Continue climbing until a bench is reached high above the creek. This bench is then followed at more or less the same height until the route obviously starts to descend.

Above this first gorge the river here runs through the lowest hanging valley and is followed up for three to four hours to a point where it forks. The western branch leads on for about two kilometres over rocky, trackless terrain to an open basin, where, high up on the left, lies a pass overlooking Lake Sutherland and the headwaters of Wapiti River. The ridge from the pass can be followed along the tops to the north until overlooking the Henderson Burn.

Half an hour up stream of the forks, the northern branch seems cut-off by a bare rock bluff. Here the creek flows down a steep cataract and a good deer trail will be found to climb precipitously on the true-left, close to the creek. Near the head of this valley at S130 634694 an easy pass above an alpine meadow leads on to the faces overlooking the north-west, McDougall, branch of the Lugar Burn. This pass also gives easy access round to the right to the eastern tops overlooking Canyon Creek and, on the other side, the headwaters of the Austral branch of the Lugar Burn.

To reach the Lugar Burn descend the dried-up creek leading down from the pass, which forms a natural staircase. Upon reaching the hanging basin halfway

The upper reaches of Canyon Creek. The creek later drops some 300 metres through a steep gorge to enter the Wapiti River. This photo was taken 100 metres below the pass into the upper Lugar Burn.

down, climb out of the creekbed and work down through scrubby bush on the true-left bank to emerge 20 minutes above the top flats in the Lugar Burn.

**Times:** *Hankinson Hut to top of gorge, 1 ¹/₂ hrs; Hankinson Hut to Lugar Burn Flats, 8-10 hrs.*

## CANYON CREEK TO NORTH-WEST ARM OF LAKE TE ANAU

A route for parties with mountaineering experience leads from the Austral Creek-Canyon Creek saddle, easily accessible from Canyon Creek. From the saddle, climb the ridge to Peak 5370 ft then descend and sidle through steep rock and possibly snow towards Smith Peak. Initially keep high to avoid an impassable canyon. A snowgrass bench at about 1200 metres offers a route around a bluffed spur from where a short, steep sidle gives access to a saddle north-east of Smith Peak. From this saddle the going is relatively easy to a large tarn and into the head basin of an unnamed creek draining into the head of North-West Arm of Lake Te Anau.

The route into a boggy flat of this head basin is on the true-right of cascades and waterfalls below the bush edge. A good deer trail can be found here on the true-left and eventually it sidles and climbs away from the creek to a ridge. The trail continues to a stunted beech and shrub covered knoll, below which the going to the lake through taller forest is bluffy. The trails are harder to find in this section. A better route may exist from the north-west side of the knoll.

From Hankinson Hut a more direct route could be found to Peak 5370 ft by the ridge above the Canyon Creek gorge by climbing up the true-left of the gorge.

**Times:** *Canyon Creek floor to Peak 5370 ft, 2 ¹/₂ hrs; Peak 5370 ft to tarn, 1 ¹/₂ hrs; Tarn to North-West Arm, 4-5 hrs.*

## EDITH VALLEY FROM LAKE ALICE

Near the top end of Lake Alice, a bush-covered promontory extends about halfway across the lake's width. Beyond, and immediately in line with the tip of the promontory, the Edith River enters. In normal conditions the true-right bank near the mouth is the most suitable landing. This locality is subject to flooding. Even the well-established campsite, five minutes up stream on the true-left bank, is submerged at times.

From the campsite continue up the south bank for 20 minutes, then cross over to the north bank where the river broadens out and cross back again where the valley narrows into a gorge just below the point where there is a difficult rock section. From here on the south bank provides the best going.

About 2 ½ hours up stream from Lake Alice a steep tributary enters from the south (see earlier). This is crossed at its junction with Edith River. Immediately afterwards progress becomes difficult for a short time as other steep streamlets on smooth rocks are encountered. Proceed very carefully here. The route improves and there are normally no other problems until a point about seven hours from Lake Alice is reached. Here the valley floor is cluttered with monstrous rocks from an old slip. At this point blazes are found near the river and, in two or three minutes, a magnificent rock shelter is reached where there is comfortable room for four or five persons and a fire, although firewood here is very scarce. This rock can be difficult to find and lies about 30 metres from the river in a grove of fuchsia.

Care is required to continue up stream over the vegetation covered rocks. Shortly the river is found to be broadened into a small lake and soon after this progress improves again. Now the valley swings steadily around to the right until it is running in almost the opposite direction. The route now crosses to the true-right and sidles gradually up through scrubby bush and clearings to the Edith Saddle.

There is a campsite between two stunted beech trees a few metres before reaching the saddle. However, this site is rather exposed to nor'-west weather. It is described further in the Glaisnock and Pitt River section. The Midnight Creek side of the saddle is swampy for about half an hour, but a good site will be found at The Forks, the junction of Midnight Creek and Glaisnock River, about one hour below the saddle. The Glaisnock Rock Bivvy is about 15 minutes further down the right bank.

**Times:** *Head of Lake Alice to Edith Rock Bivvy, 7 hrs; Bivvy to Edith Saddle, 2 hrs.*

# George River and Approaches

There are three regularly used access routes to the George River: (1) From the Glaisnock River via the George-Pitt Saddle, gained either by traversing Oilskin Pass from the Glaisnock, or by the more frequently used Edith-Pitt Saddle; (2) The less commonly used Edith-George saddle; and (3) By boat or float-plane to the sandy beach in Anchorage Cove, George Sound. The close proximity of the head waters of these four valley systems ensures exhilarating and relatively easy travel in fine weather.

The passes in this vicinity are not well labelled on the topographical maps and are:

Edith Saddle, between Midnight Creek at the head of the Glaisnock and the head of the Edith River;

Oilskin Pass, between the head of the Glaisnock and the head of the Pitt River;

Edith- Pitt Saddle, between the lake below Oilskin Pass in the Glaisnock and the Edith River;

Edith-George Saddle, between the head of the George River and the Edith River;

Upper George-Pitt Saddle, between the head of the George River and the head of the Pitt River;

George-Pitt Saddle, between the George River and the south shore of Lake Beddoes.

Edith Saddle, Edith-Pitt Saddle and Oilskin Pass are described in the Glaisnock Valley and Pitt River section. It is convenient for the routes described in this section to radiate from Swamp Clearing at the confluence of the Fourth Tributary of the George River. This spacious flat is an excellent location for a base camp.

## SWAMP CLEARING TO GEORGE-PITT SADDLE AND UPPER GEORGE-PITT SADDLE

Leaving Swamp Clearing, a small gorge is encountered just above the confluence of the fourth Tributary of the George River. It presents no problems and can be sidled low on either side. Above this the travel for the next 300 metres is reasonably good in the riverbed.

Probably the best route onto the tops above Lake Beddoes and the George-Pitt Saddle is up an old, clear 20 metre wide avalanche corridor that runs up a small creek about 50 minutes up from Swamp Clearing. It is probably easier to climb the first 150 metres in the bush on the true-left and sidle onto the avalanche

126

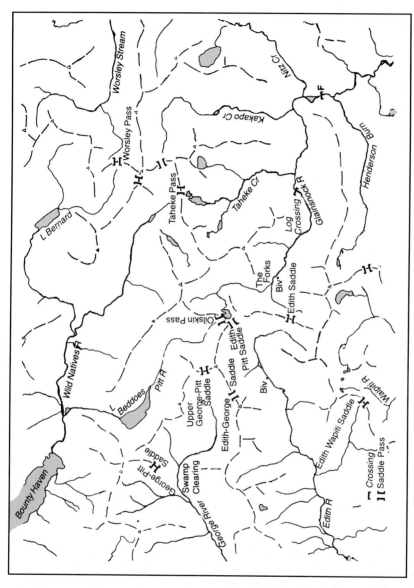

Passes and Saddles in the Wapiti Area

Head of the George River—a wapiti hunter on the tops overlooking the head of the George River. The Edith-George tops lie beyond.
*Photo: Rob Suisted.*

chute. This then provides an easy walk up on gentle open moss and grass covered slopes to the height of 850 metres. From here sidle an easy 250 metres to the left before climbing up through tussock fingers to the open tussock and obvious low point 150 metres above. The descent to the south shore of Lake Beddoes is described in reverse in the Glaisnock Valley and Pitt River section.

Continuing up the George River from the creek mentioned above it is better to travel in the open bush near to the river to the two major slips 1 ½ hours above Swamp Clearing. The best trails and least windfall is on the true-right. Upon reaching the slips it is recommended to travel on the true-left, swapping between bush and river. There are numerous small campsites near to the river in this section. It is relatively simple, but steep to climb out of the head of the George by picking a route up through the bluffs from below.

## EDITH RIVER TO SWAMP CLEARING VIA EDITH-GEORGE SADDLE

The Edith-George Saddle can be gained from the valley floor of the Edith. There are two routes, both starting at the lagoon ten minutes above the large Edith Bivvy Rock described in the Wapiti and Edith Rivers section. One route climbs directly up from the lagoon well to the east of the sizeable tributary coming from the head basin below the saddle and then veers to the left when the gently sloping bottom of this small hanging valley is reached. The bushline can be reached in about 40 minutes from the valley floor.

Alternatively, from the lagoon sidle up leftwards on to an obvious scrubby ledge. A minor deer trail leads along this steep ridge into the hanging basin and above the bushline to just below the saddle. The descent into the George is steep, direct and obvious, and the valley floor can be reached in less than an hour from the saddle. There are a few reasonable camp sites here. From the valley floor wide and obvious deer trails, mainly on the true-left bank, lead through mossy pepperwood to Swamp Clearing in about 2 $\frac{1}{2}$ hours.

## SWAMP CLEARING TO ANCHORAGE COVE

The old track from Swamp Clearing to Anchorage Cove mentioned in previous editions of this guide no longer exists. Furthermore, the deer trails are rather faint and diffuse. The route is essentially on the true-left although from time to time the travel on the other bank is easier. The gorges are all taken on the true-left.

For the first ten minutes the going is deceptively easy through open beech forest, but it rapidly becomes more constricted as it enters the top gorge. This gorge makes up the bulk of the travel between Swamp Clearing to Third Tributary and is straightforward. Sidle off the river and along at the same height for perhaps 400 metres before angling down when the river becomes quieter to emerge out onto the flats above Third Tributary.

Carry on, keeping close to the riverbed, to the middle gorge. This is again straightforward with an obvious trail that climbs slightly just after the Second Tributary and sidles before angling down and entering the riverbed 20 metres from the chasm and taking perhaps 15 minutes.

The middle gorge can normally be passed in half an hour, but below it many slips and windthrows slow the progress significantly. Struggle through these within earshot of the river. An hour or more later the bottom gorge is encountered. When descending down valley the start of the gorge is obvious. Enter the bush here and sidle along obvious benches approximately 15-30 metres above the river until an open, moss-covered waterfall gully is reached. Cross this and slowly descend to the river which enters perhaps 150 metres down from the gorge chasm proper. Travel up river involves angling up some 60 metres initially to allow for the drop of the river before sidling.

Below the gorge the valley soon widens out again and the travel is again enjoyable for an hour, or so until the tidal limit of the river is encountered, about 20 minutes below the junction with Trophy Burn on the opposite bank.

Again the route is impeded with thick pepperwood, many windfalls and only faint trails and Anchorage Cove is a welcome sight half an hour down from the tidal limit. Much of the travelling, especially in the lower reaches, is easier in the river.

*Time: Swamp Clearing to Anchorage Cove, 6 hrs.*

## TROPHY BURN TO HARRISON SADDLE

Deer trails give access up Trophy Burn starting on the true-left bank and after 45 minutes a small tributary on the same side is crossed. This tributary drains a small basin with very steep country in its head. It would require seven hours of difficult travelling up this side creek to reach the ridge overlooking Harrison Saddle, a further two hours below. The true-left bank of the Trophy Burn continues to give the better travel for a further two hours until a large rock face, covered at its base with ribbonwood, will be noticed on the opposite bank. Cross here to the true-right and continue for 1 $\frac{1}{2}$ hours until a gorge and waterfall force a crossing back to the true-left bank. A small level clearing at the top of the gorge is reached after half an hour. From here either bank provides reasonable going until the scrub covered Harrison Saddle, containing a large tarn, is reached. This saddle gives access to the limited tussock country in the area and to the west a 200 metre climb provides easy access to the Catseye Saddle. Keep to the true-right side.

*Time: George River to Harrison Saddle, 5 $\frac{1}{2}$-6 $\frac{1}{2}$ hrs.*

## SECOND TRIBUTARY

The Second Tributary enters the spectacular middle gorge by a steep cataract and the George River has to be crossed either above or below this gorge. The tributary offers rough going on either bank through dense bush and moraine boulders. A sizeable unnamed lake is reached in 2 $\frac{1}{2}$ hours from the river. From the head of the lake the left branch continues through thick scrub and above bushline an experienced party can find a route through steep bluffs giving access to McDonald Creek and a branch of Trophy Burn.

## THIRD TRIBUTARY

The Third Tributary meets the George half an hour below Swamp Clearing and provides relatively straightforward access to a large cirque with copious ribbonwood at its base. A route up through the bluffs will yield access to the ridge above McDonald Creek, but it is not possible to descend from here.

The saddle between McDonald Creek on the left and the Fourth Tributary of the George River on the right. Bligh sound lies in the distance.
*Photo: Rob Suisted.*

## FOURTH TRIBUTARY

The Fourth Tributary, the most accessible of all, enters the George just above Swamp Clearing. The best travel is on the true-right up to the first side creek before using the opposite bank for 200 metres. From here most of the best travel is in the riverbed before climbing long tussock fingers with good deer trails on the true-right to access the rocky head basin and a broad saddle just above bushline into McDonald Creek. The broad gentle ridge top provides exhilarating travel in a south westerly direction towards the head of the Third Tributary and in a north-easterly direction to Overhead Cone and the George-Pitt Saddle.

## HEAD OF STINA BURN TO HARRISON SADDLE

The ridge from the Stina Burn to Bare Cone is easy going except for the side of Bare Cone facing the Stina Burn where there are steep leatherwood guts. The ridge from Bare Cone along to Woodcutters Peak is also easy going. This ridge track is also known as Tinsleys Highway.

From Woodcutters Peak a steep wapiti trail drops down about 500 metres to a wide saddle between the Catseye and McDonald Creeks. Continue up the ridge

131

and along the open tops between the Catseye and McDonald Creeks to come out overlooking Harrison Saddle at the head of Trophy Burn. From here cut around to the true Catseye Saddle.

The route to Catseye Saddle is also fairly easy except for a section of hillside coming up the ridge from the wide saddle mentioned above which is covered in huge boulders and where it is possible to walk underground in places. At the Catseye Saddle it is important to use the true-right coming down to Harrison Saddle as the other side has thick leatherwood and no wapiti trails.

### MCDONALD CREEK

On the other side of Harrison Saddle lies a clear swampy tributary of McDonald Creek. To descend into the valley proper, move over to the right at the end of the clearing and continue the descent until limited views are obtained of the valley floor. There is no defined route, but small bush-covered bluffs can be negotiated by sidling back and forth, but keep well clear of the outlet of the waterfall from the saddle. Once on the valley floor, which offers flat and pleasant travelling, a tributary entering from the right, opposite a big slip, gives difficult access to a saddle with the Fourth Tributary of the George. From the junction of this tributary continue on the true-left bank for two hours then cross back to the true-right for the final hour to Bligh Sound. There are excellent sites at the sound for a base camp.

*Time:* *Harrison Saddle to Bligh Sound, 5 hrs.*

# Whitewater River

The Whitewater is a well-spread valley, with two major tributaries on each side contributing to a large catchment area. All of these tributaries can be negotiated to passes of varying difficulty at their heads.

At low tide a large area of tidal flats is exposed at the mouth and parties may be tempted to camp on the bush flat adjacent to the deep water of the sound. For those parties prepared to carry their gear a kilometre, or alternatively those with a small dinghy, there is an excellent rock bivvy well into the bay on the south side of the mouth. From the sound a bluff can be seen dropping to the shore here with a narrow flat strip of bush at its foot. The overhanging section of this bluff forms the bivvy which provides a spacious campsite complete with a rivulet of fresh water emerging from the base of the rock.

## GEORGE SOUND TO TOP FORKS

Access up the Whitewater Valley from George Sound is by the south bank. At low tide the bush flats 200 metres away can be easily reached, but some wading is necessary at high tide although the campsite itself appears completely safe from flooding. Once the bush flat is reached, cut across to the Whitewater on the north side of the valley. A low tide is helpful for the first kilometre or more but, if the tide is in, good going can be found in the bush close to the river.

There are three short climbs in the first hour with deer trails leading over each of them. The river then flattens out for a time and, if low, can be crossed in several places. Stay on the true-right as gorges further up stream are impassable on the true-left. After about 1-1 $\frac{1}{2}$ hours from the campsite a waterfall of ten metres, or more is reached. A trail leads up onto the shoulder of this fall and from here on the going again depends on the river level. If low it is better to travel up the riverbed for 15 minutes, but the going in the bush is quite good if this is not possible. A further half an hour brings one to the second gorge which is passed close to the river on the true-right. The valley then opens out to a large bush flat studded with swampy clearings. At this point there is little to choose between a short cut through the flats, or a somewhat drier, but longer trip following the riverbank. The first major tributary enters from the north shortly above the gorge and parties intending to visit this tributary should therefore follow the main river from the gorge.

From the junction of the First Tributary the main valley floor remains level for 1-1 $\frac{1}{2}$ hours until it gradually begins to close in. The going in the bush is good, but when the river is low, fast travelling can be made by keeping to the riverbed, crossing where necessary. Where leading spurs from both sides of the valley meet, the river becomes more confined and the Second Tributary enters from the south-east by way of a gentle watercourse. A good campsite can be found 50 metres away in the bush on the true-right side, about 50 metres up stream of a huge pool.

Continuing up the main valley of the Whitewater River, the Second Tributary is crossed just above its confluence. From here the valley begins to rise steadily, but the travelling is good for 15-20 minutes until the top forks are reached. From here the river branches into two tributaries of equal size, one of which runs to the north-west, the other to the south-east. These will henceforth be referred to as the West and East Branches.

## FIRST TRIBUTARY

The First Tributary rises steadily for approximately two hours and is negotiable on either side. It forks near its head and the westerly branch leads to a low bush saddle overlooking an unnamed bay on the coast. From this saddle the snowgrass tops above are easily reached. A leading spur above the gorge in the main river, starting below the confluence with the first tributary, provides good access to the eastern end of these tops. Travel on the south face of the tops to those above the Tasman Sea is quite good and takes four hours to do the length of them with a pack.

## SECOND TRIBUTARY

Access up the Second Tributary can be had by either bank although the true-right is initially best until past the small faces. After a few climbs around small falls, the valley levels out until near its head. This tributary runs east-west and at its head, on the south side, a difficult saddle can be reached by climbing a large steep slip. This saddle drops into a hanging basin just below grass level which in turn drops steeply to the head of the south-west arm of George Sound. This would be a difficult trip as both sides of the saddle are very steep. It is also difficult to gain the tops east, or west of this saddle as steep bluffs at both ends deny easy access.

*Time: Camp at the large pool to saddle, 6 hrs.*

## WEST BRANCH

To travel into the West Branch, cross the East Branch 100 metres above the junction. From here the going is good to the head of the West Branch, which can be crossed at will after the first half hour, with either side negotiable. Two hours from the forks a mid-level bush saddle on the western slopes connects into a hanging basin with a small lake which drains steeply down to Looking Glass Bay on the coast. A steep climb to another saddle near the head of the

134

west branch may also provide access to Looking Glass Bay. The second saddle mentioned provides good access on to the tops.

***Time:*** *Forks to head of West Branch, 3 ¹/₂-4 ¹/₂ hrs.*

## EAST BRANCH

To travel into the East Branch, cross at the same place 100 metres above the forks and proceed up the true-left bank. At this point bluffs on the true-right bank are encountered. After 30-40 minutes up the true-left bank a tributary enters from the west. This drains a hanging basin from which a steep rock slide provides access to the snowgrass. Access into the basin itself can be difficult as the stream gorges and side creeks can be confusing. It is better to climb for a while then sidle into the basin on the true-right.

Above this tributary good travelling continues up the East Branch for 30 minutes until the river begins to gorge. Access can be had on either side. On the true-left, stay high above and away from the gorge for the next half hour. The going then levels out somewhat before suddenly steepening again. Deer trails can be followed and a little scrambling is required for the climb of 10-15 minutes. Eventually the trail emerges onto a shoulder in the bush at the top of the waterfall and a large lake is suddenly reached. To avoid the steep and frustrating vegetation and side creeks on the latter part of this route, it is better to cross to the true-right when the going steepens about half way to the lake. Cross back to the true-left of the stream as it drains from the lake.

The southern shore of the lake is the only one which can be traversed. There are now no useable deer trails and the area is very overgrown and full of logfalls. Travel is better near the water's edge and is frustrating.

At the head of the valley, beyond the lake, lies a saddle with Madmans Creek, a tributary of the Stillwater. From the top of the lake there is easy going through the bush as it rises steadily until the final steep climb to the saddle. This should be reached in two hours, or about five hours from the campsite by the pool in the second tributary of the Whitewater. There is an excellent, but difficult to find deer trail on the northern edge of the saddle which is worth finding to avoid the leatherwood which makes for a difficult final haul. This saddle is just on bush-level with areas of snowgrass and scrub, and numerous tarns. To the north, access is possible on to Expedition Peak and to the south a steep climb leads onto Spot Hill. From Expedition Peak it is possible to travel a further day eastward along the tops to the Ethne Saddle and the head of the south-east arm of George Sound, making a good round trip for an experienced party.

Expedition Peak can also be reached from the main valley by climbing the steep spur on to the long leading ridge to the summit. This spur rises from the forks of the Whitewater and is very steep in places.

# Stillwater Valley

## GEORGE SOUND TO CASWELL SOUND VIA OVERLANDER RIDGE AND STILLWATER VALLEY

A daylight start for this journey is desirable, and preferably an hour before low tide. Overlander Ridge is the last ridge before the South-West Arm of George Sound. It drops sharply to an unnamed island which appears from the beach below the George Sound Hut to be joined to the mainland. The bush-clad Overlander Stream itself is negotiable to its saddle but, although more direct than the ridge, is less scenic.

Cross Katherine Stream and continue along the shore on, or near the rocks wherever possible. Do not climb too high at the impasses and keep a watch for red markers which begin at the shore in these places. Shortly before the Overlander Stream climb to about 50 metres, but there are markers to be followed.

Cross the Overlander Stream near its mouth and follow around the shore of the bay to the corner behind the short peninsula where there is a small, narrow gully. After leaving the scrub at the next bay, head around the bay to a tidal gully which leads to an area which may need to be waded amongst a few large rocks. On some large rocks, 30-40 metres on from the gully, turn into the bush at a red marker where some flax bushes have been chopped away. If the tide is unfavourable it is possible to join this track by scrambling for about 400 metres through bush and rocks from the bay.

From here the route is lightly marked and climbs diagonally for a time through large boulders. It then heads rather horizontally through a slip, about 60 metres above the water, amongst the improbable looking bluffs. Almost straight after passing a small rock gut the route climbs sharply at a point where packs may need to be passed. The bluffs are left behind now and the climb gradually lessens as the markers lead to the crest of the spur. From the hut to here takes about two hours.

The marked route up the spur is easily followed. Early in the climb an occasional old blaze indicates a slight veering to the left. After a steep section the route swings left onto a flattish shoulder. From here the route undulates southwards along the shoulder, occasionally passing through swamp, until it strikes rising ground again and climbs steadily. Eventually, after some twisting and turning, red markers swing right and somewhat uphill from a flattish section. The route is now found to be sidling onto another spur and, after a time, swings sharply left to climb steeply to the crest at 500 metres. From the hut to the crest takes five to six hours. The return journey from the hut to here takes about three hours.

The ridge is now flatter and in general the crest is followed to the top of the hill, except for an occasional divergence, usually to the left, for 50-100 metres to avoid steep sections. Normally the only place where water is obtainable on the ridge is about two-thirds way to the summit. As the bush thins out five, or six false summits are climbed until the true summit is reached. The trip to here is a worthwhile return day trip from the hut with light packs.

*Times: Hut to crest with view, 5-6 hrs, plus 3 hrs return to hut; Hut to summit, 7-8 hrs, 4-5 hrs in reverse.*

## OVERLANDER SUMMIT TO STILLWATER VALLEY

Markers are scarce after the summit into the Stillwater Valley making it a follow-your-nose route.

Head south-east, passing a small tarn on its right, and follow along a tussock tongue until bush, at the edge of a steep place, is met. Descend a deer trail which winds about 10 metres down a short, steep piece of tussock to a small mossy basin then head along the right edge of the mossy basin and pick up blazes. If tussock clearings lead to a sharp drop, head right to avoid even steeper country and follow down a scrubby track.

For a time the route follows the crest of a rocky, almost razor ridge and after a while the land on the left is noticed to be about the same height as the ground being covered. Swing hard left here, for 100 metres or more, to avoid being cut off by a steep-sided rock gully. Now follow down a rock spur which is fairly bare for a short time. Below and to the left can now be seen a basin in the bush where there is a good campsite at about 550 metres. When nearing the campsite it may be best to swing hard left from the blazed route to avoid missing the site. The saddle to the Overlander Stream now lies 30 metres above and roughly a scrubby kilometre to the north-east.

The route now follows down from the campsite in or close to the stream and eventually crosses to the true-left bank about ten metres before the stream becomes a waterfall. A few remaining red markers now indicate the route which sidles down under a bluff. Shortly it swings right and downwards to the Ethne Saddle at 250 metres.

Red markers on the saddle lead suddenly left and downwards towards the Ethne Stream. After crossing the stream keep to deer trails and in about 20 minutes the Stillwater River will be met at the outlet of its gorge. There is a walk wire here. If the track cannot be followed after the waterfall, a diagonal descent down the hillside can be taken to the walk wire.

*Times: Summit to campsite and vice versa, 1 1/2 hrs; Campsite to Stillwater walk wire, 2-2 1/2 hrs.*

## STILLWATER VALLEY BELOW ETHNE CREEK

About two hours down the true-left bank of the Stillwater River the river steepens. The route changes from swamp or silt to more bush covered rocky terrain. Almost immediately on striking the flat again the now faintly marked route veers south-west, away from the river, through swampy bush until it becomes clear that it is climbing to pass behind The Knob. Eventually the route falls and meets the Stillwater River again, a little before the lower end of a gorge, about five hours from the walk wire.

Shortly the silt river bank is encountered again and soon after, about the point where a deep silty ditch is encountered, Expectation Stream appears opposite. Immediately up stream of the junction there is the last good ford across the Stillwater River before reaching Lake Marchant.

Cross to the true-right bank here and then cross Expectation Stream. Progress may be slow and sometimes rough for a while, but the route is generally along, or close to the true-right bank. When nearing Lake Marchant the bluffs ahead appear to drop straight into the river, however the riverbank is easily negotiable.

On reaching Lake Marchant retrace the route a short distance to pass behind the backwater. The route rises to 15 metres or so as it passes the backwater and nears the lake outlet. From the outlet, follow traces of a track near the true-right bank of the river to the historic Caswell Sound Hut, ten minutes from the sound. The valley above Lake Marchant is described in the Irene Valley, Windward River, Large Burn section and is inaccessible from Caswell Sound.

*Time: Expectation Creek to Lake Marchant outlet, 2-2 1/2 hrs; Lake Marchant to Caswell Sound, 1 hr; Walk wire to Caswell Sound, a full day.*

## STILLWATER RIVER TO HENRY SADDLE

The gorge above the Ethne Stream walk wire is passable on the true-left bank. Deer trails can be easily followed to the head of the Stillwater Valley, crossing the river where necessary. If the Stillwater is running high, progress will be considerably slowed as parties grapple with pepperwood thickets and deep side streams which otherwise can be avoided. There is a particularly pleasant campsite, opposite where the valley turns sharply south, at S130 539660.

From the campsite cross the Stillwater and travel up the true-right of the stream entering from the north. The going soon steepens and the stream is crossed to the true-left. Stay away from the stream gorge until at 600 metres after which the easier travel is in or close to the bouldery streambed. There is a poor campsite below the saddle at S130 558660.

From the campsite it is a straightforward climb to the southern end of the saddle overlooking the Rugged Burn, from where the ridges to Henry Saddle are easily negotiated.

**Time:** *Twin Falls Creek to Stillwater forks, 4 ¹/₂ hrs; Forks to campsite, 2 hrs; Head of Stillwater to Henry Saddle, 3 hrs.*

# Doon Valley

## SOUTH WEST ARM TO KIWI FLAT

A now poorly marked and overgrown track exists up the Doon River commencing from a campsite on the north side of the river, about 100 metres up stream from the mouth. This track continues on the true-left bank to down stream of Pisgah Creek where it crosses to the bivvy rock there. Current opinion is that it is better to ignore the track and travel up the true-right instead.

Travel up the true-right for the first hour from the lake is slow through fern, boulders and pepperwood. However, good travel is then found close to the river on reasonable deer trails following raised levees, passing through beech forest and occasional pepperwood thickets. Opposite Pisgah Creek on the south bank, is an excellent bivvy rock. This bivvy is not easy to find and lies some 100 to 200 metres inland, facing a swampy clearing. Careful searching will reveal some of the remaining old track markers leading to the bivvy. This section of track needs to be re-marked by the next party using it.

The true-right bank of the Doon is easily reached from the Junction Burn Hut. Cross the Junction Burn at the first beach above the hut, if the river is low, and head in a north-westerly direction on a high terrace above the lake, aiming to strike the river bank about 500 metres above the mouth to avoid slow going in dense pepperwood, log falls and bog at lake level. The river can be reached in half an hour from the hut, but for the next half hour or so pepperwood and flood debris will slow progress at times.

From the bivvy rock continue up the true-right until an hour above Campbell Creek when the river becomes much steeper and better going will then be found by crossing to the true-left bank just above the junction of a small tributary entering on the true-left. From here the route will be obvious on good terraces no more than 100 metres from the creek. In dry spells the creekbed will be dry from here to the expansive Kiwi Flat. There is a rock bivvy at Kiwi Flat.

An alternative route crosses the Doon to the north bank above the Campbell Creek junction. Deer trails are then followed which climb over the ridge coming down from the north and lead to a short, sharp climb to Kiwi Flat.

***Times:*** *Lake Te Anau to bivvy rock opposite Pisgah Creek, 3-4 hrs; Bivvy to Campbell Creek, 2-3 hrs; Campbell Creek to Kiwi Flat, 1 1/2 hrs.*

## KIWI FLAT TO LAKE WAPITI

A high-level route over to Lake Wapiti at the head of Campbell Creek involves climbing up any of the numerous slips running down to the northern edge of Kiwi Flat, through the scrub and onto the glacial rock benches. From here

140

ascend by a winding, but easy route. From about 300 metres above the flat either sidle high to surmount a rock ridge on the right, or continue sidling above the lake. Do not commence the steep descent until almost level with the head of the lake.

Alternatively, in fine weather the extra climb right to the top of the ridge separating the Doon from the Large Burn is well worthwhile. Aim to join the ridge about 600 metres south of the distinctive silver-grey calcite rock peak. Follow over a small banded rock peak to reach the summit, which affords breathtaking views of Caswell Sound, the Large Burn and, a little further on, Lake Marchant and the Stillwater Valley. In the opposite direction there is a view right down the whole of the Doon Valley to Lake Te Anau. The Large Burn can be reached by traversing the slopes of Mt Donald.

From the summit of Mt Donald a relatively simple descent can be made by sidling down obvious benches, shoulders and terraces on the Lake Wapiti side of the ridge. Cut back down to the left well before the obvious pass into the Twin Falls tributary of the Stillwater River to avoid a small line of bluffs and a direct route through the short snowgrass to the basin west of Lake Wapiti will be apparent. The route passes through tussock-covered rubble slopes 100 metres or so to the left of a well cairned, dry bivvy rock. The bivvy lies about 150 metres above the flat at the head of the lake and approximately a kilometre from the lake itself. The head of the lake provides some reasonable campsites, but there is only a limited firewood.

## PISGAH CREEK

From a campsite at the junction of the Doon and Pisgah Creek, cross and follow the true-right bank until a deer trail climbs steeply away from the creek, which can be heard below cascading through a series of cataracts. After about half an hour the trail leads over a shoulder and away from the river. For a short while the track peters out, but will soon be picked up again on the up valley side of some large boulders. From this point to the head of the valley it continues up the west side of the creek and does not cross at any time. However, it is necessary to cross a fork coming away from a waterfall near the head and from this crossing a good track leads out to the head of the valley, first through beech forest and then through ribbonwood.

There is quite a large hanging basin near the head of Pisgah Creek. The basin is probably inaccessible from down valley, but can be gained from Campbell Creek. The route lies up the ridge on the east of Lake Wapiti right to the summit and then from the summit swings to the right and along the crest, from which practically the entire basin can be seen. One can descend into this basin at any appropriate point.

*Time: Doon River to head of Pisgah Creek, 3-4 hrs.*

## CAMPBELL CREEK TO LAKE WAPITI

The route up Campbell Creek starts on the true-right and crosses to the true-left about a third of the way up the creek when a waterfall comes into view. The going from here is mainly through boulders and fallen logs although there are occasional deer trails. While the going is somewhat rough the true-right looks even rougher. There is a small flat below the final climb to Lake Wapiti which provides a campsite.

From this last flat deer trails are followed until the stream steepens. Climb over and up mossy boulders to the right, aiming for the south-east corner of Lake Wapiti where the bush ends.

*Time: Doon River to Lake Wapiti, 5-6 hrs.*

## LAKE WAPITI

The most straightforward route around Lake Wapiti climbs on snowgrass from the south-east corner of the lake to an obvious terrace which is traversed to the head of the lake. An alternative route climbs very steeply up to the bench on the western side of the lake which is then easily followed to the head of the lake. This latter route would be initially very precarious in poor weather.

For the first route climb about 150 metres up the spur to the north-east where a series of terraces sidle at approximately the same altitude to the head of the lake. There are a few short scrubby patches, but on the whole the travel is good. The best descent from the terrace is some 200 metres above the head of the lake. Here there is a wide tussock basin below another hanging basin to the north-west which has an impressive looking pass to Twin Falls Creek.

The other large tussock basin on the west side of the lake, east of Mt Donald, is reached by travelling up the first basin a short distance and then angling back to climb round the shoulder of the ridge which separates the two valleys. A glance at the lie of the country readily indicates the route to follow. Out of this latter basin there is another route, over a relatively low pass, into Twin Falls Creek.

The alternative route to this latter basin crosses Campbell Creek to the true-right at the foot of the rapids falling from the lake at a point where the ribbonwood gives way to beech forest. The route then angles away from the rapids, climbing steeply through the large boulders amongst the beech trees until small, wet flats are reached. These are followed to the south-west corner of Lake Wapiti, some 100 metres from the outlet, aiming for a rusty patch low on the lakeside cliff.

Once the corner of the lake is reached, the climb begins by ascending the narrow rivulet of a scrub covered debris fan to a rubbly bare shoulder 15 metres from the lake. The route continues diagonally upwards, crossing rock ribs and using small intervening gullies to gain height, aiming to reach the glacial bench just before the bluffs proper begin. In one spot towards the top it may be necessary to haul packs for about five metres.

This glacial bench, which is clearly defined on the map, is followed above the bluffs to the western basin.

**Time:** *Traverse around eastern side of Lake Wapiti, 1 ³/₄ hrs.*

## LAKE WAPITI TO STILLWATER VALLEY VIA TWIN FALLS CREEK

Twin Falls Creek is easily accessed from both the north-west and west snowgrass basins above Lake Wapiti. The pass from the west basin is hidden by a grassy shoulder at the valley head. From the pass, Mt Donald is climbed in an hour without packs for excellent views of the surrounding valleys. Descending from this pass, stay in the creekbed to bush-level, then angle slightly left through the bush until grassy slip clearings are sighted.

Alternatively, from the north-west basin climb up to the pass until a scree slope up to the left is reached. This is climbed to almost the same altitude as the pass where a bench traverses right and onto the pass itself. The descent on the other side is through a series of spectacular snowgrass bluffs. These are easily negotiated by keeping more or less to the true-left side of the valley. There are a few campsites here. At the last bluff sidle left through some scrub and descend a streambed to the main creek. Follow down the creek bed, crossing where necessary, to the grassy flats in the middle section of Twin Falls Creek.

Progress down the middle section of the creek is best made by wading from one shingle beach to the next, if the creek is low enough. There are several grassy clearings that provide good campsites. As the valley closes in and falls away to the Stillwater River, look for deer trails on the true-left. These are followed, fairly close to the waterfall at times, steeply down to the bouldery beach at the foot of the falls. The falls are closer to the Stillwater than S130 indicates.

**Times:** *Head of Lake Wapiti to north-west pass, 1 hr; Pass to Stillwater, 5 hrs.*

# Irene Valley, Windward River and Large Burn

## COZETTE BURN TO IRENE VALLEY

From the flat at the head of the Cozette Burn follow an obvious scree fan which leads up onto the ridge between the east and west branches of the Cozette Burn to the crest of the ridge. From here sidle round the snowgrass slopes above the upper basin of the west branch and up and across to the saddle at its head. Here fine views of the Irene Valley open up and across the valley Mount Irene commands the attention it deserves.

From the saddle several deer trails lead down several hundred metres to a wide and sizeable snowgrass and swamp flat. The best trail is off the western shoulder of the saddle, about 30 metres above its lowest level and 100 metres from its western extremity (S139 398427). Care should be taken descending for the country is steep and particular note should be taken of the locality of the lead for the return journey.

There is a broad swampy terrace just above bush-level where there are excellent campsites. The route to the floor of the Irene River starts at the upper extreme westerly end of this expansive terrace at 1,000 metres, S139 393433. The descent is down a spur directly on the true-left of an avalanche cleared stream to the Irene River at S139 392444 on good deer trails. The gradient eases on the slopes to the left.

*Time: Cozette Burn head to saddle, 2 hrs; Saddle to campsite, 1 hr; Campsite to Irene River, 2 ½ hrs.*

## COZETTE BURN TO ROBIN SADDLE

Follow the route description above to the broad terrace above the Irene River. By following the terrace to the east and sidling around broken faces of snowgrass and scrub, the Robin Saddle to the south of Mount Irene and giving access to the Esk Burn may also be reached. The four bunk Robin Saddle Hut lies at the west end of the little lake on the west side of this saddle and not the north-east end as is marked on S140.

## IRENE RIVER TO WINDWARD RIVER AND GOLD ARM, CHARLES SOUND

Nearly opposite the point of descent into the upper Irene River from the Cozette Burn is a tributary which provides a difficult route across to the Windward

144

Valley. There is believed to be a better route by way of the next western tributary up stream, but no description of this is available. Deer trails climb up the true-right side of the rapids of this tributary. In a short time a slip is reached coming from the southern slopes. After about an hour some ribbonwood forest is reached. Cross the creek to the true-left side climbing away from it up a rocky trickle. Negotiate a waterfall on this stream, where a rope may be needed, and force a way from there to bushline. The saddle now lies directly above to the north, at S139 385463, reached by a 300 metre climb on steep snowgrass. The saddle has a sizeable tarn on the Irene side. In reverse, descend the snowgrass until bluffs and fern fields are seen below then sidle below the bluffs to the ribbonweed forest.

From the pass abundant deer trails lead down easy gradients to a snowgrass basin in the Windward River. Descend this basin to the bushline where deer trails are followed through open bush to swampy flats below. Continuing down stream, the valley curves north-west, a branch stream enters from the south, and shortly an attractive lake surrounded by bush is reached which is traversed on the north side. From the outlet the creek drops sharply into a gorge which is negotiated using deer trails high on the true-left. Shortly after the first gorge another, more tiring, gorge is reached. Some distance below, where tributaries enter from the south and north, there is a stretch of quiet water where the river becomes deep, black and slow moving and the valley turns to the left. Cross to the true-left for this section, which takes about an hour, passing through wide flats covered with ribbonwood and fuchsia.

From here the river falls through more rapids to flats and the main forks in the valley. Good deer trails, predominantly on the true-left bank, continue from here to Charles Sound. In its final passage, the Windward River plunges through a deep and narrow rock canyon, magnificent in its grandeur, but is easily traversed by following deer trails on the true-left. The best campsites may be found on terraces above the cataract before it drops steeply to Charles Sound.

*Times: Irene River to bushline, 3 $^1/_2$-4 $^1/_2$ hrs; Bushline to saddle, 1 hr; Saddle to boggy flats, 1 $^1/_2$ hrs; Boggy flats to top forks, $^1/_2$ hr; Top forks to lake, 1 hr; Lake to south tributary, 2 hrs; South tributary to bottom of flats, 1 hr; Bottom of flats to main forks, 2 hrs; Allow a full day from the upper Windward Flats to the sound.*

## CHARLES SOUND TO NANCY SOUND

The route from Charles Sound to Toe Cove in Nancy Sound is initially very steep on the Nancy Sound side of the saddle and a rope may be needed. Climb up to the basin southward following a small creek past a waterfall. Once over the saddle it is probably best to veer some way away from the stream on the true-left. The bush on the Nancy Sound side is harder to penetrate than on the other side of the saddle.

**Times:** *Top of last gorge before Charles Sound to saddle, 2 hrs; Saddle to Nancy Sound, 2 hrs.*

## IRENE VALLEY TO LARGE BURN

From the upper Irene Valley deer trails cross and re-cross the river to open flats and wide shingle beds about three hours from the upper junction. The pass into the Large Burn appears north-east of these flats. From the down stream corner of the flats cross the river to the east bank at S140 411483 and in a short distance a tributary ravine is met. Deer trails climbs very steeply up an obvious bluffed spur after crossing the tributary stream. There is a safe campsite here at the bottom of the spur. About 350 metres up the spur a bush knob is reached, then the gradient eases slightly up to the pass. The pass is at bushline where there are boggy campsites.

The drop into the Large Burn from the saddle is precipitous and it is necessary to move north-west of the pass, sidling at about bushline under bluffs, until a good deer trail leads down to the valley floor through open bush and easy slopes. The upper Large Burn is easy travelling and deer trails follow the true-right bank until near Lake Mackinnon where it may be necessary to ford and re-ford. Beware of camping close to the shore as the lake can rise several metres in heavy rain.

From the outlet of Lake Mackinnon very rough going in the form of windfalls, boulders and heavy undergrowth is faced until the valley levels out again. Deer trails then lead to an extensive area of scrubby swampland at a wide bend in the valley. Keep close to the river and cross to the true-left at a good ford just before a large tributary enters from the north. This stream offers high level routes into the upper Stillwater and the Doon, as mentioned below. Following the south bank of the main river, climb above bluffs where necessary and pass one section of large boulders to Lake Marchant, reached in a couple of hours from the swamps.

**Times:** *Irene Valley to Pass, 3-4 hrs; Pass to Lake Mackinnon, 6-8 hrs; Lake Mackinnon to Lake Marchant, 6 hrs.*

## LAKE MARCHANT

The precipitous sides of Lake Marchant render it impassable by foot and thus the lake poses a problem for routes into the Stillwater. Such routes have in fact been crossed by way of the north tributary of the Large Burn, which enters at the swampy flats above Lake Marchant, but these are only recommended to experienced mountaineers.

## EMELIUS ARM, CHARLES SOUND TO IRENE VALLEY

The Irene River is tidal for about five kilometres from where it runs into Charles Sound and a boat of some description is therefore a help to travel this section. There is a campsite near the mouth of the river, on the north side, but a much more attractive place will be found at the tidal limit on the south side, just opposite Marjorie Falls. From this latter site a track on the south side of the river will give access to the Upper Irene. About two hours up stream a small clearing provides a good campsite from which the tops in the vicinity may be explored.

The tops between the Irene Valley and Lake Marchant can be reached easily by way of the ridge which can be seen to the north-east from the campsite at the tide limit. This ridge commences to the east of the mouth of a stream which enters the Irene about half an hour above Marjorie Falls, the Irene being forded just above the junction.

**Time:** *Charles Sound to head of Irene River, 2 days.*

## LARGE BURN TO KIWI FLAT, DOON RIVER

A straightforward crossing to Kiwi Flat from the Large Burn starts about two kilometres below Lake Mackinnon. Although this route has never been popular, it is interesting to note that it formed MacKinnon's original 1888 route. From S130 463583 cross the valley floor on the true-right in open beech forest which undulates over rock and bare shingle to S130 464586 and from here climb on strong deer trails through open hina hina (whiteywood) and fuchsia north-east onto a prominent knoll at S130 466586, which is not obvious from the valley floor. Here an imposing vertical sided and ended spur covered with rata will appear above the bushline. Proceed along the spur for about 300 metres to S130 471589 to cross a small creek and head south-east across the slope, climbing slightly when another small stream will be encountered at S130 474586. Climb this stream which is enclosed in scrub and bush for a short distance when a moss and leatherwood valley will be found at S130 475587. Carry on north-east up to S130 476593 where a clear view of Kiwi Flat and the Doon Valley, overlooked by the shaly rock face of Mt Donald, will be gained.

Kiwi Flat is surrounded by a forested cirque above which there is a broad undulating bench which leads to an easy descent through light scrub on the north side to S130 487597. It is probable that a direct descent to Kiwi Flat could also be made.

**Time:** *Large Burn to Doon River, 8 ½ hrs.*

# SOUTH OF THE MURCHISON MOUNTAINS AND WEST OF LAKE MANAPOURI

## Camelot River and Cozette Burn

Above Tuaraki Stream the Camelot River becomes the Cozette Burn. From Elaine Stream there is access to the Awe Burn and from Tuaraki Stream the Freeman Burn and Gorge Burn can be reached. From the head of the Cozette Burn there are routes into the Forest Burn and Irene River.

### FOWLER PASS TO BRADSHAW SOUND VIA TUARAKI STREAM AND CAMELOT RIVER,

Fowler Pass can be reached from either the Gorge Burn or the Freeman Burn and the routes are described in those sections. To continue down into the Camelot it is necessary to climb about 100 metres or so south of Lake Tuaraki to the top of a small gully which saddles with a rock chimney which is then descended to the outlet of the lake. The route now swings almost horizontally to the left, travelling at first close under the small bluffs. After about 200 metres it then heads directly downwards to the corner of the forest, where the track becomes more defined and soon leads down to a swampy clearing which is skirted on the left. At the end of the swamp, if weather and time permit, it is well worth while to leave the track and cross to the somewhat barer shoulders on the other side of the stream. From these, commanding views can be obtained which will assist parties to appreciate more clearly the significance of many of the details which follow. It is also possible to reach below this swamp from Macpherson Pass via Lake Tuaraki, as described later in this section.

Shortly after passing the swamp the track swings sharply left, leading down and round to a small tributary which enters steeply from the south. This may be crossed and the valley can be followed down either bank, until it levels out on a 200 metre long clearing. Faint signs of the old track will be found which climbs out of the gully and generally follows down the crest of the spur to a group of fallen trees. It is here necessary to swing a little to the right and cross some streamlets formed by the Tuaraki, which has divided. These streamlets are followed down their true-right bank and the track, although faint, becomes more apparent and is worth re-locating if lost.

Soon after the valley levels out, the Torre Stream enters from the right and the Tuaraki should be crossed to the true-left bank above the junction. Around the Tuaraki-Torre junction the deer trails are exceptionally prolific and the travel is good. From here the route continues down the true-left bank of the river, which suddenly becomes a long, steep cataract dropping to join the Cozette Burn. The best policy is to leave the Tuaraki shortly after the going becomes difficult and, climbing up, sidle high around to above the Camelot. It is straightforward to work down through the bluffs into the Camelot 100 metres down stream of the Tuaraki-Cozette Burn confluence.

A crossing is made above the confluence to the true-right bank, although it is possible to travel down either side of the river to the Pre-Raphaelite looking Bedivere Falls. At Bedivere Falls a few punga floorboards and some cooking utensils can be found, being the sole remains of Murrell's tourist hut.

From Bedivere Falls the route follows the true-left bank of the river, which swings from one side of the valley to the other. The Elaine Stream, a bouldery rapid which enters from the south, may be difficult to ford if high. As the track no longer exists the shortest route, if the river is low, is to cross wherever convenient, returning ultimately to the true-left bank to go down the final placid stretch of river to the sound. The sound cannot be reached on the true-right of the river. A good campsite can be found at Bradshaw Sound, around to the southern end of Shoal Cove, by a small creek.

***Times:*** *Outlet of Lake Tuaraki to 200 m clearing, 3-3 ¹/₂ hrs; Clearing to Cozette Burn, 2 ¹/₂-3 hrs; Tuaraki-Cozette Burn junction to Bradshaw Sound, 6 hrs.*

## MACPHERSON PASS TO TUARAKI STREAM VIA TORRE STREAM

The route from Macpherson Pass to Tuaraki Stream is described in the Gorge Burn section.

There is an alternative route from Macpherson Pass, if approached from the Gorge Burn, round the north and west side of Lake Tuaraki. Climb about 120 metres up a gully, then sidle above the lake round to a hanging basin with a small tarn. Here a spur leads down to the Tuaraki Stream below the swamp described in the Fowler Pass route.

## AWE BURN TO ELAINE STREAM

The Elaine Stream can be approached from the Awe Burn via Anehu Pass, which in turn is accessible from West Arm. This route is described in the Mica Burn, Oonah Burn, Awe Burn section.

***Time:*** *Anehu Pass to junction of Elaine Stream, 3-4 hrs; Junction to Camelot River, 5-6 hrs.*

## COZETTE BURN

It is possible to reach the upper Cozette Burn from the Gorge Burn head basin which is described in the Gorge Burn section. The route into the Irene River is described in the Irene Valley, Windward River and Large Burn section.

About half an hour above the Tuaraki junction cross to the west bank and keep to this side as much as possible to the head of the valley. In another half an hour a waterfall tributary is crossed and further up ribbonwood flats are reached where it may be necessary to cross and re-cross the river. At the head of the flats the valley climbs steadily to Hidden Lake. Ascend on the true-right of the rapids and pass the lake on the west side. Continue up valley through bush, scrub and boulders until a waterfall is encountered. A steep climb 100 metres to the west leads to the cirque above the waterfall. The scrub here is very thick and it is best to follow the stream bed where practicable until the upper flats are reached.

*Time:* *Tuaraki Junction to head of Cozette Burn, 1 day.*

# Gorge Burn

The Gorge Burn, which enters the head of the South Fiord of Te Anau, gives access to two passes: Fowler Pass which leads southwards to Lake Manapouri via the Freeman Burn and westwards to Bradshaw Sound via Tuaraki Stream and the Camelot River; and Macpherson Pass which leads to Torre Stream and Tuaraki Stream. A more difficult route across the tops leads northwards into the head of the Cozette Burn which in turn provides access to the Irene Valley.

The Gorge Burn itself consists of a series of cataracts with a number of bush flats broken by short, steep faces over which the stream falls from the level above. Each level contains its small lake. There are good campsites on the small flats at the head of Lake Cecil, the lower end of Lake Boomerang and the clearings at the head of the second valley-level above Lake Boomerang, some three kilometres above Lake Boomerang.

## LAKE TE ANAU TO LAKE EVA AND MACPHERSON PASS

The route commences up the short tourist track leading to the Gorge Burn Falls and follows this side of the river, the true-right, all the way to Lake Boomerang. There are two tarns in the lower reaches of the valley before coming to Lake Cecil. From here it is another 1 1/2 hours to Lake Boomerang, situated beneath the hanging valley which leads to Fowler Pass. The shape from which this lake takes its name diverts the valley in a north-westerly direction towards Macpherson Pass.

Cross the burn just below the outlet of Lake Boomerang and negotiate the northern shore. The scrubby growth provides slow travelling and easier routes will be found some distance above on the hillside and through stunted beech and bog-pine. Sidle around the lake until an open slip is reached from which the upper shore of the lake may be gained. At the head of the lake cross to the true-right and follow this side until a clearing is reached two levels of the valley further on where there is good camping. At this clearing cross to the true-left and follow through the scrub. A short climb up a bush face leads into the tussock basin of the upper valley which contains Lakes Eva and Ione, with Macpherson Pass lying to the south.

Sidle left through sub-alpine scrub to drop back to Lake Eva at the mouth of the creek coming down from Macpherson Pass. From here easy travel through tussock and scrub clearings leads to the pass.

From Macpherson Pass sidle left across two streams and descend on the true-left of the second. A short, steep final descent, to the left of a waterfall, opens out to the open shingle riverbed of Torre Stream. From here very good deer

151

trails on the true-left lead to where the stream enters the Tuaraki Stream. It is possible to cross over Macpherson Pass and return via Fowler Pass. The remainder of the route down Tuaraki Stream is described in the Camelot River and Cozette Burn section.

*Times: Lake Te Anau to Lake Cecil, 4 hrs; Lake Cecil to Lake Boomerang, 1 ¹/₂ hrs; Outlet to head of Lake Boomerang, 1 hr; Head of Lake Boomerang to Macpherson Pass, 3 ¹/₂ hrs; Macpherson Pass to Torre Stream, 1 hr; Torre Stream to Tuaraki Stream, 1 ¹/₂ hrs.*

## LAKE BOOMERANG TO FOWLER PASS

As mentioned above, Fowler Pass is gained by way of a hanging valley entering rather obscurely from the true-right, south of Lake Boomerang. It will be clear that the waterfall is not the route to Fowler Pass. While access into the hanging valley is not obvious going up valley, the reverse route coming down from Fowler Pass is straightforward.

Aim for the spur to the south-west of the Lake Boomerang outlet rising to the west. Follow round the south side of the lake for about 200 metres crossing all the branches of a little stream entering from the south to reach this spur. On the west side of this stream is the foot of the bush spur. Climb up the slip at the foot of the spur and sidle up and around the foot onto the spur. Climb for 300 metres to a bare shoulder, then left again up a steep zig-zag deer trail to another clear shoulder. After climbing another 60 metres the stream draining the hanging valley will be crossed onto the foot of a snowgrass tongue and then a further short climb will reveal, above bush-level, the hanging valley. Fowler Pass lies at the head of this.

*Times: Lake Boomerang to Fowler Pass, 1 ¹/₂ hrs; Lake Te Anau to Fowler Pass, 6 ¹/₂ hrs.*

## LAKE EVA TO HIDDEN LAKE, HEAD OF COZETTE BURN

From the outlet of Lake Eva, follow round the eastern side of the basin, keeping the lakes to the left until directly below a snowgrass fan to the west of Lake Ione which leads up through thick alpine scrub to a steep rock face. Leading steeply to the left, a slope runs upwards to the high ridge above Lake Ione and the head of the Gorge Burn basin. The best route is found by hugging the rock face, the ground being a little less steep here than out on the snowgrass slopes. Cross a scrubby gully at the head of Lake Ione and head up a snowgrass spur on the left. From the summit of the ridge west of the lake, sidle towards Te Au Saddle. There are splendid views from the top of the ridge with several small tarns immediately to the west.

The ridge provides easy travelling until a rock peak blocks the way and the party is on a saddle between the Cozette Burn and the Adams Burn, the latter flowing into Lake Te Au. Descend to the west of the peak gradually losing height towards the bushline, sidling slowly into the upper valley. As soon as a travelling level is reached, about 30 metres above the bushline, the prominent ridge which drops into the Cozette Burn at the far end of this stretch of tops, visible from where the descent was made from the ridge, should be clearly noted. This is the ridge down which the descent is made into the east branch of the Cozette Burn. There is a fine view of Coronation Peak from this stretch of tops.

Once this ridge is reached, S140 4083391, descend into the valley, ensuring that the route followed will take the party to a point above the lip over which the stream cascades down towards a swampy lake and the forks of the Cozette Burn. This entails a short descent from the bush edge of 30 to 60 metres and a sidle north on the 850 metre contour for a one and a half kilometres in thick bush. To proceed around the tops beyond this ridge would lead the party into further trouble for here steep bluffs and faces drop suddenly into the valley floor, so every effort should be made to ensure the correct ridge is selected. On reaching the valley floor proceed up valley until the upper flats are reached where there are good camping sites.

**Times:** *Lake Te Anau to Upper Gorge Burn, 1 day; Upper Gorge Burn to Upper East Cozette Burn, 1 day.*

# Freeman Valley

The Freeman Burn provides access to the Gorge Burn and Bradshaw Sound from its head. The Kepler Track can be reached via Lake Herries and the head of the Delta Burn.

During the 1930's L. Murrell of Manapouri opened up a tourist track through the Freeman Valley to Fowler Pass and thence down the Camelot River to Gaer Arm, a branch of Bradshaw Sound. He also constructed huts at the North Arm of Manapouri, at Lake Minerva, and at Bedivere Falls. However, the war years intervened and upkeep on the track became so neglected that it is now very difficult to find in places.

## FREEMAN BURN HUT TO FOWLER PASS

From the 12 bunk Freeman Burn Hut at the North Arm of Lake Manapouri the track leads up the east bank for about an hour before deteriorating to a route. A derelict cage across the river is reached about three hours from the hut. Cross to the west bank at the first good ford. The route is now more difficult to follow, but in half an hour or so open swampy ground will be reached where log corduroys indicate traces of the old track. Good views of the surrounding country are obtained here for the first time.

From opposite the Steven Falls continue up the main Freeman Valley. On the northern side of the swamp clearing the remains of the old tourist track can be found and followed quite easily for half an hour to the remains of the Mid Hut Camp. From here the route continues up the true-right bank for about $1\frac{1}{2}$ hours to a point where the river forks and rises into two impassable gorges. The track is overgrown in this area and deer trails close to the river should be followed. The main Freeman Burn is the north branch and the stream entering from the west is the Gilmour Stream.

After fording about five minutes below the forks, above a small island in the river, the route leads away from the river and sidles slowly upwards round the south side of sunless bluffs. A small stream will be noticed, or heard to the right while the main river is on the other side of bluffs to the left. About 40 minutes from the river, about ten minutes above a point where it is obvious that the route is climbing under bare rocky bluffs, a blaze will be found marking the point where the route climbs to go hard against the bluffs and on to a long spur running north with the river away below on the left. The bush from the ford in the river to this point is crossed with deer trails. Some of these, however, head too high and too soon to the left and if followed will lead under small bluffs on the river side where further progress becomes impossible. Should this happen,

154

work back towards the small stream mentioned before and head up until the high, bare bluffs are seen above to the left.

The track along the spur, northwards from S140 423243, is easy to follow being defined by chopped-away trees. At the end of the spur the track drops about 60 metres to a small grassy flat. From here it is five minutes through the bush to the Freeman Burn just above the junction of the Omaki Stream entering from the west. Follow closely along the east bank of the Freeman Burn for 45 minutes until it becomes necessary to leave the river then climb up and around the side of the valley for about two hours crossing over a series of rocky slips coming in from the right. The Ranfurly Falls, which drain Lake Freeman, will be seen on the left and after a short climb through stunted bush, the lake itself will be observed below, almost at bush-level.

The track follows round the east side of the lake and drops some 15 metres down to clearings at the northern end. The stream is crossed to the west bank and after a climb of some 20 metres through sparse bush Lake Minerva is reached, 45 minutes from the head of Lake Freeman. The remains of the collapsed Minerva Hut will be found just inside the bush near the north-west corner of the lake.

From here about 1 1/2 hours' open travelling leads through the head basin of the Freeman Burn and on to Fowler Pass. There are two obvious routes up to the pass, but the one up the gut and streambed seen to the left is the easier. At the top of this gut Lake Tuaraki will be seen below while Fowler Pass lies above to the right. The pass gives access down the Camelot River to Bradshaw Sound, and also into the Gorge Burn and down to the South Fiord of Te Anau.

***Time:*** *Freeman Burn Hut to Mid Hut camp, 5 hrs; Mid Hut camp to Minerva Hut site, 6-7 hrs; Minerva Hut site to Fowler Pass, 1 1/2 hrs.*

## STEVEN FALLS TO IRIS BURN VIA LAKE HERRIES AND DELTA BURN

The Steven Falls thunder down out of a hanging valley on the east side of the Freeman Burn. The Steven Burn is entered by climbing the steep bush face to the north of the waterfall and the large pear shaped Lake Herries will be reached, almost on bush-level, about four hours from the main valley. The outlet of the lake flows underground and large moraine boulders around this part of the lake make for very slow travelling. The last half hour up the Steven Burn before reaching Lake Herries is hard going. The lake edges are steep except for a white sandy shore at the outlet and where a valley enters from the north-west.

From the outlet angle high around the lake until upon the mouth of the north-west valley and then drop directly down to it. Travel up this valley until the bush is left behind and climb directly up snowgrass slopes to a saddle 60 metres above a small lake at S140 468277. This saddle overlooks the saddle between the northern stream leading into Lake Herries and the Delta Burn. Descend easily to this saddle and sidle around above the bush to the top of the waterfall draining the prominent lake in the Delta Burn head. Carry on to the head of this lake and up the stream entering it to reach the flat area that is the saddle between two tributaries of the Delta Burn. Veer right and a stream will be seen leading out through a prominent 'V' notch in the ridge. This stream offers steepish although easy access into the head of the Iris Burn. From the Iris Burn the 'V' is also very obvious. From here it is straightforward, if a little swampy, to continue down the Iris Burn on the true-right. Just before crossing the Iris Burn to join the Kepler Track there is a steep, but easily negotiated descent through bush beside the Iris Burn waterfall. Cross to the true-left below the waterfall.

**Times:** *Freeman Burn Hut to Steven Falls, 3 $^1/_2$ -4 $^1/_2$ hrs; Steven Falls to Lake Herries 4 hrs; Outlet of Lake Herries to North-west Valley, 2 hrs; North-west Valley to head of Delta Burn, 5 hrs; Head of Delta Burn to Iris Burn Hut, 4-5 hrs.*

## DELTA BURN

The Delta Burn offers good travel from the South Fiord of Lake Te Anau to the open flats at its head. Travel is up either side of the river. A short bluffy section is encountered when passing through the scrub just before the flats. However, there are routes on the true-right and a short scramble through the scrub leads to the flats. From the head a hanging valley to the left gives access to the Iris Burn.

**Time:** *Lake Te Anau to valley head, 1 day.*

# Kepler Track

The Kepler Track offers a popular mixed alpine and bush tramp that makes a round trip from Te Anau. It is usually completed in two to four days and generally in an anti-clockwise direction to get the strenuous part of the trip over and done with as soon as possible. The whole track is benched, well graded and easy to follow for its entire length and has good hut facilities. It also provides access to the Freeman and Delta Burns which are of a much more rugged nature. There are wardens at each hut during summer.

The section of track between the Mt Luxmore Hut and Iris Burn Hut is very exposed to the weather and is far enough to make it a serious undertaking. Although the track is well defined, parties should be very cautious if attempting this stretch in bad weather. Certainly, stormproof clothing is needed to carry on in safety in doubtful weather and party members should know the symptoms indicating the onset of hypothermia and how to deal with it. The track becomes drifted over with snow in winter and spring and under these conditions parties will find the travel very slow. From Luxmore Hut avalanche conditions may exist at these times. Parties attempting this section when there is snow on the tops must be competent to deal with the conditions that will be encountered.

## CONTROL GATES TO IRIS BURN HUT VIA MT LUXMORE

The Kepler Track starts at the Lake Te Anau outlet control gates, reached in ¾ hour by the pleasant walking track from the Fiordland National Park Visitor Centre in Te Anau. Alternatively, various concessionaires run transport to and from the track from Te Anau.

From the control gates the track follows the lake shore to Brod Bay, which is an attractive camping site. There are toilets here and this is the last campsite before the Iris Burn. Halfway along the Brod Bay beach the track leaves the lake and climbs steadily to some prominent limestone bluffs some two hours away. The track is well graded and should present no difficulties. From the limestone bluffs it is an hour to the bushline followed by a board walk up and across the tussock tops for ¾ hour to Mt Luxmore Hut (40 bunks). From the tops there are impressive views of the Murchison Mountains and the Te Anau Basin through to the Snowdon, Earl and Takitimu Mountains.

From the Mt Luxmore Hut the benched track is well graded and follows the ridge, passing just below the summit of Mt Luxmore to the Hanging Valley Shelter, passing the Forest Burn Saddle Shelter on the way. Another open, exposed ridge is followed down to the bushline and a series of zig-zags through

Kepler Tops. On a clear day, the views from the Kepler Mountains are extensive. However, bad weather can quickly set in. Note that snow drifts have completely filled in the track which follows the ridge, making for slow progress.
*Photo: Susan McNeill*

the bush leads into Hanging Valley and shortly to the Iris Burn Hut (40 bunks), sited in a large tussock clearing. There are campsites near the hut. The Iris Burn Waterfall, ten minutes from the hut is worth visiting.

*Times: DoC Information Centre to control gates, ³/₄ hr; Control gates to Brod Bay, 1 ¹/₂ hrs; Brod Bay to Mt Luxmore Hut, 3 ¹/₂ hrs; Mt Luxmore Hut to Iris Burn Hut, 5 hrs.*

## IRIS BURN HUT TO CONTROL GATES VIA MOTURAU HUT

From the Iris Burn Hut, the track climbs over a low saddle and carries on through mixed forest down the Iris Burn and past an impressive slip formed during heavy rain in 1984. Below Rocky Point the track sidles through a gorge, coming out onto river flats near the mouth of the Iris Burn. Near Lake Manapouri, the track heads left to follow the lake shore around Shallow Bay to Moturau Hut (40 bunks).

Half an hour after leaving the Moturau Hut a signposted track leads to Shallow Bay Hut (six bunks) ten minutes away. The main track continues to cross a kettle bog on board walks and then the Forest Burn, just above its outlet into Balloon Loop. There is a short side trip to Kettle Lake before Balloon Loop. The main track follows the Waiau River terrace to the swing bridge at Rainbow Reach. While many parties finish the tramp here there is an interesting track along the river bank back to the control gates.

*Times:* *Iris Burn Hut to Moturau Hut, 5 hrs; Moturau Hut to Rainbow Reach, 1 1/2 hrs; Rainbow Reach to control gates, 2 1/2 hrs.*

## SIDE TRIPS FROM THE KEPLER TRACK

Around Mt Luxmore are several cave systems and there are good directions in the hut to one nearby. This system contains pretty formations and delicate crystal pools. Take extreme care not to damage the formations and do not leave graffiti as it will become embedded into the cave permanently. Take at least two independent light sources— say, a torch and a candle.

From Luxmore Hut, good deer trails lead to Forward Saddle along the ridge top. Here there are good views into South Fiord that are otherwise not seen.

From the tops, competent parties can climb out onto the Jackson Peaks for good views, but only in good weather. Leave the track exactly half way between the two emergency shelters and follow the ridge for half an hour for good views into Lake Manapouri.

There is also good travel along the ridge from the second shelter for two hours to Peak 5075 ft, and could probably be followed on to Peak 5140 ft. It is possible to traverse the tops all the way to Fowler Pass. Access to the Delta Burn and Freeman Burn from the head of the Iris Burn is described in the Freeman Valley section.

# Mica Burn-Oonah Burn-Awe Burn-Elaine Stream

## MICA BURN

From the Deep Cove Road a deer trail follows the true-left bank of the Mica Burn, close to the river. After about ³/₄ hour it is better to cross to the other side at an obvious ford. Open flats are reached in a further 30 minutes and from there good deer trails along the stream bank lead to where the valley steepens and swings to the east at the confluence of the Disaster Burn. From the waterfall near here, the going becomes steeper and broken and the best travel through the gorge is well above the river on fainter deer trails. At the head of the valley ribbonwood flats providing good campsites. The saddle ahead can be climbed easily by ascending a stream falling from a gut to the north then sidling across above the scrub.

*Time: Deep Cove Road to head of Mica Burn, 4-5 hrs; Head of Mica Burn to Mica Burn Saddle, 1 hr.*

## MICA BURN SADDLE TO OONAH SADDLE

From the Mica Burn Saddle it looks as if it may be feasible to descend directly to the Oonah Burn through steep bush. An alternative high level route climbs up the spur towards Mount George to 1,200 metres. From here sidle easily across a series of ledges on the eastern slopes of Mount George, above the Oonah Burn, and slowly descend to the outlet of a small lake at 1,060 metres. In about an hour the dispersed remains of a hut will be seen at the outlet of this narrow lake seated in a deep basin. The lake is traversed via a bouldery scree on the east side to the pass at its head, then the ridge is followed north of the lake to a low saddle between the Elizabeth Burn and the head of the Oonah Burn.

Alternatively, cross the pass at the head of the narrow lake. Veer left during the descent to reach a much larger lake draining into the Elizabeth Burn. From here sidle around the east shore then climb up snowgrass to the north to the well defined saddle mentioned above.

From the saddle descend through the snowgrass basin of the Oonah Burn to bushline and through the bush to the head of one of two attractive lakes in the valley below where there are poor campsites. It is possible to sidle via scrubby guts directly towards the Oonah Saddle from the snowgrass basin. The climb up to the Oonah Saddle from the lake shore is straightforward and is started by taking the bushy spur at the north-east end of the lake which rises to a prominent knoll. A lower saddle that leads to a branch of the Elizabeth Burn is seen on the left during the climb.

From the Oonah Lakes the Oonah Burn can be descended to its mouth in the West Arm of Manapouri. It is also straightforward to descend from the saddle between the Oonah Burn and the northern tributary of the Elizabeth Burn to Doubtful Sound following deer trails, taking between eight and ten hours.

*Time: Mica Burn Saddle to Oonah Lakes, 5-6 hrs.*

## OONAH SADDLE TO AWE BURN

From the top of the Oonah Saddle the obvious, steep spur immediately east of a deep gully gives access to the Awe Burn. It is straightforward to turn all the bluffs to connect the bush-free clearings higher up the spur. Problems may well be encountered lower down the ridge as route finding becomes difficult and the map is not sufficiently accurate to be useful. It is possible to descend the last bluffs to the left, down a slip.

An alternative, but improbable route off the saddle sidles above the steep gully mentioned above and drops down onto the ridge in front, finding the bluffs mentioned. A lead can be found into the gully about halfway to the valley floor. A ledge formed by an ancient slip and the use of solid tree roots for hand and foot holds allows good access to the opposite side of the creek. It is then a clear scramble down to the valley floor.

*Times: Allow a full day from the head of the Mica Burn to the Oonah Saddle and at least 3-4 hours down into the Awe Burn.*

## AWE BURN

The Awe Burn can be followed without difficulty from the North Arm of Lake Manapouri to where it can be ascended to Lake Annie. Although either bank of the river can be followed, the true-left offers consistently good travel on deer trails close to the riverbank. From Wekawai Stream the valley rises only slowly through pepperwood thickets, ending in open bush and swampy flats. About 400 metres down stream of the flats there is a large isolated rock with a big overhang providing very good shelter.[1]

Beyond the swampy clearings, travel on the open shingle river bed and deer trails on the true-right almost to the junction of the two upper branches of the river. From the shingle flats it is possible to scramble up with some difficulty through the bush and scrub to the Oonah Saddle and then drop down easily to the Oonah Lakes.

*Time: North Arm to Shingle flats at head of Awe Burn, 7 hrs.*

---

[1] This description is probably insufficient to find the bivvy and the editor welcomes a more detailed one.

## NORTH BRANCH AWE BURN TO LAKE ANNIE

The North Branch of the Awe Burn provides easy travelling except in flood conditions. Follow the riverbed on the east bank from the junction. The route then crosses the river about 500 metres up stream to climb the side of an avalanche gully on the true-right for 20 metres to reach good deer trails. From here the route follows up the true-right bank through scrub, ribbonwood and beech forest and finally up the streambed to the point where the creek swings from the east down a series of cataracts. Climb up the obvious bare rock rib to a prominent knoll. From here traverse to the right, into and out of an open creek to a second rock knoll 20 metres higher than the first. From here a careful appraisal up valley will show a fault-line slanting steeply upwards from left to right, close to the cataracts and ending at the outlet of Lake Annie. Angle towards this and, in about $^3/_4$ hour, this old overgrown fault will lead to the lake outlet.

From the clear snowgrass Mt Soaker, an excellent vantage point, can be climbed by following round the ridge which borders the cirque below Lake Annie. Although not obvious from the outlet, Lake Annie itself can be traversed via the western shore. After the first 200 metres have been traversed near the lake edge, travel is straightforward. A short swim may be necessary for this first section. Higher ledges that appear to promise better travel are hopelessly bluffed further around the lake.

*Time:* North Branch Awe Burn to Lake Annie, 4-5 hrs.

## LAKE ANNIE TO CAMELOT RIVER VIA ANEHU PASS AND ELAINE STREAM

About a kilometre further on from Lake Annie a prominent scree slope to the north leads up to the Anehu Pass. Near the top progress is difficult because of loose and precariously placed boulders. On the other side lies an attractive snowgrass basin containing a large mountain tarn. Cross its outlet then climb onto a ridge and follow the curve of the basin on the true-left side of the creek to bushline and swampy flats further down. Below the flats a very steep step in the valley is negotiated on the true-left and a tributary stream crossed where the valley swings west. While descending this steep step take care not to get between the two streams. Move to the left, as the two converge into one smooth-sided waterfall. Shortly another steep drop in the valley is reached and also descended on the true-left, a little distance away from the stream which plunges down a rather spectacular chasm, ending in a waterfall near the junction of the Elaine Stream. A left sidle of 150-200 metres along the bluffs above the waterfall will lead to a small, but generally dry steep sided watercourse, overgrown and boulder strewn. Follow this down to the base of the waterfall.

Follow down the true-left of the Elaine Stream to an attractive lake which may be skirted on the west side. Keeping to this side of the valley, or crossing over to the true-right, Lake Norma is reached in a further 30 minutes. This lake is best negotiated on the east side. From the outlet, continue on the true-right. After reaching the gorge and the first main waterfall about two hours down river, veer further right to get above the bluffs then sidle slowly right over a small hump and descend carefully to the Camelot River. On no account descend down river past the first waterfall as progress at the bottom of the gorge is barred by a huge bluff and a smooth water chute.

***Times:*** *Lake Annie to Anehu Pass, 2-3 hrs; Anehu Pass to junction of Elaine, 3-4 hrs; Elaine to Camelot, 5-6 hrs.*

# Garnock Burn Area

A network of tracks in the general area of the Garnock Burn is accessible from two points of entry. Boat owners may travel to Hope Arm and base themselves at Hope Arm Hut. However, most parties row across the Waiau River at Pearl Harbour to the landing that leads to the start of the Circle Track. Rowboats may be hired from Manapouri Motors.

## PEARL HARBOUR RETURN VIA THE CIRCLE TRACK

The Circle Track, which offers some of the best views of any track in the area, follows up river from opposite Pearl Harbour, then along the lake shoreline in open bush until the end of a ridge is met. Here the track forks and the left-hand branch which leads up the ridge is the Circle Track. Height is steadily gained past several lookouts until the climax is reached at the viewpoint at 600 metres. Excellent views from this point include Hope Arm, The Monument, Back Valley, Mt Titiroa and the Garnock Burn. The return to the landing on the Waiau River is by a steep track on the north flank of the ridge followed by 15 minutes of flat walking.

**Time:** *Round trip, 3 1/2-5 hrs.*

## THE MONUMENT

A short exhilarating climb of 290 metres to the summit of The Monument provides a magnificent viewpoint of Lake Manapouri and surrounding areas. The climb begins from the beach at the head of the bay to the north of The Monument in Hope Arm. From the beach climb fairly steeply up through open beech forest to the main leading ridge, then follow the ridge up to bushline. Exercise extreme care on the exposed crumbling rock and narrow ledges, both on the ascent and descent, and remember that the temperature above the bushline can be considerably lower than that in the bush. If the lake is low and there is walking access around the beach past the mouth of the Garnock Burn, The Monument can be climbed from Hope Arm. From the base of The Monument, bush bash up to the leading ridge where markers on the other access route can be picked up. Take care on the return not to follow the markers down to the beach as there is no foot access to it.

**Time:** *2-2 1/2 hrs return.*

## PEARL HARBOUR TO HOPE ARM

To reach the 12 bunk Hope Arm Hut from Pearl Harbour the route is along the Circle Track to the fork at the foot of the ridge where the right-hand branch is now taken. A short sidle leads to Moraine Spur and after 15 minutes of downhill travel the track again branches. Follow the right-hand track through flat forest covered swampland to the Garnock Burn and after crossing the river on a three-wire bridge the track follows the true-left bank to the beach at Hope Arm. The hut is sited at the far end of the beach.

**Time:** *Pearl Harbour to Hope Arm, 2-3 hrs.*

## HOPE ARM TO SOUTH ARM

It is possible to travel from Hope Arm to the head of the South Arm in one day via Waiwaiata Stream. Avoiding the gorge where the river enters Hope Arm, climb about 150 metres and follow up the north side, crossing over and back where necessary. After climbing out on the right side at the head of the valley, follow along the ridge to the head of the South Arm where a lightly-blazed trail will be found leading down an obvious spur. Another route from the upper valley leads out over Poachers Pass to a tributary of the Garnock Burn (see below).

An alternative route onto the tops is via Bicycle Spur. Follow around the west of Hope Arm to the first creek. After crossing the creek look for markers on the bush edge. Follow the markers to the main ridge and then on to the bushline. From above the bushline there is good travel in many directions. Take water.

## HOPE ARM TO UPPER GARNOCK BURN AND SNOW WHITE CREEK

The track to the Upper Garnock Burn and Snow White Creek leaves from behind the hut and at the fork the right-hand track is followed up a small tributary valley. The swamp at the head of the valley is crossed to a short descent to the Garnock Burn. The marked track ends here as travel is easy through open tussock flats and the junction of Snow White Creek, the first tributary on the north bank, will be reached in about an hour. There was formerly a small hut on the south bank, opposite the junction, but this has now been demolished.

The next tributary from the north rises from a basin with two saddles. The saddle to the left leads into the other head of the Garnock Burn, with another saddle beyond providing a good route down to the head of South Arm. The saddle to the right rises to a steep, narrow saddle known as Poachers Pass which leads into the upper valley of the Waiwaiata Stream.

Returning to the main valley of the Garnock Burn, the northern branch at the head saddles with the other tributary mentioned previously, beneath the summit of Flat Mountain, while the southern branch, which contains two small lakes, saddles southwards into the Borland Burn. Refer to the Borland Valley section for details.

**Time:** *Hope Arm Hut to Snow White Clearings, 3-3 ¹/₂ hrs.*

## MT TITIROA

Opposite the point where the track from Hope Arm first meets the Garnock Burn, described above, is the steep bush covered northern end of Mt Titiroa. Although steep, it is best to climb straight up on to the spur directly opposite the track exit. Once on top follow the ridge along towards Titiroa. It soon levels out and when the snowgrass is reached a reliable stream will be found. This provides a good camp area, but beware of fire danger in dry, or windy conditions. Water is scarce in the long ascent through the open tops. On a fine day there are some extensive views on the eastern side from Stewart Island in the south to the Eglinton Valley in the north. Wind erosion has sculptured many unusual shapes from the rocks of Mt Titiroa and these alone make the visit well worthwhile.

*Time: Allow two days from Lake Manapouri to the summit and return, using the campsite, as described, on the descent.*

## BACK VALLEY

Two tracks, one on each side of the Garnock Burn, lead to Back Valley Hut (four bunks). To reach the hut from Pearl Harbour proceed along the track to Hope Arm to the track junction as described above and take the left-hand track. The route meanders through open ribbonwood forest and podocarp stands where long grass may obscure the track during some seasons.

To reach Back Valley Hut from Hope Arm Hut follow the Garnock Burn track starting behind the hut to a fork. The left-hand fork leads through open forest to the lower Garnock Burn which is crossed at this point on a three-wire bridge. Five minutes further on Back Valley Hut is reached. A good round trip from Hope Arm Hut is to Back Valley Hut by this track and return by the track on the true-right of the Garnock Burn.

From Back Valley Hut another track follows up Stinking Creek to Lake Rakatu where there is a dinghy available for public use. There is a good campsite on the west side of the lake towards the head. The dinghy must always be returned to its site at the end of the track.

*Time: Pearl Harbour to Back Valley Hut, about 2 1/2 hrs; Back Valley Hut to Lake Rakatu, 1 hr; Hope Arm Hut to Back Valley Hut, about 1-1 1/2 hrs.*

# Doubtful Sound

## DOUBTFUL SOUND TRACK

From the Portal a section of the original walking track to the sound leads up valley on the true-right of the Lyvia River to the bridge over the Stella Burn. From across the river a zig-zag track gains height to meet the road after an hour's easy walking.

## HELENA FALLS VALLEY

Cross to the true-right berm of the tailrace by the track across the Portal and follow a rough trail that leads up the talus slope on the true-left of the falls. Rising steeply from here there is a rough track that leads to the top of the falls and gives access on the true-left side to the valley beyond. From the road end to the top of the falls takes about 1 $\frac{1}{2}$ hours.

## STELLA FALLS TRACK

About two minutes' walk up the road from the top of the Doubtful Sound Track there is a cairn marking the start of the Stella Falls Track. The track is well defined, rises steadily and takes approximately 20 minutes.

## MT TROUP TRACK

Follow a track up the true-right side of the Wanganella Stream climbing steeply into the lip of the valley. Keep heading up until a small stream is crossed. Then cross the Wanganella Stream to find the track on the true-left bank. Climb up steeply for 30 minutes to an old slip where the cut track ends. Open country leads easily to the top of the ridge. Standards mark the route from the old slip onwards.

## LYVIA VALLEY TO UPPER SEAFORTH AND SPEY VALLEYS

This is a trip for experienced parties only. Starting from the Deep Cove Road, the Lyvia Track is marked through to the top of the gorge 45 minutes later. The track finishes on level ground beside the river and further travel is best close to the river, keeping on the same true-right side. Lake Colwell is reached about four hours from the road. This section is not easy with swampy areas and at times thick vegetation with few deer trails.

It is better to cross the outlet of Lake Colwell and proceed along its true-left side. Otherwise, if the river is too high, the true-right is possible although there is a short, difficult bluff to negotiate.

At the head of Lake Colwell the route proceeds up steeply on the true-right of the South Branch stream. Travel here improves with height and after about two hours a tussock and scrub clearing is reached with a good campsite amongst a group of beech trees in the centre of the clearing.

From this clearing the route goes up the true-right bank, first through scrub, then tussock, then large boulders until small tarns are passed. The route turns sharply right up the true-right of a small waterfall about 500 metres from the head of the valley. This gives access to a basin containing large tarns and easy travel over tussock and rock. From the west side of the most western tarn proceed in a south-westerly direction and climb the tussock gully heading to the pass.

From the pass the upper Seaforth basin can be gained by traversing left and then down via scree slopes. From the basin the route up to MacKenzie Pass is straightforward through small clearings and old deer tracks. From here on refer to the description in the Seaforth Valley section.

*Time:* *Road to Pass, 8hrs.*

## DAGG SOUND TRACK

From Haulashore Cove at the head of Crooked Arm the track starts on the true-right of the creek. After five minutes' travel cross to the true-left for a further five minutes before leaving the creek to veer to the west side of the valley. The track, which is well marked, then follows along the foot of the hill to Dagg Sound, taking 30 minutes. For particulars of the route onwards to Vancouver Arm of Breaksea Sound see the Dusky Sound section.

## DEAS COVE HUT

This 12 bunk hut will be found in the forest about 30 metres back from the beach. A short track connects Deas Cove and Neck Cove, ensuring access from a sheltered anchorage depending on the weather quarter. There is no overland route to this hut.

## SECRETARY ISLAND

Secretary Island now has no special status within the national park. There is a hut and a number of tracks on the island.

# Dusky Sound Track

This track has become popular over recent years and links a chain of huts from Lake Hauroko through to Supper Cove at Dusky Sound and then back to finish at the West Arm of Lake Manapouri. The track is normally walked from the head of Lake Hauroko to Loch Maree where provisions can be cached. From here the return trip to Supper Cove is undertaken. From Loch Maree the track to Centre Pass leads out to Lake Manapouri. Experienced parties sometimes join the track at Lake Roe from the Florence, or the Jaquiery valleys and these routes are described in the Grebe Valley Section.

While it is an easy day's walk to go from one hut to another it is hard work to do two huts in one day. The best strategy is to take time out to enjoy the track and do one hut a day. This area is not for inexperienced, or poorly equipped parties, or those who dislike three-wire bridges. Note that the Seaforth valley floods regularly with heavy rain and can become impassable for days and this should be allowed for when planning the trip. During winter deep snow and avalanche danger may make the tops impassable.

## HAUROKO BURN HUT TO LAKE ROE HUT

The well marked track leaves the ten bunk Hauroko Burn Hut at the head of Lake Hauroko and follows the west bank of the Hauroko Burn. Where the track crosses a rocky stream in time of flood a walk wire will be found down stream. When the valley narrows to a canyon, the track climbs for 150 metres and near the top of this climb the mist from the Hauroko Falls can be seen rising above the tree tops. The track drops back to the river and in a short time the first river crossing is reached, prior to the Gardner Burn. A walk wire can be used if the river is high, but the ford is usually quite shallow. After the river is crossed the track rises very steeply for quite a distance to keep above a deep canyon and then drops in an easy grade back to the stream. A small clearing is passed and later the track enters a larger clearing. This point is about halfway to the saddle. The 12 bunk Halfway Hut is located at the south end of this clearing.

The track re-enters the bush at the far end of the clearing and bears away from the river. After crossing a rocky creek and following around a low ridge, it comes back to the river and after a short distance reaches the last river crossing. A large, fallen tree makes a handy bridge if the river is high. From here on the track follows the west bank of the stream until the open tussock is reached. Orange snow poles lead to the Lake Roe Hut (12 bunks) at the northern end of Lake Laffy, on Furkert Pass.

## LAKE ROE

Easy rolling tops extend in all directions, so that a day or two can be enjoyed in this area exploring the surrounding country. It is only a 20 minute climb up the scrubby ridge to the east to come out onto the tussock above Lake Roe. From the low ridge to the south of this lake almost the whole length of the Hauroko Burn can be seen. To the east of Lake Roe is the Merrie Range with a prominent, rough ridge which leads up to a high pass connecting with the Florence Stream (see Grebe Valley chapter). From the tops to the west of the hut there is a magnificent view of the surrounding country. The bare, grey mountain to the left of Supper Cove is Mt Solitary. Immediately in front of it is the ridge to the east of Roa Stream. Either this ridge, or the Roa Stream itself gives an alternative route from Supper Cove back to Lake Hauroko by way of an easy saddle into the head of the Gardner Burn and down to the Hauroko Burn.

## LAKE ROE HUT TO LOCH MAREE HUT

From Lake Roe Hut the track to Loch Maree follows the marker poles up the ridge to the west and then around the south shore of Lake Horizon, which drains into the Jane Burn. After passing this lake the track climbs upwards and swings left along the top of the Pleasant Range. The track follows down off the end of this range and drops steeply and without let-up for 600 metres through the bush to meet the Seaforth River at the top end of Loch Maree. The Seaforth can usually be forded here and a long, high three-wire bridge has been provided should the river be high. The Loch Maree Hut is located three minutes from the crossing, just over the rise, and can accommodate 20 people.

## WEST ARM TO UPPER SPEY HUT

The track commences from West Arm of Lake Manapouri and follows the Wilmot Pass Road until 20 minutes past the Mica Burn and there drops down to the Spey River at a signposted track. The Spey is an open ribbonwood valley for most of its distance. The track is initially of very good standard being the old Doubtful Sound Walking Track as far as Dashwood Stream. There are two walk wires across this stream and the track continues up the true-left of the Spey until this is crossed to the true-right by another walk wire a short distance past Waterfall Creek. A large swampy clearing is then reached, where the route is marked by yellow pegs. The Upper Spey Hut (12 bunks) is at the top end of the clearing.

## UPPER SPEY HUT TO KINTAIL HUT.

From the hut the track climbs steeply to the head of the Warren Burn and the route over Centre Pass is marked by standards, which are particularly necessary

Dusky Sound Track. A tramper on the Dusky Sound Track nears the mouth of the Seaforth River.

in snow conditions. The presence of snow on this pass can, incidentally, be gauged roughly from the lookout point at the Dashwood Corner on the Deep Cove Road. There is a short, steep pitch on the east side of the pass and once off the tops a very steep descent on the west side through bush to the Kintail Stream. From the pass itself there is an impressive view of Tripod Hill in the Seaforth beside Gair Loch. If the weather is fine it is worth leaving packs at the pass and climbing 20 minutes to the summit of Mt Memphis. The Seaforth itself is crossed by a walk wire just above the Kintail junction and the Kintail Hut (20 bunks) is situated five minutes up stream along a signposted side track.

## KINTAIL HUT TO LOCH MAREE HUT

From Kintail Hut the track follows the true-right side of the valley past Gair Loch which is easy going apart from a swampy area at the top of the loch and a large slip. The track is rough underfoot through a gorge to the Kenneth Burn, which is crossed by a walk wire. From here on it is flat going to the Loch Maree Hut (20 bunks). Watch for track markers on the opposite bush edges of the clearings. This section of track crosses several deep river guts which fill deeply with water and become difficult to cross, or even may need to be swum if river levels are high. The track is rough underfoot and susceptible to flooding between Deadwood Creek and Loch Maree Hut.

## LOCH MAREE HUT TO SUPPER COVE

From Loch Maree Hut follow around Loch Maree and down the Seaforth Valley on the old track which was cut by working parties in 1903. Some of their abandoned tools lie beside the track below Loch Maree. Loch Maree itself can become impassable for a day or two at a time. The rule of thumb is that if the tree stumps in Loch Maree are underwater then the track is impassable. The old hut at Supper Cove can still be used, but the newer 14 bunk hut 1 $\frac{1}{4}$ hours further on is far more comfortable. The going is rougher on this last section and it is easier to walk on the beach where possible rather than clamber over the hillside track.

Blue cod can be caught from the shore and groper in the Sound. There is a dinghy at the hut for public use and better fishing. Take extreme care when using the boat as rough sea conditions can develop without warning.

*Times: Lake Hauroko Hut to Halfway Hut, 4-5 hrs; Halfway Hut to Lake Roe Hut, 3-4 hrs; Lake Roe Hut to Loch Maree Hut, 4-5 hrs; West Arm to track head, ³/₄hr; Track head to Upper Spey Hut, 4 ¹/₂ hrs; Upper Spey Hut to Kintail Hut via Centre Pass, 5-6 hrs; Kintail Hut to Loch Maree Hut, 4-5 hrs; Loch Maree Hut to Supper Cove, 6 hrs.*

# Side Routes from the Dusky Sound Track

## PILLANS PASS

From the Spey Valley, a little down river from the Upper Spey Hut, climb the ridge on the true-left bank of the Cockburn Stream for about 150 metres and then, still climbing steadily, sidle up through the bush parallel to the stream and about the same distance above it. After about 1 $\frac{1}{2}$ hours a large basin will be seen above and to the left of the stream which swings to the right up through a steep gorge. Keep climbing towards this basin and after about 2 $\frac{1}{2}$ hours from the Spey a stream will be heard tumbling over cliffs at the lip of the basin. Lake Earnshaw (not Earnslaw as spelt on some maps) will be reached in open country a few minutes above the lip of the basin.

The route lies west across this basin past patches of scrub and bush and then climbs steeply up through more bush and scrub past rock bluffs and out on to a rocky tussock shoulder. Although the pass cannot be seen from the basin, the route is the only obvious way out from the basin which is surrounded at its head by high vertical faces. Climb up the rocky shoulder moving to the right and keeping high above the main gorge of the stream which is now below and to the right. Soon the pass will be seen ahead in a narrow gap between peaks. A small tarn will be found on the pass.

Follow down the Kintail Stream, keeping at first to the true-left, then crossing to the true-right before entering the bush, generally keeping a bit away from the stream until a tributary entering from the south is passed. Still on the true-right bank of the Kintail, the route now angles away to the right a little, but tends generally to follow close to the stream in the flatter parts and a little away where the terrain is steeper. The track from the Centre Pass route will then be joined a short distance above the Seaforth junction.

***Time:*** *Spey Valley to Pillans Pass, 4 $\frac{1}{2}$ hrs; Pass to Kintail Hut, 4 $\frac{1}{2}$ hrs.*

## MACKENZIE PASS

From the Upper Spey Hut cross the Warren Burn Branch of the Spey, which comes from Centre Pass, and follow up the south bank of the West Branch. The old blazed track should be found here and followed up till it crosses to the north bank when the river becomes fairly small and partly lost underground. The blaze now leaves the stream, not by any means for the first time, and ceases when it returns to it again about 20 minutes later. (On the return journey follow down the stream from Mackenzie Pass until these old blazes are picked up about 20 minutes below the bushline on the left bank.)

Following up the true-left bank of the stream, there is a sharp rise in the valley where a deer trail about 20 to 30 metres from the stream offers reasonable going. Keep beside the stream to the bushline which leads round to the right to Mackenzie Pass. There is no indication of the position of the pass until this point is reached. The stream itself should not be followed any further past the bushline unless the party is making for Murrell Pass which lies at the very head of the valley about half an hour away. After turning right the highest point of Mackenzie Pass is reached in half an hour. On the way three cairns will be noticed– these lead past a point where, on the return journey, there is a danger of taking a left turn which runs out into a nasty gut.

The descent from the pass to the valley takes about half an hour, and the going is then fairly level for another half hour, except for one small drop. (On the return journey look for a cairn on the true-right bank and two more on the true-left bank near the head of the valley. The latter two give a line to an oval shaped prominence, passed to the right, in a gully which leads through the lowest point in the upper bushline to Mackenzie Pass.)

At the end of a small flat, follow down the left bank of a tributary which enters from the right and cross it at the junction with the main stream. A few metres on begins a blaze which leads down a steep gorge, keeping a fair distance from it most of the way, and the next flat will be reached in about 45 minutes. (On the return journey the blaze leads in from the true-right bank just a little below the first waterfall in the gorge.)

In another ten minutes a stream enters from the right, larger than the one so far followed, and parties travelling in the reverse direction must be very careful not to follow it. It is another half hour of fairly flat going to the next big drop and a crossing must then be made at a convenient point to the left bank as there is an impassable tributary gorge on the right. The journey down this gorge takes an hour. Keep close to the stream until forced out a little by a bank which runs out on the next flat. (When returning, turn right at a prominent blaze on the true-left bank about ten minutes below high falls at the bottom of the gorge. The bank begins about 40 metres into the bush from this blaze and is followed round the top until it meets the gorge just above the waterfall. Care should be taken not to get above any other banks and to keep close to the gorge from here up, as there is a maze of banks above.)

After 40 minutes along the flat two more streams enter, one from each side, and the main stream is crossed between here and the next stream entering from the right, an hour further on. The next big drop in the valley comes 40 minutes later, and keep within about 40 metres of the true-right bank to reach the next flat in about 45 minutes. The Kintail Hut is then reached in another 20 minutes.

## MURRELL PASS

This route is more direct than Mackenzie Pass or Pillans Pass but care must be taken on the descent on the Seaforth side. For the approach to the pass from the Spey follow the Mackenzie Pass description above. From the top of the Murrell Pass move left to a bank which is followed round to a long spur running right down into the valley. The Mackenzie Pass route is then rejoined at a point between the first and second gorges described above. Do not descend directly from the pass as numerous steep bluffs will be encountered here.

## LYVIA VALLEY TO DUSKY SOUND TRACK

For a description of a route from Deep Cove to the Upper Seaforth and Spey valleys see Doubtful Sound chapter.

## LAKE ROE TO FLORENCE OR JAQUIERY

The route to Lake Roe from the Florence and Jaquiery Rivers, described in the Grebe Valley section is difficult to follow in reverse from the west, particularly in poor visibility. Many parties have encountered problems in route-finding and a west-east crossing of the Merrie Range should therefore be undertaken only by experienced trampers and in fine weather.

## LAKE ROE HUT TO KINTAIL HUT VIA KINTAIL STREAM

There is a difficult, but fairly direct route via the scrubline of the Merrie Range to the Kintail Stream on the upper Seaforth Valley, but this should be used by experienced parties only.

From Lake Roe Hut head north towards Lake Bright, cross the stream below Clark Cascade and climb up to terraces on the right. Follow these through mixed scrub and snowgrass to a deep intercepting gully. Keep high, near bluffs, then sidle down to a rocky slip that gives access to beech forest near the bottom of the gulch. The climb out is obvious, up a snowgrass slope, then there is a rough section negotiating steep guts and scrubby pockets. Next there is a fair distance of easy snowgrass before another intercepting gully. Climb out of this gully to a shoulder then sidle carefully keeping as high as possible before descending a bouldery fan into the head of Deadwood Creek just above scrubline. This traverse from Lake Roe is by no means easy as there is much scrub, bluffs and sharp ravines to negotiate. It might actually be preferable to descend into Deadwood Creek from Lake Bright and then climb up that valley to the head.

The pass ahead into the Kintail is easily reached, but the northern aspect of the saddle is very steep and bluffed. From the top descend a little to the left and shortly a flat terrace is seen at the bushline. Look carefully for deer trails that lead through scrubby bluffs to the boggy terrace. To the right of this terrace an almost vertical deer trail penetrates the difficult bluffs to the valley floor where there are good campsites adjacent to open flats. Excellent travel is afforded from here to the forks of the Kintail Stream and Kintail Hut.

*Time: Lake Roe Hut to Kintail Hut, allow a full day.*

## DINGWALL MOUNTAINS

From Mackenzie Pass descend into the extensive parkland basin of the Seaforth River and cross to a junction of streams near the lip of the hanging basin on the right. Climb the spur on the true-right side of the creek falling steeply from the north until the top of the ridge between the Lyvia, south branch, and the Seaforth is reached. The beautiful lake deep in the Lyvia Valley below is Lake Louise. The ridge is easily traversed to a saddle between this lake and a hanging basin of the Seaforth.

A base camp could be set up at the head of the Seaforth and the tops of the Black Giants, Matterhorn Mountains and Dingwall Mountains explored. The north-south ridge of the latter range of mountains may be followed to a saddle between Mounts Thornton and Menteath and a descent made into the upper reaches of the Kenneth Burn, a large tributary of the Seaforth River.

About an hour down valley from the head of the Kenneth Burn are large open flats where a good campsite may be established. Alternatively, a tent may be pitched near bushline and the higher mountains of the region, Cusack, Nantes and Crowfoot explored. A prominent 'V'-shaped pass at the head of the Kenneth Burn should give easy access into the long valley leading down to the head of the Hall Arm. The Kenneth Burn falls in three major drops in its course to the Seaforth River. Deer trails can usually be found on the true-right side. Allow about three hours from the flats down to the Dusky Sound Track.

# Dusky Sound Area

Overland access to Supper Cove in Dusky Sound has been described in earlier chapters of this guide book. It remains now to describe a number of routes in the region of the sound itself, all of which require access by boat or aircraft.

## DOUBTFUL SOUND TO BREAKSEA SOUND

The initial portion of this route, from Crooked Arm to the head of Dagg Sound, has been described in the Doubtful Sound chapter. The route continues round to the heel of Dagg Sound and then follows up the true-right bank of the stream entering here, swinging southwards to a low saddle, well below bushline. The track, now less distinct in parts, then drops directly down another stream which is followed at first on the true-right bank, then the true-left, and then the true-right again to its mouth in a bay to the east of Third Cove in Vancouver Arm of Breaksea Sound.

*Times: Crooked Arm to the heel of Dagg Sound, 1 ¹/₂ hrs; Heel to the saddle, 3 hrs; Saddle to Vancouver Arm, 3 hrs.*

## DUSKY SOUND TO EDWARDSON SOUND

There is a route from Cascade Cove, Dusky Sound, to the head of Edwardson Sound in Chalky Inlet.

*Times: Cascade Cove to pass, 6 ¹/₂ hrs; Pass to Edwardson Sound, 6 ¹/₂ hrs.*

## WET JACKET ARM TO SUPPER COVE

Another unmarked route lies up Herrick Creek in Wet Jacket Arm and down the Henry Burn to Supper Cove. From a good campsite about 30 metres in from the mouth of Herrick Creek, follow up the south bank of the stream to a small lake, reached in 20 minutes, which is passed on the south side. About a third of the way round there is a sheer drop into the lake which usually requires wading. From the head of the lake follow a series of boggy clearings, with forest and scrub, now on the north side of the stream. About an hour above the lake the valley swings south-east. A steep rocky gully with a stream enters here from the true-right and this should be climbed for about 50 metres, then sidle back towards the saddle rising slightly all the way. There is a small campsite on the saddle itself. The drop into the Henry Burn is straightforward, following the stream on the south bank and from here on there is easy going down the east bank of the Henry Burn all the way to Supper Cove. If travelling in reverse, take care to pick the correct tributary leading to the saddle with Herrick Creek. The Henry Burn itself can also be followed easily to its head, and from here the tops can be gained to the east of Tussock Peak.

*Time:* *Mouth of Herrick Burn to Supper Cove, approximately 6 hrs.*

# Grebe Valley Area

## GREBE VALLEY

The lower Grebe Valley is accessible on foot up the road from the South Arm of Manapouri, or across the saddle from the Borland Valley. Refer to the notes in the Lake Monowai and Borland Burn section regarding road access.

The shortest access route into the Jaquiery River lies from the Borland Road up the Grebe instead of the higher level route via Island Lake and Clark Hut[1]. However, there is no proper track and the going is rough. Leave the road at its nearest point to Shallow Lakes and follow the edge of the bush southwards, keeping above the valley floor. A deep creek is crossed and the Grebe River itself is reached in bush at the top, south end of the clear flats. An alternative route, if the valley floor is reasonably dry, is to cross the flat directly over to the Grebe above Shallow Lakes and then follow up the firmer ground on the bank of the river. The Grebe River itself, if high, can usually be forded above Shallow Lake, about two hours upstream from the Florence junction.

Lake Roe. Trampers descending to Lake Roe from the Merrie Range.

[1] Note that Clark Hut is sometimes incorrectly spelt as Clarke Hut

A rough track continues up the east bank of the Grebe to the flats below the Jaquiery junction where there are good campsites. If continuing up the Grebe rather than the Jaquiery, Clark Hut, near the top end of the flats, can be reached in one hour, keeping to the west bank of the Grebe and at most times away from the river, close to the bush.

***Times:*** *Borland Road to flats below Jaquiery junction, 3 hrs; Borland Road to Clark Hut, 4 hrs.*

## PERCY SADDLE

Percy Saddle is normally only traversed by cyclists and mountain bikers wishing to traverse the Borland Road to the Percy Saddle Road and West Arm of Lake Manapouri.

From the end of the Percy Saddle Road at the ECNZ radio hut traverse 50 metres, under the power pylons, on a faint track. A line of marker poles lead down a scree and tussock slope to scrubby bush. With care a further marker pole and plastic ribbon markers can be followed through the bush and out to the Borland Road.

***Times:*** *Downhill, $^1/_2$ hr; Uphill, 1 hr.*

## FLORENCE STREAM TO LAKE ROE, SOUTHERN ROUTE

This route is now normally used in preference to the route up the Jaquiery. A DoC A-frame hut in poor condition is situated near the Florence Junction 20 minutes from the Borland Road. Follow track markers from the "Florence Hut" signpost. For an approach from Clark Hut, follow in reverse the route description above.

The south bank of the Florence Stream is followed to the junction of the main north branch, the third large tributary on the north side of the valley. Swampy flats on the way are best skirted by keeping to the firmer ground on the river bank. From the large, swampy clearing on the north side of the main river, above the junction of the north branch, a small south branch will be seen ahead. Continue up the main valley to the junction of this south branch, staying within earshot of the river. Follow it, initially climbing steeply through a line of bluffs from close to the river. Travel up the west side, past numerous tarns on a terrace above the bushline, to the ridge between the Florence and the Russett Burn. From here on the route to Lake Roe is the same as from the Jaquiery.

***Times:*** *Grebe junction to ridge between Florence Stream and Russet Burn, 8 hrs.*

## FLORENCE STREAM TO LAKE ROE, NORTHERN ROUTE

A very seldom used and more spectacular route than the one described above involves a high, but not difficult, pass. Above where the North Branch enters the Florence Stream, cross to the north bank and climb through the bush in a north-westerly direction, following the best route the contours will allow. After crossing a small bush ridge a small bush lake is reached, about half a kilometre long. Pass this on the east side then cross to the west at the head. Intermittent bush leads to a massive cirque where there is a good campsite.

At the head of the cirque a steep cataract can be readily climbed on its eastern side. This leads to a slightly larger lake which is passed on its eastern side which in turn leads to another slightly larger lake which is also passed on its eastern side. Then climb a further cataract at the head to arrive at the outlet of a fourth lake at an altitude of 1090 metres. From the outlet climb to the west, past small tarns lying to the south, until the main divide is reached at about 1520 metres. From here the view to Dusky Sound is comprehensive. The descent to Lake Roe Hut is straightforward. It is possible to continue westwards past the south end of Lake Bright and along the Pleasant Range on the north side of Lake Horizon before dropping to the Seaforth River above Loch Maree instead of descending to Lake Roe.

## FLORENCE STREAM TO KINTAIL VIA EMERALD STREAM

The main North Branch of the Florence is the third tributary on the north side of the valley. From its junction with the Florence follow up this valley and after passing the small gorge and waterfall, sidle and climb a spur on the west bank dropping down to open flats, at the head of which the valley takes a right-angle turn to the west. This takes about four hours from the Florence. Continue round this bend, climbing past two gorges and passing a waterfall to reach the top flats, where a glacier fed tributary enters from the south. Reasonable going will be found on the south side of the first gorge and the north side of the second. From the flats continue up through open tussock, past some tarns and climb a steep scree slope to the pass at the head of the valley. The route from the pass into the Emerald Stream is straightforward and Lake St. Patrick may be visited by following down stream, keeping to the true-left above a gorge.

At the head of the Emerald there is an easy saddle, lower than the previous one from the north branch of the Florence, which leads into the head of the major tributary of the Kintail Stream. Reasonable going will be found down to the junction with the Kintail, which is a good day from Lake St. Patrick, thus joining with the Pillans Pass route described in the previous chapter. Alternatively, a party with mountaineering experience might be able to follow

The head of the Jaquiery River. This view is from the pass overlooking the Russet Burn.

a high-level route northwards along the tops to join the route near Pillans Pass itself.

*Times: Florence junction to top flats, 1 day; Top flats to pass, 2 hrs.*

## FLORENCE STREAM TO SPEY RIVER VIA THE TOPS

The first main tributary of the Florence Stream leads over the tops to Lake St. Patrick and makes for pleasant travel. The descent to Lake St. Patrick is steep, working down through bluffs on the true-right of the waterfall that joins Emerald Stream below the lake.

Crossings are possible from Lake St. Patrick to the Spey, skirting the western side of Mt Watson to drop steeply on a spur between Diamond Creek and Shott Stream to join the track. Travel down Emerald Stream from Lake St. Patrick is not possible in high water.

## JAQUIERY RIVER TO LAKE ROE

This is an interesting trip, but can be made hazardous by fresh snow on the Merrie Range which is crossed at over 1400 metres and with steep slopes on both sides. It should only be attempted by experienced parties. Fog can also cause delays in the vicinity of Lake Roe and the Pleasant Range and parties should make allowance for this in planning trip schedules.

Leaving Clark Hut, follow open swampy flats down the Grebe River on the true-left side of the valley till the mouth of the Jaquiery is reached in about one hour. The junction can also be reached in about three hours from the Borland Road.

The route leads up the south bank of the Jaquiery with good going about 30 metres above the stream until in 1 $\frac{1}{2}$ hours the junction with the north branch is reached. The main stream is crossed below the junction and the route follows up the true-left bank of the north branch, keeping away from and above the stream until a waterfall, which can be heard in the gorge below is passed. Gradually move closer to the stream until about an hour from the junction the stream is crossed where the going is obviously easier on the opposite bank. Continue on the true-right bank until some swampy clearings are passed and cross back to the true-left bank where the river swings left and the head basin is revealed in the distance. The grade steepens and the route follows deer trails away from the stream until after passing another waterfall when the easiest going lies close to the stream until the bushline is reached. Keep in the streambed for a few hundred metres after leaving the bush to avoid difficult scrub and until open grassy flats are reached where good camp sites are readily available.

Merrie Range. Looking across the head of the Florence River towards the high pass above Lake Roe from the ridge between the Florence and Jaquiery Rivers. The Russet Burn lies to the left.
*Photo: P.D. Orange.*

The Jaquiery Saddle is visible from this point, above a shingle slide far above at the head of the valley. It is reached by climbing up through two basins, the first being gained by climbing up the true-right of the stream to the first basin. The stream is crossed here and the way is straight up the centre of the basin and through a narrow gut to the second basin. The shingle slide is now directly ahead and is climbed up through a narrow neck and then, with a short scramble up loose rock and bare rock ribs, the saddle is gained.

From the saddle move to the right, dropping about 60 metres past a small snow-fed tarn and then sidle north over rough slabs and shingle towards a prominent shoulder at about the same level. This is reached in 30 minutes from the Jaquiery Saddle. The route descends steeply from this shoulder to the low hummocky saddle ahead which divides the Russett Burn on the left from the West Branch of the Florence Stream on the right.

There are two low saddles separated by a steep rocky knob, which is climbed with assistance of tussock hand-holds. From the second of these saddles ascend steeply up the large rocky prominence which leads towards the main Merrie Range. When starting to descend again, bear to the right past some small tarns and then up a rocky defile which leads north-west and right in under the range. Commence to sidle upward across a shingle slide which drops steeply from the main range down through a narrow gut to the large deep blue lake below. After passing out above this lake ascend the solid rock ridge which provides good climbing directly toward the high point in the range above. When close to the top a small niche in the ridge will be visible a short distance away on the left and across a small permanent icefield. From this niche a vast panorama of rolling tussock and tarns is visible to the west, with Lake Roe prominent in the foreground below.

Directly in front and below is Prominent Knob with the large basin containing Deep Snowy Lake, not visible, to the right. Drop steeply down and to the right towards the lowest point in the ridge leading to Prominent Knob. If the weather is clear the best route is over Prominent Knob and directly down to Lake Roe. Alternatively, pass through the low point in the ridge and descend steeply to Deep Snowy Lake which is followed to the left around the shore to the outlet. From here climb steeply down over large unstable boulders and follow the outlet stream westward over a couple of low tussock ridges until Lake Roe is reached. If the weather is foggy keep to the right under steep bluffs until the lake can be seen close at hand and on the left.

Follow around the northern end of Lake Roe toward the low country directly westward which forms the divide between the middle branch of the Hauroko Burn and the Deadwood Creek. Drop down through patches of stunted beech to

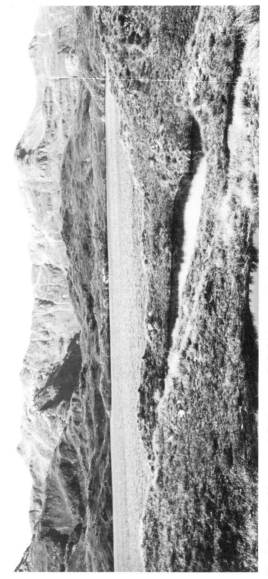

Merrie Range. Looking across Lake Roe towards the high pass to the Florence River. The route sidles from the pass to Prominent Knob and descends either as shown, or further left behind the Knob to Snowy Lake.
*Photo: S.R. Allen.*

the Lake Roe Hut at the northern end of a small tarn named Lake Laffy. For the remainder of the route from here on to Dusky Sound refer to the Dusky Sound Track section.

*Time: Jaquiery junction to flats, about 5 hrs; Flats to Jaquiery Saddle, about 2 hrs; Jaquiery Saddle to main Merrie Range, about 3 hrs. Total time from campsite at head of the Jaquiery to Lake Roe Hut, 8-9 hrs.*

## WEST BRANCH OF JAQUIERY RIVER

An earlier edition of this guide book referred to this valley as an alternative route to Lake Roe, joining the north branch route again at the saddle between the Florence Stream and the Russett Burn. This can be done, but is not very direct by comparison. However, the saddle at the head of the valley does give access to the Russett Burn at a point across the valley from Lake Story.

*Time: Grebe junction to saddle, 1 full day.*

# Lake Monowai and Borland Burn Area

The ranges of the Hunter Mountains, which are visible from most parts of Southland, form a pleasant and familiar background to the view towards the west. The road to the foot of Lake Monowai provides quick access to within a few hours of the open tops. These tops, compared with the country further north, are by no means high and during the summer months are usually clear of snow.

## BORLAND ROAD

The Borland Road, owned by DoC, enters the national park by the Borland Lodge and goes as far as the Percy Saddle. Access to the road is unrestricted to traffic during summer. The gate is kept locked between 31st May to 1st October although the key may be hired from DoC at Tuatapere, Te Anau or Invercargill. The road is unsealed, narrow and steep in places. There are shelters on the road at Borland Saddle, start of the Green Lake Track, Florence River, bottom of the Percy Saddle and at South Arm.

## CARPARK TO RODGER INLET AND MONOWAI HUT

The Rodger Inlet track starts at the Fiordland National Park entrance sign 300 metres before reaching the end of the road at Lake Monowai. Climb the terrace and follow the track through manuka in a westerly direction. Little trouble will be experienced in keeping to the track. After about half an hour the track forks and the left-hand route leading down to Walkers Creek should be followed. The track then crosses an old river delta, which tends to be very boggy during wet periods, before reaching the shores of Rodger Inlet. This point is 20 minutes away from the six bunk Rodger Inlet Huts.

From Rodger Inlet Huts a steep climb to the open tops is rewarded by great views of Lake Monowai and the mountains of Southern Fiordland. The track deteriorates to a route and leaves the open tops to descend to the head of the lake and Monowai Hut.

**Times:** *Monowai carpark to Rodger Inlet Huts, 3 ¹/₂ hrs; Rodger Inlet Huts to Monowai Hut, 7 hrs.*

## CARPARK TO MT CLEUGHEARN, GREEN LAKE AND THE UPPER GREBE VALLEY

Half an hour along the Rodger Inlet Track mentioned above, a signpost indicates the start of the Green Lake Track. This track climbs steeply to a saddle between Mt Cuthbert and the ridge leading to Mt Burns, overlooking Green Lake.

To ascend Mt Burns from this saddle, climb northwards steeply through heavy snowgrass to the top of the ridge and follow this steadily for about four hours to the summit, traversing a subsidiary peak on the way. A simple descent on open tops then bush can then be made to the Borland Saddle carpark.

To reach the site of the derelict Ryans Hut, sidle southwards from the track to the left of Mt Cuthbert until a spur runs down to the east where the old hut site will be found. The summit of Mt Cuthbert, overlooking Green Lake, is easily reached up snowgrass slopes and, further to the south, Mt Cleughearn can be climbed in about two hours from the Ryans Hut.

The most interesting route to the top of Mt Cleughearn is by following along the narrow ridge to the south of Mt Cuthbert and from here excellent views are obtained of the ranges on all sides. Continuing along the ridge a small, deep lake called the Devils Punch-bowl is seen in a straight drop below on the eastern side. The ridge narrows and climbs steeply up the Devils Staircase onto Rocky Top and from here, after a slight descent, leads up the north ridge of Mt Cleughearn.

To reach Green Lake itself from the gap between the Mt Burns Ridge and Mt Cuthbert, continue along the marked track across a swampy section above the bushline, which descends gradually across bush clad slopes to the lake shore. The four bunk Green Lake Hut is located on the western side of a large tussock flat.

From Green Lake Hut continue through tongues of bush northwards up onto a spur from which Island Lake clearing will be seen. From a clearing before Island Lake, the Borland Road track junction is met. Tussock clearings, marked by poles, and beech covered saddles lead to the road.

The track skirts the top of the clearing and travels on round to the outlet. The Island Lake outlet is the source of the Grebe River and is followed downwards to a small clearing. The river then goes through a small gorge and drops down to another clearing. Passing to the left of the island of bush, follow down through this clearing and the track will be picked up on the bush edge, 200 metres to the left of the main creek. The track continues through a gap in the hills, then follows downwards, keeping the river below on the right. In less than an hour from the last clearing the river comes out onto the Grebe Flats. Pushing through scrub the Grebe Swamp is reached and across the valley will be seen Clark Hut above the junction of Fowler Stream. The river is crossed and Clark Hut will be found well into the bush. During heavy rain the Grebe Swamp becomes very boggy and the river difficult to cross.

From Clark Hut the track traverses the bush edge and crosses the Grebe River. It then enters the bush to gain a saddle before descending gently to Lake Monowai. In reverse, approach the head of Lake Monowai by boat to land at Boat Harbour to the west of the stream mouth. From the hut, the track leads some 300 metres through the bush to a small clearing. Directly across the clearing a good marked track leads all the way to Clark Hut.

**Times:** *Carpark to Green Lake Hut, 6 ¹/₂ hrs; Green Lake Hut to Borland Road, 2 ¹/₂ hrs; Green Lake Hut to Clark Hut, 4 hrs; Clark Hut to Monowai Hut, 4 hrs.*

## BORLAND VALLEY

All tracks in this area are well marked with permalat strips and school pupils based at the Borland Lodge use the track system extensively. The lodge was donated by the then Electricity Department to the Southland Youth Adventure Trust in 1972. Accommodation is available to the public, but school groups have priority over other bookings.

The track to the North, Middle and South Branches of the Borland enters the bush to the right of the Borland Road gate on the Fiordland National Park boundary. Pig Creek is crossed by a swing bridge and the track carries on to reach the Borland and follows up the true-right bank to the junction of the South Branch which should be reached in about an hour. This point may also be reached by a track that descends steadily from the Borland road about six kilometres up from the lodge. After crossing the South Branch by a walk wire the track continues for half an hour to a good campsite where there is a large, dry bivvy rock.

Continuing from this point the track shortly comes to the foot of a high white rock which can be seen from Monowai and in about ten minutes from this point the forks of the North and Middle Branches are reached.

**Times:** *Borland gate to Borland south branch, 1 hr; South branch to bivvy rock, ¹/₂ hr; Bivvy rock to Borland middle branch, ¹/₄ hr.*

## NORTH BORLAND BURN TO MT TITIROA

After crossing the middle branch of the Borland Burn by a walk wire, the North Borland track leads on an angle up a steep hill and for about 45 minutes climbs through totara and celery pine trees to the edge of a deep gorge and then continues on for a kilometre to a clearing. Mt Titiroa will now be seen to the north-east. After a further hour's travel through bush covered ridges a long tussock clearing is reached and about half an hour later the two bunk North Borland Hut will be found on the true-left bank of the river.

The rest of the way to the head of the valley is all clear going. The river has its source at a small lake in a basin on an unnamed mountain peak and looking back east from this lake the saddle leading over into the Garnock Burn will be seen. Continuing along the ridges towards Titiroa, a splendid view of Lake Manapouri can be obtained, appearing like numerous separate lakes, with Lake Te Anau further on in the distance.

To cross to Manapouri do not go to the head of the valley, but follow up the first small creek joining the river from the north a short distance above the hut. This leads to the saddle over to the Garnock Burn. From the saddle follow a creek down to the bushline, then angle left and follow a spur down to the valley floor. The route from here to Hope Arm and onwards to the Waiau River at Manapouri is described in the Garnock Burn section.

*Time:* Borland middle branch to North Borland Hut, 3 hrs; Pig Creek to North Borland Hut, 5 $^1/_2$ hrs; Hut to head of valley, 2 $^1/_2$ hrs.

## SOUTH BRANCH OF BORLAND BURN

The South Borland track branches off 100 metres before the crossing on the North Borland Track is reached and continues to climb up the terraces following the stream for about 45 minutes. It then rises away from the river and traverses below a spectacular sand-stone outcrop. Another ten minutes brings one out on to the transmission line road 1 $^1/_2$ hours from the Lodge. This track, walked in reverse from that described above, is a pleasant family outing of four to five hours and is sign-posted where it leaves the road.

## MIDDLE BRANCH OF BORLAND BURN

The Middle Borland track commences 100 metres upstream from the confluence of the Middle and North Branches. It initially follows the south bank then crosses to the north bank until the small clearing below Borland Peak is reached after approximately 1 $^1/_4$ hours. From this clearing the track follows up the south bank ending at the gorge midway between the confluence with the North Branch and the head of the valley. Should the river be too high to cross it is possible to follow the south bank from the confluence to this point although the terrain is rougher. The large tussock clearing above the gorge is best reached by continuing up the south bank and while the route is poorly defined some blazes from the original cullers' track remain. A good campsite can be found halfway along this clearing, on the south bank, approximately three hours from the confluence. From here it takes another three hours to reach the lake at the head of the valley, the south bank still providing the easiest travelling.

191

Crossings to the Grebe Valley and to the Garnock Burn are possible from the head of the valley, and the tributary joining from below Peak 4,870ft (1484 metres) provides easy access to the tops and to the saddle with the South Branch.

*Time: Pig Creek to start of Middle Borland track, 1 hr; Start of track to head of valley, 6 hrs.*

## BORLAND SADDLE TO ISLAND LAKE

A 3 1/2-4 hour walk up the Borland Road from Borland Lodge leads to the Borland Saddle which gives easy access to the Hunter Range. Prior to reaching the saddle an A-frame shelter is situated just off the road in the South Borland Valley. The Island Lake track commences from the road about 20 minutes beyond the saddle and proceeds due south to join the Green Lake-Clark Hut track at the head of Island Lake, one hour from the road. Along this track, at the first clearing, Pyramid Lake is traversed along the eastern perimeter then through an opening to another small clearing. The track will be located along the eastern side and heads away at the southern end. Archies Clearing is the only other clearing which is crossed. Head straight out, slightly left of the obvious draining exit. On the left an orange marker at bush edge indicates the track.

As an alternative to this route, follow directly up onto the ridge from Borland Saddle until overlooking Green Lake on easy tops. The second obvious shingle slide offers the best descent to Green Lake. The track mentioned above can then be followed to Island Lake.

## MT ELDRIG

A short track from the Borland Road leads to the bushline on Mt Eldrig. About 1 1/4 hours from the lodge follow the spur road indicated by the track sign to the highest pylon at the end of that road. From there it takes another hour through the bush to the tussock tops of Mt Eldrig. One can then continue westwards to Mt Burns and descend to the road near the saddle.

# THE SOUTH COAST

# Lake Hauroko

Lake Hauroko is the nearest of the southern lakes to Invercargill, lying approximately 110 kilometres from the city. At the end of the road there are picnic facilities, a jetty and a launching ramp. The lake is aptly named Hauroko, Sounding Wind, and the greatest care must be taken by parties using boats as there are very few sheltered spots where a boat can be beached when a storm arises. As the lake can become dangerously rough very quickly, small boats are not recommended.

As a caution, it should be noted that not very far south of the lake from the car park, the streams run to Foveaux Straight and not back to the lake. The age-old practice of following a stream out has resulted in more than a few hunters spending unplanned nights out on the strength of this geological phenomenon. A compass should be carried in this area.

A track from the jetty climbs from the north end of the bay to the top of a high bluff 1 ½ hours away, from which there is an excellent view of the lake, the sea to the south and the plains to the east.

### HAUROKO CARPARK TO TEAL BAY HUT

At the south end of the lake the 12 bunk Teal Bay Hut is located on the east side, approximately two kilometres from the outlet. This hut is opposite the island in Teal Bay and can be reached either by boat or by the track from the Hauroko picnic area, or by the Bluecliffs-Hump Track described later.

The track starts from the picnic shelter and follows the lake shore south to the far end of South Beach. There the start of the track is easily found and this leads over a peninsula to a secluded beach. From the far end of this beach the track continues on the ridge to the south end of the lake where it descends steeply to the lake edge and the 12 bunk Teal Bay Hut.

*Time: Car park to Teal Bay Hut, 10 hrs.*

### TE WAEWAE BAY TO TEAL BAY HUT VIA THE HUMP

The Hump Range lies to the west of Te Waewae Bay and rises to a height of 1067 metres. On a fine day a magnificent view is obtained of southern Fiordland, overlooking Lakes Poteriteri and Hauroko and the vast area of country beyond the range stretching towards Long Sound and Preservation Inlet.

From the end of the Bluecliffs Beach, access to which is described in the Te Waewae Bay to Preservation Inlet section, find the old logging road above the beach. Take the first old road which branches off to the right, just across the Hump Burn. This road continues for approximately five kilometres and is joined by several side roads, but the main track is obvious to follow. The start of the Hump Track from this road is signposted. The track is obvious, muddy, is not blazed and leads to the remains of the New Zealand Deerstalkers' Association Hut. The hut was burnt down in 1994, but there are plans to rebuild it. The hut site is a little east of where it is marked on S167, being at S167 478328.

For the next half hour from here the track is through light bush to about halfway up a spur and then climbs up the steep open spur to the top of the range. Orange marker poles show the route across the alpine section but they may be difficult to follow in poor weather. Parties with time to spare may like to walk southwards for some distance along the ridge to view the remarkable rocks there.

The highest point on the range, marked by a trig station, is reached from the ridge to the right through a saddle and the tops can then be followed in a north-westerly direction until Lake Hauroko comes into view. The track continues from the most north-westerly tussock tongue and leads down the prominent ridge to the lake shore at a point 20 minutes south of the Teal Bay Hut. The start of this track off the tops is well marked as it enters the bush. It is 15 minutes to the walk wire over the Wairaurahiri River, some 200 metres down stream from the outlet from the point where the track reaches the lake. A DoC sign on the Hauroko boundary track indicates the start of the track beside the lake.

*Time: Te Waewae Bay to Hump Hut site, 2 hrs; Hump Hut site to Teal Bay Hut, 4 1/2 hrs; Teal Bay Hut to Hump Hut site, 7 hrs; Hump Hut site to Bluecliff road end, 5 hrs.*

## THE HUMP TO WAIRAURAHIRI HUT

There is a route off the south end of the Hump Ridge, down to the Wairaurahiri Hut on the south coast. Follow down the ridge dividing the two branches of the Kaituna Stream and then the south side of this stream, after the branches join, to its junction with the Wairaurahiri River. Continue down the east bank of the Wairaurahiri to Rabbit Flat, then on to Lookout Bluff and down to the Wairaurahiri Hut.

*Time: Hump Hut site to Wairaurahiri Hut, two days.*

# Hauroko and Poteriteri Watersheds

The routes described in the immediately preceding chapters are, for the most part, properly formed and well-marked tracks, with huts located within reach of each day's journey. However, the remote regions west of Lake Hauroko should be tackled only by experienced parties properly equipped for rough country and for weather conditions which are often much worse than those further north in Fiordland. The valleys and ridges here are traversed infrequently and, in the absence of any real tracks, the route descriptions leave much to the initiative of individual parties.

## LAKE HAUROKO OUTLET TO LOWER LAKE POTERITERI VIA RATA BURN

The Rata Burn joins the Wairaurahiri River below the swing bridge at the outlet of Lake Hauroko. From the site of the former deer-stalkers' hut at the southern end of Lake Hauroko head due west along a small gully and the Rata Burn is reached in about 20 minutes. Continue up valley to the forks and take the south branch. The valley soon steepens and it is necessary to climb a few hundred feet above the gorge on the north bank. Take the right fork, looking up stream, where the stream splits about an hour above the gorge and from here climb up to some open flats just below bushline. From here climb up the snowgrass basin which curves leftwards to a low rise overlooking a large attractive tarn to the north. Its outflow plunges down a steep scrubby gut into the Rata Burn basin. Further to the south there is a small two bunk A-frame hut known as Waps Bivvy.

From the head of the tarn mentioned above climb steeply to an obvious ledge that gives access to a pass above, then descend on the right side of an eroded gut and down steep bush to the upper reaches of an unnamed stream that leads down to Lake Poteriteri. There are some large swampy clearings to cross and then the valley falls in fairly steep drops. In about two hours the valley assumes the characteristics of a canyon and the lip of an impressive waterfall is reached. At the same time a deeply gorged tributary enters from the west and it appears that the route has struck a dead end. However, a deer trail sidles on the right some distance into this tributary then climbs back above the chasm of the main stream. If the river is high the canyon can be negotiated on the true-right though the country is exceedingly rough and progress is very slow. Below the gorge the river turns sharply to the west and Lake Poteriteri may be reached in an hour by following an old blazed trail on the true-left bank.

There is probably an easier route from the South Rata Burn, or adjacent spurs, by climbing and traversing the Beatrice Peaks southwards to a bush knob at

S166 363363 from where a descent should be found to the bush flats below the gorge.

*Time: Outlet of Lake Hauroko to forks, 2 hrs; Forks to bushline, 4 hrs; Traverse of pass, 3 hrs; Head of Rata Burn to Lake Poteriteri eastern shore, 1-2 days.*

## LAKE HAUROKO OUTLET TO HEAD OF LAKE POTERITERI VIA CAROLINE BURN AND PRINCESS MOUNTAINS

It has been suggested that this route is harder than following up the Rata Burn and then heading north on the tops. However, the Editor has no description of this route. From the outlet of Lake Hauroko follow the shore or terraces where possible to the steep bush slopes north of the Rata Burn delta. Climb fairly high and sidle using deer trails until above the very deep ravine through which the Caroline Burn takes a plunge into Lake Hauroko. Select a gradual route of descent into the Caroline Valley above the gorge. Allow a full day to reach this valley from the foot of Lake Hauroko. If a boat is taken to the mouth of the Caroline Burn climb high on the south side of the ravine.

Above the gorge the south bank provides good going for about an hour to where a large tributary joins from the north. Then the valley narrows again, though the north side may be traversed without too much difficulty. After about an hour of rough sidling the valley widens and the open though often swampy nature of the forest floor allows fast progress to the upper valley. In a couple of hours from the gorge a number of small grassy clearings are reached, before the valley forks. Taking the west branch more open boggy ground is crossed then the valley climbs steadily and swings to the north. The size of the stream dwindles in about two to three hours from the forks and a narrow swampy clearing indicates the low saddle between the Caroline and Unknown Valleys.

Cross the saddle and descend a short distance into the bush to where a small stream cascades down from a basin to the west. This basin can be seen from the pass, but a direct ascent can lead into problems. Follow good deer trails alongside this stream until above the bush, then climb to the ridge that encloses the basin. Lake Poteriteri now appears 1000 metres directly below with a surfeit of rugged mountains surrounding it. Proceed northwards along the ridge traversing a small peak (1220 metres) then sidling along the west slopes of a larger peak to descend to a prominent terrace at bushline. This flat provides an excellent campsite, having recourse to a small tarn and a shelter of trees.

From the northern end of the terrace a steep spur leads about 300 metres down towards to the Princess Burn, but seems to fade out above a gorged creek. Sidle towards the left looking for deer trails that descend through steep bluffed slopes to the valley floor. The intertwining swamp forest at the head of Lake Poteriteri must then be crossed to reach the Princess Burn at the far side of the valley.

**Times:** *Foot of Hauroko into the Caroline Burn, 1 day; Caroline Burn, 1 day; Alpine crossing and descent to Lake Poteriteri, 1 day.*

## PRINCESS MOUNTAINS

The Princess Mountains are straightforward to traverse from the head of the Rata Burn to End Peak. From End Peak there is an easy descent to Hay River below Sphinx Lake. As the river enters a gorge to enter Lake Hauroko, follow a bush ledge to the north which leads to the head of the lake. Descend to the lake shore just before the Hauroko Burn Hut.

**Time:** *Head of Rata Burn to Hauroko Burn Hut, allow 2 days.*

## LAKE HAUROKO TO HEAD OF LAKE POTERITERI FROM UNKNOWN BURN

Access to the mouth of the Unknown Burn, which enters Lake Hauroko to the north-west of Caroline Peak, is by boat. Head into the bush from a bay to the south of the actual mouth, which is swampy. Deer trails lead close to the south bank and there are open clearings. In about an hour a fork in the valley is reached and the west branch, which swings around in a wide curve, is taken. The top part of the stream affords good travel in the river if it is low enough. Travel close to the stream bank through thick stunted bush until a huge slip on the south side is approached. This slip gives direct access to the open tops of the Princess Mountains, but above 600 metres the gradient becomes very steep. At about 750 metres sidle south-west across the slip towards bushline then force a way through bluffs and chasms to a snowgrass basin. Climb out of the basin towards the peak to the south. From the summit descend the south ridge, cross the head of a snowgrass gully and follow a spur that leads west to the bushline terrace as described in the previous section. The descent to Lake Poteriteri has been described above.

**Time:** *Head of Unknown Burn to Lake Hauroko, 1 day.*

## LAKE POTERITERI TO LAKE KAKAPO

A large tributary of the Princess Burn joins from the west a short distance above the head of Lake Poteriteri. This tributary enters from a hanging valley which contains the large and rarely visited Lake Kakapo. Cross the Princess

197

Burn where it splits into channels above the confluence of the Kakapo Burn and follow the north bank of the latter. Soon it is necessary to climb up steep moss and scrub-covered rock above a deep gorge. At the top keep a good high level gradually working down into the valley floor. Keep to the north side past a swampy lagoon and on to Lake Kakapo.

**Time:** *Princess Burn to Lake Kakapo, 3-4 hrs.*

## LAKE ROE TO HEAD OF LAKE POTERITERI VIA HEATH MOUNTAINS

The traverse of the Heath Mountains from Lake Roe to the saddle between Roa Stream and the Long Burn stays fairly close to the ridge top all the way and is straightforward given good visibility. In poor weather there are bluffs which could catch a party out. There are feasible camping areas at Lake Jane and at the bushline in the south fork of the Jane Burn. If descending from the Heath Mountains to the head of the Jane Burn keep traversing until reasonably near the saddle between the Jane Burn and the Gardner Burn. There are excellent campsites at tarns on the saddle between Roa Stream and the Long Burn.

From the head of the Long Burn sidle above the bushline passing two tarns north-west of Kathryn Peak. Keep sidling above the bushline until a small tarn south of Sea View Peak is reached, then sidle and drop to the saddle above Lake Hay. There are flat camping sites south of Lake Hay, but the area is swampy.

From the south end of Lake Hay climb directly to the saddle to the Princess Burn through subalpine scrub and tussock clearings. There are some small rocky outcrops and bluffs, but they are easy to avoid. The upper reaches of the Princess Burn provide fast travel through open bush. Stay close to the river. There is a small, 15 metre waterfall which is easy to negotiate about halfway between the saddle and the forks.

The route from the forks to the head of Lake Poteriteri is straightforward, but is sometimes extremely slow going through windthrow, swamp, supplejack and pepperwood thickets. There are, however, sometimes good deer trails on raised levees on the banks of the river.

**Times:** *Lake Roe Hut to Long Burn-Roa Stream saddle, 10 hrs; Saddle to south end of Lake Hay, 4-5 hrs; Lake Hay to Princess Burn Saddle, 1 $\frac{1}{2}$ hrs; Saddle to Princess Burn Forks, 4 hrs; Forks to Lake Poteriteri, 8-9 hrs.*

# Long Burn and the Dark Cloud Range

## WEST OF LAKE KAKAPO

The north shore of Lake Kakapo is easily traversed though it becomes a little steeper near the head. The valley above the lake is a quagmire filled with scrubby forest and heavy undergrowth and is unpleasant to negotiate. However, by following the general course of the valley it should be possible to reach the Long Burn in a day. The two watersheds are linked by a scarcely noticeable bush saddle. In about an hour beyond the head of Lake Kakapo a tributary enters from the west. This saddles with the Dunlop Stream and provides a fairly direct route to Lake Widgeon. Continue up the main valley the gradient steepens and large boulders are encountered. Soon the valley forks and the smaller, north-west, branch gives access to the Long Burn. The larger, north-east, branch may be followed to a large unnamed lake at 656 metres, immediately south of Cone Peak.

## HEAD OF LAKE KAKAPO TO THE RICHARD BURN AND LONG SOUND

From the head of Lake Kakapo force a way across the swampy tangles and backwaters to the south side of the valley to where a side stream descends steeply from a gorge. A good deer trail climbs up the true-left side of this tributary keeping high above the gorge. The track leads onto a spur covered with stunted beech and the route swings gradually towards the west. After an hour's climbing a clearing is reached giving a good view of the way ahead. Deer trails and narrow openings in the dense, dwarf forest give easy access to the lip of the plateau which is the low saddle between Lake Kakapo and the Richard Burn. Assuming a dry campsite could be found, this extensive and attractive parkland saddle would make a good base for further exploration. From here it is possible to reach the Dunlop Stream by climbing over a ridge to the north, or Lake Monk by traversing open tops to the south-west. To the south another saddle of about the same height leads into the watershed of Lake Mouat.

On descending from the outlet of a crescent shaped lake situated at the top of the saddle try to keep out of the scrub as much as possible. Below bushline the Richard Burn is easily followed to where a large tributary enters from the north. Across this stream there is a large rock overhang that would accommodate several people. Progress down the true-right bank becomes hampered by massive boulders until the valley widens and a stream enters from the south. Here the river splits into innumerable channels, no doubt rendering this section difficult in wet conditions. Further down stream the valley narrows again and the river falls in rapids to Long Sound. Deer trails lead down on the true-left and the river cuts into some remarkable chasms on its plunging course to the Sound. From the mouth of the Richard Burn it is probably possible to climb above Cascade Basin to Lake Widgeon and force a way around the east side of the lake into the Long Burn or the Dunlop Stream.

*Times:* Lake Kakapo to saddle, 3 hrs; Saddle to Long Sound, one day.

## DUNLOP STREAM

From the pass at the head of Dunlop Stream, reached either from the tributary above Lake Kakapo, or across the tops from the Richard Burn Saddle, rapid progress can be made down the upper basin through scattered scrub and boggy meadows. In about an hour the valley narrows, but deer trails lead through the gorge until the creek cascades down rocky slabs. Cross over to the true-left and keep high above the stream following deer trails where possible. Conditions improve down the final 300 metres. Possibly a better route could be found on the north side high above the gorge. Dunlop Stream passes through a large lagoon flanked by dense scrubby forest before entering Lake Widgeon about halfway along the east shore. It runs into the lake adjacent to the Long Burn which has formed a prominent spit at its mouth. It is possible to reach this spit by hugging the beech forest bordering the swampland and crossing the neck deep, sluggish Dunlop Stream near the mouth.

The Lake Widgeon environs consist mainly of an almost impenetrable tangle of swamp forest. The lake level is subject to large fluctuations.

## LONG BURN

The Long Burn is one of the most isolated and least visited valleys in Fiordland. From Lake Widgeon it takes two long days to reach the head and the going is often arduous through swamp and scrub, windfalls and gorges. The river, during its long course, passes through several impressive chasms and these may block during floods, resulting in widespread damage to trees along the bank.

From the spit at Lake Widgeon keep close to the east bank of the river, following an avenue of taller bush. In an hour up stream a large tributary enters from the west and the main stream takes a sharp loop. Leave the river bank at this point and follow a deer trail that rejoins the river above a gorge. About half an hour further on is a small rock bivvy that would sleep four people, but although reasonably high above the river it may be prone to flooding. If commencing from the west side of Lake Widgeon, the Long Burn can be forded about 1 1/2 hours up valley, 50 metres below a large half-rounded boulder in the middle of the river.

Continue up valley on the true-left until a large tributary from the east is shortly reached which gives access via a low bush pass to Lake Kakapo. Immediately ahead is the first of a series of lakes which appear to be passable on the east side of the valley. If the river is crossed below the lake try to keep to the beech forest as much as possible as the valley flats ahead are scrubby swampland. Indeed, many hours may be spent in the wallows trying to regain firm ground above the lakes.

The valley eventually begins to climb gradually and the riverbed is followed closely until the valley forks, some 1-1 $\frac{1}{2}$ days from Lake Widgeon. The main branch from the east is followed to where it issues from a dramatic gorge. This is traversed by climbing 150 metres above the ravine on the true-left and keeping a good level until a very steep-sided tributary is reached. Considerable difficulty may be experienced in crossing this obstacle, but there is a way about 30 to 40 metres above the main river. The tributary itself leads to Lake Hay and the Hay River via a low bush saddle. After crossing this tributary keep sidling high until it seems possible to descend to the main river above the gorge. Progress now resumes a more respectable pace and when the banks become scrubby the riverbed is followed. In about two hours from the gorge a prominent loop in the stream is reached and then at the head of the valley scattered scrub and tussock slopes are encountered.

Good campsites are available in pockets of beech close to the stream above a short climb in the valley. A low pass ahead with a number of small tarns give easy access to the Heath Range. Assuming fine, clear weather Lake Roe may be reached in a day following the main ridge in the north-east direction. Routes may also be found to link with the Gardner or Hauroko Burns and the Roa Stream provides direct access to the Seaforth River.

As an alternative route to that described above, some parties have climbed up on to the Dark Cloud Range from Lake Widgeon and followed the tops all the way before descending to the campsites at the head of the valley. This takes three days, or more and is essentially a fine-weather route.

## PRESERVATION INLET TO LONG BURN VIA DARK CLOUD RANGE

There is straightforward navigation via tarns and tops, including Treble Mountain, from Southport and Seek Cove to Last Cove in Long Sound. The best route down to Last Cove from the tops is down the spur to the east until a flatish area short of point 451 metres is reached. From here descend a gut to north of this point to the shoreline.

From Last Cove cross over a scrubby ridge to Cliff Cove and around the exposed shoreline to Two Cove Head. Gradually sidle upwards to eventually climb onto Two Cove Head Spur at approximately 180 metres. The final climb onto the spur is very steep. Follow the spur up to south tops of the Dark Cloud Range through easy going open bush. There is a beautiful tarn and campsite north of the top of the spur at S166 010504.

The tops of the Dark Cloud Range are humpy, but traversable as far as Needle Peak where the gradient steepens. To continue northwards, drop into the stream south-east of Needle Peak and follow it down into the valley. Sidle and climb upwards to the saddle at the head, to the north. Drop into Cascade Creek, always sidling left, to emerge at the first of some small tarns. The descent is through thick bush and is sometimes steep.

Cross boggy ground to the second and larger tarn at the head of the creek. This tarn is rounded on the northern side and then an obvious ramp is climbed on granite slabs to the saddle north-east of the tarn. From the saddle climb up a short steep gut to rejoin the Dark Cloud Range tops north of point 1,164 metres. Follow the tops in a north-west direction, sidling knobs on the eastern side, until, swinging north, a flat area containing three tarns is reached. Here the tops become too steep to traverse and the best route drops down west to the top tributary of Carrick River. It is possible that the tops may be traversable in dry weather, but this is not known. At the junction of this tributary climb eastwards again through thick bush to rejoin the Dark Cloud Range tops at an unnamed tarn at S157 065634. This tarn can be negotiated with considerable difficulty on the northern shore and a saddle is crossed to a larger tarn at 701± metres. Swing north again to follow Oho Creek through stunted bush and clearings to Lake Mike.

Climb the leading spur back to the Dark Cloud Range and travel through undulating tussock flats to Prong Lake. Head towards the obvious saddle to the north-east and on the west shore of a large unnamed lake at 780± metres. Climb through bush and tussock to the end of the ridge north of the lake where a panoramic view of the Long Burn and environs is gained on a good day. Drop off the ridge down a north easterly spur to the Long Burn which is gained with some difficulty. The spur is steep at times and no best route is obvious although this is the only feasible route. Avoid the bluffs at 300 metres. The river is swampy and the best campsites are further back from the river.

# Aan River- Big River Area

The routes described below are comparable in difficulty with the routes west from Lake Hakapoua described in the previous chapter. Parties must be well equipped and prepared for a type of travel in total contrast with the easy south coast track from Te Waewae Bay to the foot of Lake Hakapoua.

## AAN RIVER TO HEAD OF LAKE HAKAPOUA

Leave the south coast track before crossing the swing bridge over the Aan River and follow the terrace of this creek until it becomes convenient to travel closer to the river bank. After three to four hours watch closely for the valley junction as the outflow from Lake Innes could easily be missed. The main stream, which is not followed, soon issues from a steep gorge. From the junction take a compass-bearing across a wide, swampy gully to Lake Innes, reached in about 30 minutes. Good campsites can be found at the foot of this large attractive lake enclosed by bush clad hills.

The head of the lake is reached in about 1 ½ hours by scrambling along the west bank, then a gully is climbed through dense stunted forest to a low saddle which gives access to Lake Hakapoua. The descent is short and sharp to swampy Lake Marshall. Progress down stream from the outlet remains relatively slow through bush entanglements. About 20 minutes below the lake it is best to sidle northwards away from the creek, over a low spur and into another gully which also drops to Lake Hakapoua. If this gully is followed down almost to the lake a large rock will be noticed to the right of the gully about 15 metres above the lake. This is an excellent dry bivvy rock to sleep four people and with ample room for a fire.

Keeping a course 30-50 metres above Lake Hakapoua, look very carefully for a ledge which remarkably traverses a series of vertical bluffs. This natural passageway, which is used by deer, must surely be one of Fiordland's most impressive features. Do not drop down to the lake after emerging from the ledge, but sidle and climb over further bluffs before making the descent to the stony shore at the head of the lake.

***Times:*** *South Coast track to Lake Innes, 4 hrs; Lake Innes to Head of Hakapoua, 5-6 hrs.*

## BIG RIVER

Big River enters Lake Hakapoua at the western extremity of the beach. Follow the riverbank through dense fern until gravel beds provide good going. In

1 ¹/₂ hours the river cascades through a short gorge which is easily followed on the true-right. Above the rapids the valley swings to the west and opens up, revealing a huge slip on the eastern slopes. After crossing through a devastated forest and swampy ground on the true-left ford the river again and proceed towards the junction.

The west branch of Big River probably provides the best route to the Cameron Mountains or the head of Lake Monk. After three hours of fairly easy going the valley narrows and travel becomes rougher. The crux of the gorge is reached after the valley swings due west and if the river is high it may be necessary to climb 100 metres or so on the true-left to get past. The final exit of the canyon is via a tumble of windfall debris down to bush flats and pepperwood swamps and further on to large swampy clearings. It is possible to reach these flats in one long day from the head of Lake Hakapoua.

Continue up stream. Conditions vary, but nowhere assume the difficulties of the gorge. It may be desirable to cross the river in several places. A further series of flats is reached in about three hours, then a tributary enters from the west and the main stream falls from a higher level in the valley. Climbing a deer trail on the true-left keep fairly close to the rapids until the upper valley and more open flats are reached. A low scrubby pass to the north gives easy access to the Cameron Mountains. Tongues of open swampy ground alleviate, to a certain extent, the toil of scrub-bashing and the 150 metre climb takes about half an hour.

From the head basin of Big River, where there is an attractive lake, it is possible to traverse a low saddle to the south-east and reach the head of Lake Monk.

## CAMERON MOUNTAINS

From the low pass east of Arnett Peak force a way through the scrub to the bushline, then climb up to the main ridge of the Cameron Mountains which may be followed in a north-easterly direction to the region of Lake Kakapo. The high points of the ridge are Rugged Mountain and a slightly higher unnamed peak, the latter being traversed on the east side. Views from the ridge are exceptional with numerous tarns, park-like basins and deep ravines. The approach to these tops from the head of Lake Poteriteri, via Lake Kakapo, has been described previously.

*Time: Pass east of Arnett Peak to Lake Kakapo, 1 long day.*

# Te Waewae Bay to Preservation Inlet

The track to Port Craig is well marked and graded. From here on to Big River the track is on the whole good, if rather boggy between Wairaurahiri and Waitutu. All the viaducts are in good order. The route from Big River on to Preservation Inlet, however, is entirely different with no formed track and should be attempted only by stoical, experienced parties.

Parties are encouraged to make a donation to the Southland Port Craig Viaduct Trust, PO Box 857, Invercargill towards the upkeep and maintenance of the Port Craig viaducts. For a description of the Hump Track and routes to the south end of Lake Hauroko and the Wairaurahiri River, see the Lake Hauroko section.

## BLUECLIFFS TO PORT CRAIG

From Tuatapere turn off onto the Papatotara Road and follow the signs to Bluecliffs Beach. Cars may be left at the carpark, or in front of the Rarakau Station homestead on the hill above the carpark, but first notify the farmer.

From the Bluecliffs carpark the old road is followed along the base of the cliff though in some places it has been washed out and small boulder banks must be crossed. At low tide it is best to walk along the beach. Deduct 2 hours 20 minutes from the Bluff tide tables for Port Craig tides. The Waikaou River, an hour from the carpark, may be forded, or crossed by footbridge and either the beach or track may be followed for another 6 ½ kilometres to the end of the Bluecliffs Beach. From the end of the beach follow the main ex-logging road for a kilometre and cross the washed out bridge over the Track Burn.

The track to Port Craig commences from a signpost just across the Track Burn and is well graded for about ¾ hour when it forks so that Flat Creek can be forded at low tide or crossed using the swing bridge. From here travel on the beach apart from two short sections which cross headlands. Half and hour from Flat Creek, at Breakneck Creek, the track resumes to follow up the true-right bank to head inland. This track is used if it is above half-tide as otherwise the beach may be followed instead. The only route back onto the track after Breakneck Creek is at The Whata, a well signposted, steep scramble up a bank at the western end of the bay. The old Port Craig Schoolhouse lies two kilometres farther which is now used as a 15-20 bunk hut. The schoolhouse is a building of high historical significance and parties should treat it as such. Even if parties have no intention of continuing from here, it is worth while making the short trip to the first of the viaducts described below.

*Time: Carpark to Port Craig, via beach , 5-6 hrs; Carpark to Port Craig, via track, 6-7 hrs.*

Swing bridge. This one, across the Waitutu River, is a standard NZFS design.

## PORT CRAIG TO WAIRAURAHIRI, WAITUTU AND BIG RIVERS

From the Port Craig Schoolhouse the track heads south across a small creek next to the hut, then the old logging tramline provides a well graded track for the next 15 kilometres, almost to the Wairaurahiri River where there is a 12 bunk hut. About 1 1/2 hours from Port Craig is Sandhill Point which is *tapu* to the local Maori— please do not leave the track here. Beyond Sandhill Point are four viaducts on the old tramline, all of which have been re-decked. At the end of the tramline the track enters unlogged forest and drops down three terraces to the clearing beside the hut. As an alternative route the coast can be followed from Sandhill Point, but the trip should be timed for the tide halfway out between the Francis Burn and the Wairaurahiri.

A swing bridge crosses the Wairaurahiri River at the hut and the track continues on through tall podocarp forest for 13 kilometres to the Waitutu River. The track is inland from the coast and is less well defined than the earlier section. There is a walk wire over Crombie Stream and swing bridges over the Angus Burn and Waitutu River. After crossing the Waitutu follow up stream about 200 metres to find the 12 bunk Waitutu Hut.

The track to Big River commences at the western end of the hut and again follows the remains of the Puysegur Point—Orepuki telephone line. All that can be seen now is some wire, insulators and trees sawn off about two metres above ground that were used as telephone poles. There are swing bridges over the Grant Burn and the Aan River, but no more huts past the Waitutu River, which also marks the start of Fiordland National Park. On reaching Big River follow the river up until opposite a little island. Ford the stream to this island and, provided the main channel is not in flood, continue straight over to the other side of the river. A camp can be made here on the site of an old hut, demolished some years ago.

***Times:*** *Port Craig to Sandhill Point, 1 1/2 hrs; Sandhill Point to Wairaurahiri, 4-6 hrs; Wairaurahiri to Waitutu, 5 hrs; Waitutu to Big River, 5-7 hrs.*

## BIG RIVER TO HILL E

From Big River there is no formed track and travel is through diabolical, dense, slimy, scratchy, stunted bush which is difficult to push through. Nylon over-trousers are recommended to protect the legs from scratches. In the past it has been the usual practice to try and follow the old telephone line to Puysegur Point. However, as considerable extra time can be wasted in trying to locate the line of the old track, which tends anyway to be replaced by dense regeneration, it is probably better to work out your own route by topographic map and compass.

Head up stream from the Big River Hut site and skirt the shoreline of Lake Hakapoua for a distance of about two kilometres from the hut, S173&174 141228. From here head west to cross the saddle into the Cavendish Valley and follow the East Branch of the Cavendish River down to its junction with the main river, which is a suitable crossing place. Unless there has been high flooding there is normally no problem in crossing the Cavendish, nor the next river, the Fred Burn, although it does flood easily. By following the Cavendish up from the junction for about a kilometre a direct east-west approach can be made to the Fred Burn saddle. From the saddle continue in the same general direction to cross the Fred Burn at the junction of its north and west branches and follow along the south bank of the latter, occasionally meeting with the phone line. Now climb gradually out of the valley and sidle round the northern slopes of Kakapo Hill, where the remains of an old P&T maintenance hut may be seen. From here continue west to ascend a ridge leading up to the summit of Hill E (1,468 ft, 447 metres) for the inland route that continues NNW along the line of the old gold miners' trail to Cromarty. Parties choosing the easier coastal route can either head for Hill E, or for the saddle between Hill E and Hill K.

*Times: Lake Hakapoua to Hill E, allow 1-1 ¹/₂ days.*

## HILL E TO KISBEE BAY, PRESERVATION INLET VIA THE INLAND ROUTE

Old maps show that the goldminers' route headed more or less straight from Hill E to the outlet of Lake Kiwi. Although this route has not been checked since its use in the 1890's, a bearing a few degrees north of this to about halfway along the eastern shore of Lake Kiwi has been traversed recently and would seem to cross easier contours. From here there are good deer trails leading round the shoreline to the Kiwi Burn which is reached about four hours from Hill E.

The outlet of Lake Kiwi lies in a small flat area and the Kiwi Burn is crossed easily under normal weather conditions. From the small beach on the far side climb straight up the steep slip to the west to reach a flat area on top. This is a suitable place to camp and probably safer than the beach which could flood. From here head in the direction of The Knob, which can be seen clearly from the tussock flats when they are reached. Although there is a certain amount of open country here, there are also some patches of dense scrub which have to be traversed.

Aim to cross the Wilson River at the junction of its north and east branches. Do not descend into the Wilson gorge south of the junction as this is very steep.

There is a good ridge leading down to the junction and after crossing the river a deer trail leads straight up through the bush to the open country of The Knob. Continue round the north side of The Knob to strike the Cromarty-Golden Site tramline which provides excellent travel and thence carry on down to Kisbee Bay. There is a shelter at Te Oneroa three hours further down the inlet, or 2 $\frac{1}{2}$ hours if the tide is low.

*Times:* *Hill E to Kisbee Bay, 2-3 days. Lake Kiwi to The Knob has been walked in a long day but probably more time should be allowed, particularly if the Wilson River is in flood. The tramline is excellent going and it takes only about 2 hours down to Kisbee Bay.*

## HILL E TO PUYSEGUR POINT VIA THE COASTAL ROUTE

Descend from the saddle between Hill E and Hill K and sidle across to the Andrew Burn and drop down steeply into it. Follow the stream to the sea where, on the east side of the stream mouth, there is a huge cave, complete with fire, seats and table.

Carry on along the beach to Green Islets, which has beautiful rock formations. Seals and penguins may be seen in the caves near the seaward point. Climb up a steep bank at S173&174 022175 and cross the peninsular by way of a gully and drop down to the beach at the Grace Burn. At S173&174 0081880 climb up a slip and into the bush again to pick up the phone line almost immediately. It is now difficult to follow the phone line so the best alternative is to follow a compass bearing to the Kiwi Burn mouth. Here the Kiwi Burn can only be crossed at low tide. At other times the first ford is about 600 metres up from the mouth.

From the mouth, travel along the beach to Long Reef, taking care to avoid any quicksand at the Gold Burn. A side trip to Long Reef point is worthwhile. Climb back into the bush at approximately S173&174 947193 to cross through open bush, picking up the phone line more easily to drop into Gates Boat Harbour. The harbour is pleasant and sheltered in most conditions and provides fishing when the tide is out.

A marked track starts on the true-right of the creek, which is shown on the geological map of the area, and can be followed through to Wilson River. From here on the old pack track can be followed to Macnamara Creek and Sealers Creeks 1 and 2, the latter offering great campsites. The track to the lighthouse road begins just above the first bend in the creek, about 200 metres up. When the road is met, turn left and about quarter of an hour later the lighthouse station buildings will come into view. Now that the station is unmanned, parties must expect to remain independent here. Parties can stay in the goods shed originally used for lighthouse stores in Otago Retreat.

Puysegur Point—the south-west tip of Fiordland.
Photo: D.L. Homer, Institute of Geological & Nuclear Sciences.

To carry on to Te Oneroa and the three bunk A-frame bivvy, return up the hill from the store a little way and pick up a marked track. Alternatively, the shoreline is negotiable at low tide.

*Times:* Hill E to Puysegur Point, 4 days; Puysegur Point to Te Oneroa, 4-5 hrs; Te Oneroa to Kisbee Bay, 2 hrs.

# EAST OF FIORDLAND

# Eglinton Valley

Routes are described here in the same order of sequence as encountered on the Milford Road from Te Anau. All the routes described in this chapter are excursions for a full day or more.

### BOYD CREEK AND HENRY CREEK TO UPUKERORA RIVER

A track from the Boyd Creek picnic area leads onto the tops of the Countess Range while another heads south-east to the Upukerora River from which access to the Whitestone and Mararoa rivers can be gained. The track from Henry Creek bridge meets the Upukerora River further down valley. These tracks are fully described in the Snowdon Forest section.

### EGLINTON EAST BRANCH TO CASCADE CREEK AND GREENSTONE VALLEY

From the East Eglinton road bridge, the marked track commences on the north bank and continues to where it strikes the East Branch above the forks. Follow the river on the true-left to the first flats in the upper valley, six hours away. Follow up the west bank to the head of this clearing, taking about an hour, and then climb up a spur in bush, between the main stream and a smaller creek coming in from the west. This is followed to the upper flats and in about an hour from where bushline is reached, the forks in the river should be seen. The western branch of the river is now followed along its true-left bank, climbing slowly away from the stream until the open saddle is reached, two hours from the forks. This saddle overlooks the headwaters of Cascade Creek while Lake Gunn, in the Eglinton Valley, can be seen to the west.

To reach the saddle at the head of the left branch of Cascade Creek work round to the right and thus avoid peat swamps near the stream. Keep climbing steadily until nearly on a level with the saddle ahead, then follow deer trails for the rest of the distance. About two hours is occupied in moving from the East Eglinton saddle to the Cascade-Greenstone saddle. From the latter, or from points to the north or south, a good view is to be had of Lake McKellar and of the Hollyford, Caples and Greenstone country.

To reach the Greenstone flats, work round to the right, overlooking the Greenstone, then descend to scrubline and locate the beginning of the cattle track near the head of a prominent bluff. This track is steep, but well opened out and the descent to the Greenstone will take an hour with packs on. From the foot of the hill, follow old blazes to the main Greenstone Track. These commence about 200 metres inside the bush from where the Greenstone track emerges on the first flat below Lake McKellar. The blazed track is overgrown on the flat and a careful watch should be kept for the old marks.

*Times:* *Milford Road to first flats, 6 hrs; First flats to Greenstone Track, 8-10 hrs.*

## EGLINTON VALLEY TO GLADE HOUSE VIA DORE PASS

Dore Pass is more direct than the once-used Birley Pass which crossed from a southward branch of the Murcott Burn into Nurse Creek. The bush track from there to Glade House has long been completely overgrown.

The Dore Pass track is not a tourist track and should be attempted only by parties who have New Zealand alpine experience. Other than in summer, it is likely that an ice axe will be needed, especially on the Glade House side. The Eglinton River is forded up stream of the carpark, just below the Murcott Burn junction, which stream flows out of the narrow defile in the range ahead. The track enters the bush on the south side of the steam and leads to the foot of the spur which it climbs very steeply. After about an hour it sidles back towards the Murcott Burn, which can be heard below on the right in a deep gorge with steep cliffs on the other side. The track soon crosses a little stream, rises up a bank and then descends across the hillside and leads out onto the small flats of the upper Murcott Burn.

After crossing the stream, the route lies on the north side to the top of the gorge and then bears to the left up steep snowgrass slopes. Follow occasional snow poles and when high up the easiest way can be chosen to the pass. From the pass little can be seen of the Eglinton, but there is a fine view of the head of Lake Te Anau, Glade House and the Clinton Valley. Continuing, bear round to the right above scree slopes and under bluffs, initially at the level of the pass for about an hour until arriving at the spur which leads straight down to Glade House. If mist is encountered on the pass, it should be remembered that it will take nearly an hour going round the top of the rocky gullies, dropping slightly at first, then ascending steadily before reaching the leading spur; the turning point on this spur is a little higher than the pass itself. However, the route here is well marked with snow poles and would only be dangerous if the mist was very dense. Any short cuts down from the track above the bush line are cut off by bluffy guts further down. After the track reaches the Glade Burn a good track starts about 50 metres down stream on the opposite side and from here it is about 20 minutes to Glade House.

When the trip is commenced from Glade House, the track enters the bush directly behind the house and is well marked. Above bush-level it skirts around on the right towards the pass, which can soon be seen. After about two hours three deep gulches will be seen ahead and to reach the pass one must pass round to the left of these. On reaching the scree, keep as high as possible with the easiest travel being found right up under the bluffs. For the descent from the pass to the Eglinton, follow the description above in reverse.

*Times:* *Eglinton to Dore Pass, 3 hrs; Dore Pass to Lake Te Anau, 2 hrs.*

## HUT CREEK

The track up Hut Creek is fairly rough, but is marked to the head of the valley. Commencing from the 'Earl Mountains Walking Track' signpost, a walk wire leads over the Eglinton. After fording Mistake Creek make for the 'V' of Hut Creek where the sparsely marked track commences on the north bank and after 1 1/2 hours leads up to the first clearing where the stream is crossed to the south bank. From here on the route is reasonably well marked with stone cairns. Before reaching this clearing the track leaves the bush for a scramble up a sizeable creekbed which could be a problem in heavy rain.

Where the track descends to the bush at the other end of the clearing, there is a sparsely marked track through the bush which keeps well to the true-right of the creek. The entrance into the bush is marked by a stone cairn on the true-right bank. After 20 minutes open slopes are reached which lead up towards Glade Pass. Where the track leaves the bush towards the head of the valley, two orange plastic pack liner strips have been tied to tree branches, but they are not easy to find. An alternative to the track is to follow up the true-right bank although this may not be advisable in heavy rain.

Directly opposite Glade Pass can be seen U Pass which leads to Mistake Creek. This is a straightforward trip, providing the route down the waterfall in the south branch of Mistake Creek is known, described in reverse below. A third route from the head of the valley climbs southwards over another pass east of Triton Peak into the head of Waterfall Creek, providing a round trip back to the Eglinton about two kilometres down valley from the walk wire.

## HUT CREEK TO GLADE BURN VIA GLADE PASS

Glade Pass is severely eroded and bluffed on the Hut Creek side and is not as easy as previous editions of this guide and map S122 would imply. Follow the creekbed at the top of Hut Creek up towards Glade Pass until well into the gut below the pass. The better route is up a vegetated strip between two slips on the true-right of the stream. The vegetation provides good handholds in all but one location where care is necessary to negotiate a narrow ledge around a large rock about halfway up. The slope becomes more gradual after this and becomes and easy wander up to the actual pass.

Finding the route in the reverse direction down to Hut Creek is not obvious. Traverse well to the right of the pass and sidle along and down the tussock covered slope for a while, until the lower portion of the route can be seen through the bluffs.

The descent from Glade Pass down the Glade Burn is straightforward, down easy slopes until the bush starts where the easier going is close to the stream. Deer trails are not very evident and it is a matter of picking the easiest terrain to follow. The lower reaches may prove impassable in heavy rain where the streambed becomes a gorge and travel would be confined to the true-left.

Once out of the gorge, the Dore Pass track crosses over the stream and is well marked on both banks.

*Times: Eglinton Carpark to Glade Pass, 4-4 $^1/_2$ hrs; Glade Pass to Dore Pass Track, 4 hrs; Track to Glade House, 20 minutes.*

## MISTAKE CREEK TO HUT CREEK VIA U PASS

Cross the Eglinton as described above, but be careful not to cross Mistake Creek itself, thus entering Hut Creek in error. Turn hard right from the walk wire and initially follow up the east bank of Mistake Creek, then ford to the west bank. The track is marked all the way to the open flat near the head of the valley where the south branch from U Pass joins the main steam. However, considerable sections of track were lost in the January 1994 floods. There are pleasant campsites at the flat from which it is an easy walk to the head of the main valley.

To cross over into Hut Creek, follow up the true-right bank of the south branch of Mistake Creek until the waterfall is reached. Here a bluff cuts off the lower valley from the upper valley and some care is required. The best route up the waterfall follows up the true-right. Angle up through the fern 150 metres or more before the waterfall to follow up through the steep rocky ledges. At the head of the valley the pass to Hut Creek lies straight ahead, obviously part of the local fault line.

*Times: Eglinton Carpark to flats at head of valley, 3 hrs; The round trip from the Eglinton takes about 9 hrs.*

## CASCADE CREEK.

This route provides probably the most direct route into the upper basins of Cascade Creek and the East Eglinton. From the road bridge, the south bank of Cascade Creek is followed and in about ten minutes a small shingle beach is reached. Continue on the south bank from here for a further 1 $^1/_2$-2 hours to the

Flats at the head of Hut Creek. The Mistake Creek-Hut Creek round trip is a moderate two day tramp from the Eglinton.

forks. If the creek is low it is possible to cross and re-cross to avoid some steep slopes. From the forks, follow up and cross the south, true-left, branch about 100 metres from the junction, where a blazed trail leads up the edge of the blue bluff above the main valley and then on up the ridge dividing the South and East Branches for about two hours, until the bushline is reached on a clear grassy strip. Follow up this clearing through large patches of scrub and then sidle out to the right, climbing steadily up snowgrass slopes to the saddle at the head of the East Eglinton. This saddle is very swampy and it is advisable to keep above it. On reaching the bush at the forks in the valley of the East Eglinton, a shelter rock will be found in the true-left branch, on the south bank.

## MISTAKE CREEK TO FALLS CREEK

There is a route from the head of the north-east basin of Mistake Creek to Falls Creek below the bushline. The descent is very steep and joins with the Melita Creek to Falls Creek route described below.

## MELITA CREEK TO FALLS CREEK

From the campsite at the top end of the Lake Gunn, travel around the true-right of the lake to Melita Creek. The going is rough. Cross to the true-right of the creek and follow up an old track, climbing steeply at first then out to a relatively small open basin. Follow up through scrub on the true-right, heading for the head of the basin and the low point of the saddle. From the saddle there are two routes for getting into Falls Creek. The first descends slightly to the right for ten minutes then heads left to bush bash steeply down to the valley floor. The alternative route descends slightly to the right and then carries straight down through the bush on the spur. The Falls Creek track will be picked up shortly on the true-right of the valley.

*Times:* Campsite to Melita Creek, 2 hrs; Campsite to saddle, 4 hrs.

## KEY SUMMIT TO GREENSTONE VALLEY VIA TOPS

From The Divide on the Milford road or from Howden Hut, the Howden track should be followed to the highest point, just on the bushline, where a post marks the turn-off to Key Summit. A good track ascends by several easy zig-zags to the open top of the Key Summit ridge. There is a fairly well-defined track running south along this ridge, commencing at first towards the west side of the ridge, overlooking the Eglinton Valley, but once through a small patch of bush veering back to the east, or Greenstone side. It is now possible to travel south without gaining, or losing much height and in about two and a half hours from Key Summit turn-off a point overlooking Lake McKellar should be reached, with Mt Bonpland in the Humboldt Mountains visible through the low saddle across the valley. From here it is necessary to climb to avoid bluffs and the saddle at the head of Cascade Creek will then be seen straight ahead with Williamsons Track climbing steeply up the spur from the outlet of Lake McKellar. Once on the saddle the directions given earlier should be followed in reverse to reach the East Eglinton.

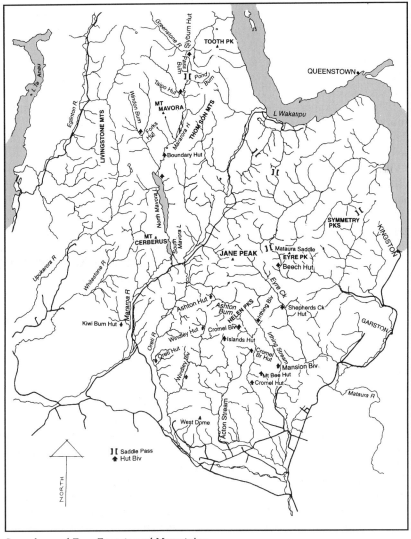

Snowdon and Eyre Forests and Mountains

# Mavora Lakes and Snowdon Forest

The Snowdon Forest extends from immediately east of Lake Te Anau, across the northern edge of the Te Anau basin and through to the Upukerora, Whitestone, Mararoa and upper Oreti valleys. The Eyre Forest lies to the east of the Snowdon Forest, across the Oreti Valley, and Fiordland National Park abuts to the north.

With its gentle topography and park-like flat open grassed valleys the area is particularly suited to family parties and relaxed tramping and hunting. The neck between the North and South Mavora Lakes at the head of the Mararoa River is popular with campers in summer. DoC maintain a self registering camping ground here with limited facilities. The Mavora Lakes lie at the far end of 39 kilometres of metal road from the Centre Hill turn-off and 37 kilometres from the Burwood turn-off on State Highway 94.

With a comparatively low rainfall, forest and scrub fires are a constant threat in the area, especially when high temperatures and strong drying winds prevail. Take care to observe all fire safety rules.

Legal access is confined to a metalled road into the Mavora Lakes and an easement to the boundary between DoC and Takaro properties. Access is from Kakapo Road, east of Te Anau, into the Whitestone and Upukerora valleys. There is also a short road off the Mavora Lakes Road leading to the Kiwi Burn swing bridge. Entry to the forest can also be made from the Milford Road near Te Anau Downs. Permission to cross private property should be obtained from the adjoining land owners.

## MAVORA-GREENSTONE WALKWAY

This is an easy but long tramp, linking the Mavora Lakes camping area with the Greenstone Track. Earlier this century this track was commonly used, in conjunction with the Greenstone Valley, to drive cattle from Martins Bay to Mossburn. Part of the walkway passes through Elfin Bay Station and is closed between the beginning of May and Labour Weekend in October. Cars can be taken to about a kilometre up from the outlet of North Mavora Lake and four-wheel drive vehicles can be taken to Boundary Hut. The huts all have eight bunks and do not have any cooking facilities.

From the camping area follow the four-wheel drive track around the lake edge to the head of North Mavora Lake. Just before the head of the lake is the four bunk Careys Hut. At the lake head the track branches with the left hand track leading up the Windon Burn to the Forks Hut. Continuing on the right hand branch the track climbs above the Mararoa River to some fine views. The track then sidles the hill, dropping back to the river and on to Boundary Hut.

The North Mavora Lake—from the start of the Mavora-Greenstone walkway

From the hut, cross the swing bridge and follow marker posts on the true-right of the Mararoa River. The track enters Elfin Bay Station, crossing small terraces and flats, sidling above the Mararoa River. Another swing bridge gives access to Taipo Hut.

Leaving Taipo Hut, the track enters the Pond Burn valley by following the toe of the hill on the western side. After passing the top pond the track veers west into the forest and continues to the saddle of Pass Burn valley. The track heads down the Pass Burn, crosses the stream and sidles around to the Sly Burn Hut. The hut is sited in a bush clearing above the Greenstone-Sly Burn confluence.

The Greenstone River is crossed by a swing bridge and is followed down to the carpark. This stretch of the route is described in the Greenstone Track section more fully.

***Times:*** *North Mavora Lake to Forks Hut, 3 hrs; North Mavora Lake to Boundary Hut, 4 hrs; Boundary Hut to Taipo Hut, 3 ³/₄ hrs; Taipo Hut to Sly Burn Hut, 3 ³/₄ hrs; Sly Burn Hut to Greenstone Road End, 3 ³/₄ hrs.*

## MARAROA RIVER TO KIWI BURN HUT FROM KIWI BURN SWING BRIDGE

A metal side road passes through a gate exactly 2.0 kilometres beyond Hikurangi Station and 5.0 kilometres before the Mavora Lakes turn-off on the

Mavora Lakes Road. The side road leads to a carpark and the Kiwi Burn swing bridge. From the bridge, one track heads inland directly to the mid reaches of the Kiwi Burn, another leads up the true-right of the Mararoa River to the South Mavora Lake swing bridge and the track to the Kiwi Burn Hut heads down the true-right of the Mararoa River. All the tracks are marked with permalat markers and are well graded.

Follow down the Mararoa for ³/₄ hour until just before the Kiwi Burn confluence. The track to the Kiwi Burn then follows up the true-left of the Kiwi Burn through the forest, emerging near the bottom of the extensive flats. The 12 bunk Kiwi Burn Hut is on the true-right on a terrace away from the river, shortly before the river veers to the north.

From the hut, follow up to the top of the flats, at first on the true-right and then when the river veers to the north on the true-left. At the head of the flats the track leading into the Whitestone River is picked up, entering the bush on the true-right. Just as the forest closes in, a cairn on the true-left bank shows the start of the alternative track back to the swing bridge. This track climbs immediately up from the riverbank to enter the trees.

*Time: Kiwi Burn swing bridge to Kiwi Burn Hut, 1 ¹/₂ hrs.*

## KIWI BURN SWING BRIDGE TO WHITESTONE RIVER VIA UPPER KIWI BURN

An alternative, permalat marked, track to the head of the Kiwi Burn and the upper reaches of the Whitestone River heads inland from the Kiwi Burn swing bridge. It starts by following a small creek until the edge of an open flat is reached. Here the track continues in the forest and climbs up onto a ridge to emerge a little way up another flat fifteen minutes later. The route here is through open scrub and a bearing on the far side of the flat should be taken before crossing it. Shortly the track reaches an even bigger flat and this is skirted in the southern bush edge. A low saddle is crossed and the track enters the bush to drop down into the very top of the Kiwi Burn Flats mentioned above.

From here the track sidles the western side of a pretty gorge before skirting a large scrub and tussock flat which is on its western side. The track continues to slowly gain height and the broad forested saddle between a side stream coming off Mt Cerberus is reached. Descend on a zig-zag track, coming out of the forest onto the top of a burnt-off slope from which extensive grassy slopes give access into the Whitestone proper.

Following the Whitestone down stream, a permalat marked track is picked up on the true-left which leads to the bush edge opposite the tussock bite that leads to the Upukerora River described below.

Kiwi Burn. A hunter enjoying winter conditions in the upper Kiwi Burn. The Snowdon mountains are especially popular with family parties and instruction groups.

Up river of the side stream descending from below the Kiwi Burn saddle is good travelling to the forks. A rough tarpaulin bivvy can be found on the true-left just before the forks. The eastern fork leads up some more grassy flats until below a side stream coming down from the north slopes of Mt Cerberus. From here the going is more difficult through a steep-sided gorge which is traversed on the true-left until emerging onto flats below Mt Eldon.

*Times: Kiwi Burn swing bridge to Kiwi Burn, 1 hr; Top of Kiwi Burn Flats to Kiwi Burn Hut, ³/₄ hr; Top of Kiwi Burn Flats to Whitestone River, 2 hrs.*

## TRACKS FROM THE SOUTH MAVORA SWING BRIDGE

From the swing bridge at the outlet of the South Mavora Lake a well formed permalat marked track leads down the true-right of the Mararoa River to the Kiwi Burn swing bridge. The track is pleasant and the gorge is pretty.

A track may be found leading up a well defined spur leading to the south-east ridge of Mt Cerberus about ³/₄ hour down stream of a side stream running down from the top of the mountain itself. The top of the track traverses Peak 1055 metres and is ill-defined through windthrow and is non-existent for the last few hundred metres. The track leaves the bushline 180 metres to the south-west of trig station 'G' and as it is not marked a good note of the exit should be noted for the return. The views from the trig station and Mt Cerberus, an hour further along the ridge, are impressive.

Another track continues up the west side of the South Mavora Lake to the outlet of the North Mavora Lake where another swing bridge crosses to the true-left.

**Times:** *South Mavora Lake swing bridge to Kiwi Burn Hut, 3 hrs; South Mavora Lake swing bridge to North Mavora Lake swing bridge, 1 1/2 hrs.*

## BOYD CREEK TO UPUKERORA HEADWATERS

As the Milford Road turns and starts to descend to the Boyd Creek culvert a rough shingle road leads off to the right to the Southland Boys High School Lodge. Two hundred metres down this road a carpark and picnic area is reached, followed by a locked gate. Follow the road past the lodge and 200 metres further on the permalat marked track begins as it enters the bush. Forking shortly afterwards, the left fork climbs to the Boyd Creek tops. From here the track passes through a low saddle at D42 206493 and descends a bushed ridge for half an hour until reaching the Upukerora River. Down stream there is an airstrip on the true-left riverbank. The valley is predominantly open and by travelling up stream a low saddle may be crossed into the East Branch of the Eglinton River via Annear Creek.

## BOYD CREEK TO UPUKERORA RIVER VIA DUNTON SWAMP

The right-hand fork of the track mentioned turns left and stays in the bush for a short time. It then skirts a clearing and crosses a series of terraces until reaching Retford Stream.

Within an hour of the Retford the track comes to a clearing. Two-thirds of the way across the clearing the track re-enters the bush on the right. Several kilometres later Dunton Swamp is reached. Through the swamp, travel is open to the Upukerora Valley and up to the Army Hut a little down river from the Snowdon Slip. The quickest and easiest way up Snowdon Peak starts in the Upukerora Valley by climbing up the southern side of this slip.

Passing the slip, the track to the Upukerora Headwaters follows the bush on the true-right side of the river for about three hours before reaching open tussock country where an airstrip is established. Beyond this a tussock saddle gives easy access to the North Mavora Lake.

Half an hour down stream from the Army Hut, a track heads east. It enters the bush through a very low saddle, then out into an open tussock bite that runs down into the Whitestone Valley. The bush edge on the left of the valley offers the quickest travel. The open tussock and river flats in this vicinity are part of Mount Prospect Station and permission should be sought before crossing it. Note that the chain-wide river reserve may be travelled freely.

*Times: Boyd Creek to Retford Stream, 3 hrs; Retford Stream to Dunton Swamp, 2 hrs; Dunton Swamp to Army Hut, 2 hrs; Army Hut to Snowdon Peak top, 2 hrs; Army Hut to Upukerora headwaters tussock flats, 3 hrs; Army Hut to Whitestone River, 3 1/4 hrs.*

## HENRY CREEK TO UPUKERORA RIVER

From the Milford Road, a track commences on the south side of Henry Creek bridge. It passes through old, cutover forest and scrub for 1 1/2 hours until virgin forest is reached. Entering the forest by a cluster of bluegums, the track comes out onto Te Anau Downs station in the vicinity of the Retford Stream. If this open country is crossed an old pack track can be found entering the public conservation estate. The track goes through to land owned by Takaro Properties at the Upukerora River. Permission is required to cross this land although a chain river reserve with free access exists beside the river to Dunton Swamp.

# Eyre Mountains

The Eyre Mountains lie south-west of Lake Wakatipu and to the east of the Snowdon Forest. The public conservation estate extends from West Dome and the Oreti River in the south and west to the headwaters of the Mataura River and Robert Creek in the north, including the Ashton Burn catchment and the upper 18 kilometres of Eyre Creek.

The infrequently visited Eyre Mountains form an attractive backdrop with Eyre Peak and Jane Peak both rising to over 1800 metres and worth climbing in their own right. The area offers considerable scope for "remote experience" recreation. Much of the area is very eroded and there are large areas of scree all through the tops of the range.

The area is considered dry by Southland standards, but heavy rain can soon make even small streams impassable. Once the rain eases the rivers drop very quickly. The mountains are usually free of snow for most of summer, but snow may fall at any time of the year and sudden changes in weather do occur. Fire is also a risk in the area as the clearings in the lower Cromel are evidence. Take particular care with fires.

Legal access is confined to the Acton, Cromel, Irthing, Oreti, Eyre Creek and Mataura catchments at present. Elsewhere access is over private roads or run land and permission must be first obtained to cross it. The roads providing access to the Acton and Windley both have two fords that have to be crossed.

The Five Rivers sector of the forest is well served by plastic triangle and permalat marked tracks. Each major catchment has either a hut or bivvy in it, generally sited about two to three hours from each other.

## ACTON HUT TO CROMEL HUT

The six bunk Acton Hut, owned by the people of Mossburn, but available to all, is located about 350 metres along the outside bush edge of the Acton Stream at the road end. Contact Lyn or Lex Lawrence, phone 0(3)248 6030, before using the hut.

The well marked track enters the bush about 20 metres north of the Acton Hut. The entrance markers are visible from the hut door. A clearing is reached after about five minutes and the track then rises steeply up the ridge to a saddle. After sidling to the north-east for 300 to 400 metres the track descends down a ridge to the south-east. An old burnt off area is passed after 30 to 40 minutes and the track drops to the Cromel Stream which is crossed about five minutes north of the Cromel Hut.

*Times: Acton Hut to saddle, 1 hr; Acton Hut to Cromel Hut, 2-2 $^1/_2$ hrs.*

225

## ACTON HUT TO CROMEL BRANCH HUT

Where the Acton Stream enters the forest a track can be found leading up the true-left bank. Continue past the Islands Hut track turn-off, 20 minutes later, to a large clearing. The track follows around the clearing on the bush edge and continues up the valley. The track soon begins to climb up to a low saddle between the Acton and the Cromel Branch Stream, passing a track branching off to the right which leads to the lower Cromel Stream and Cromel Hut. From the junction the track climbs to the beech covered saddle before descending through several damp tussock covered clearings and some beech forest. The four bunk Cromel Branch Hut is situated on the true-right of the valley, about an hour further on, above the junction of the Cromel Branch Stream and clear of the bushline.

*Time:* Acton Hut to Cromel Branch Hut, 4-5 hrs.

## ACTON HUT TO ISLANDS HUT

About 20 minutes along the Acton Stream track from Acton Hut, follow a track branching off and leading across to the true-right bank. From here it climbs very steeply to the ridge top, which it follows through two old burn clearings, to the open tops. From there, cross the head of a small gully on the true-right of the ridge and climb over a low saddle into a gully and descend to the stream below. Follow up stream until a small patch of beech can be seen in a tributary on the true-left bank. Islands Hut (four bunks) is located on a terrace set back into the bush. It is not visible from the steambed although it can be easily seen from across the valley.

It is possible to travel across the tops from Islands Hut to Windley Hut, Cromel Bivvy and Cromel Branch Hut.

## CROMEL HUT TO CROMEL BRANCH HUT

In the lower Cromel there is an area of private native forest which extends about three kilometres up valley from the lower bush edge. Above this is public conservation estate and an old logging road carries on out of the private forest for a further three kilometres through several old burns. The six bunk Cromel Hut is situated near this track.

Follow a former four-wheel drive track from below the hut through forest and grassy clearings. After about 20 minutes cross the Cromel to the true-right bank to pick up the track which generally follows the river. About ten minutes later the remains of an old post cutters' hut will be passed and then 10-15 minutes later the track starts to climb steadily through red beech forest. The track then sidles along the ridge before crossing a saddle and dropping down to meet the Acton-Cromel Branch track, approximately two hours from the start of the climb.

From here the track climbs to the saddle between the Acton and Cromel Branch and descends to the Cromel Branch Hut described above.

*Time: Cromel Hut to Cromel Branch Hut, 3 1/2-4 hrs.*

## CROMEL BRANCH HUT TO CROMEL BIVVY

From the Cromel Branch Hut, head diagonally across the valley to the bush edge on the true-left where the start of the track will be picked up, about ten minutes from the hut. The marked route then makes its way through the forest, keeping to the true-right of the Cromel throughout. After 2 to 2 1/2 hours a small waterfall is passed and about 20 minutes later a damp tussock and cushion plant clearing is reached. The two bunk Cromel Bivvy is found tucked behind beech regrowth in the upper left corner of this clearing. From here access can be readily gained to the head of the valley and the foot of the impressive Helen Peaks.

*Time: Cromel Branch Hut to Cromel Bivvy, 2 1/2 to 3 hrs.*

## CROMEL BRANCH HUT TO IRTHING BIVVY

About a kilometre above the Cromel Branch confluence a track leads up to a bush clad saddle on the Mt Bee ridge. A short distance on the other side of the saddle a track leads off along the Mt Bee ridge, which provides high level access from the road. The other track descends to the two bunk Irthing Bivvy.

## IRTHING STREAM

There is a picnic area on a small riverside clearing in the lower Irthing, gained by an all-weather road off Irthing Road. From the picnic area, a track leads up the true-left riverbank, crossing to the true-right after an hour. Twenty minutes further on there is a small clearing and a two bunk bivvy known as "The Mansion". Up stream the river becomes gorged and the travel is difficult to the two bunk Irthing Bivvy, which is situated in the last stand of trees on the true-left bank of the stream. The alternative routes to this bivvy are better than travelling up the gorge.

## MT BEE RIDGE

A private road leads off Irthing Road and climbs up Mt Bee to a group of huts (eight bunks) two to three hours walk from the Irthing Valley road end. Check with the Burdon Brothers in Irthing Road before using the road, especially in spring. This road continues along the ridge for another six kilometres and stops at a saddle. During summer it is possible to travel along the Mt Bee ridge and into the headwaters of either the Irthing or Cromel.

From the Mt Bee huts it is possible to reach the Cromel Branch Hut by walking along the ridge until opposite the Cromel Branches valley and dropping off the ridge, down a scree slope and through bush to the Cromel Stream. From here continue up the valley to the hut, described above. In good weather the hut can be seen from the Mt Bee ridge.

## WINDLEY RIVER

A metal road traverses around the south of West Dome, arriving at the Windley River 2 1/2 km above the Oreti River. The Windley Bivvy is in a clearing on the true-left, about 20 minutes up stream from where the Windley River leaves the forest.

From the Windley Bivvy, follow up the rather overgrown track on the true-left for about one hour until the forks are reached. Cross the river and follow the north branch on the true-left bank. This track crosses and recrosses the stream many times, but is easily negotiated except in times of flood.

After a further three hours travel some clearings are entered. The Windley Hut (four bunks) is located in a sunny clearing 90 metres up the true-right bank. Travel to Lincoln Bivvy and the Oreti River can be made from here.

An alternative route climbs the spur opposite the forks and traverses the tops until above the Windley Hut. This is a faster and drier route. The track between the Acton Hut and Windley Hut described in the 1978 NZFS booklet for the area was never completed and cannot be trusted.

## ORETI RIVER

Access to huts in the Oreti Valley is either from the Mavora Lakes Road, or from the Mossburn-Five Rivers road on the opposite side of the Oreti River.

An hour's walk up stream from the Windley-Oreti confluence is the four bunk Oreti Hut. Further up the Oreti valley is the Lincoln Bivvy, situated on the bush edge near a mustering hut.

In the Ashton Burn there is the four bunk Ashton Hut on the upper bush edge. Travel is best made on a broad open ridge which leads away from the Oreti-Ashton junction to the tops as the stream is gorged. The hut can be seen from the tops and is on the true-left side of the valley, below a face of pine trees, of which half have been cut down.

*Time:* *Oreti-Ashton junction to Ashton Hut, 2 1/2-3 hrs.*

## MATAURA RIVER TO BILLY SADDLE AND EYRE PEAK

The head of the Mataura River consists in the main of interesting open tussock landscapes well served with four-wheel drive tracks and features spectacular bluffs and mingled scrub thickets. DoC prefers that vehicles are not taken up the Mataura past the Robert Creek confluence. Vehicles are not permitted beyond the fence 1 ¼ kilometres past The Bowels of the Earth.

Travel up the Mataura from the Robert Creek confluence on a good four-wheel drive track on the true-left which continues to the stream draining The Bowels of the Earth. To reach Billy Saddle ascend the spur to the west of the stream entering the Mataura from Billy Saddle, starting 200 metres up river of the stream mouth. At first climb due west to avoid scrub in the stream until opposite the side stream draining the saddle. Cross this stream here to the west bank and climb the spur leading directly up to Eyre Peak. After about an hour sidle down into the stream when the creek widens out to form the top half of a hanging valley. Billy Saddle lies at the head of the now bouldery stream bed. Eyre Peak is a rewarding short, steep scramble from the shingle slide leading up from Billy Saddle.

***Times:*** *Robert Creek confluence to mouth of Billy Saddle stream, 2 hrs; Mouth of Billy Saddle stream to Billy Saddle, 3-4 hrs.*

## MATAURA RIVER–LOCHY RIVER–LONG BURN–ROBERT CREEK

To travel up the Mataura to Mataura Saddle and out to Halfway Bay via the Lochy River makes for a long two day tramp or an easy three day tramp. A four day trip returns to Robert Creek. Permission to travel in the upper parts of the Lochy River should be obtained from Walter Peak Station, while permission should be sought from Halfway Bay Station for the lower parts.

Carry on up the Mataura river bed from the stream draining The Bowels of the Earth, described above, to the large patch of bush near the valley head. Beech Hut is a restored musterers' hut at the start of the bush and is owned by DoC. As it has beech pole bunks and no mattresses it is advisable to take sleeping pads.

The route to Mataura Saddle is obvious and the travel down the Lochy River is good. The four-wheel drive track that starts before reaching Cascade Creek climbs quite high to enter Cascade Creek and should be abandoned before too much altitude is gained. The four bunk St Marys Hut is owned by Walter Peak Station and is halfway between Cascade Creek and Killiecrankie Creek. There is another hut two kilometres up Killiecrankie Creek that makes a useful overnight shelter if heading out to Walter Peak Station via Killiecrankie Saddle and McKinlays Creek.

There is more good travel down the Lochy to the Long Burn where there is a popular DoC owned fisherman's hut. From here it is an easy five kilometres to Halfway Bay. Alternatively, cross to the true-right of the Long Burn and travel up river on a four-wheel drive track which eventually peters out. It is best to travel high on steep sheep tracks, about 300 metres above the river, to keep out of the scrub below. Siberia Hut (four bunk) is on the true-left opposite Symmetry Creek and is not easy to find. It is incorrectly shown on S142. Follow up the creekbed for the last two kilometres before the hut.

From the hut climb up the spur leading to the peak to the north of Lambing Saddle and sidle up to the saddle. Head south along the ridge from Lambing Saddle, making for the start of Way Spur which is descended to the confluence of Ross Creek and Robert Creek. Follow a good station track which starts about a third of the way down the spur. A four-wheel drive track down the true-right of Robert Creek leads back to the start of the trip.

## ROBERT CREEK

From the carpark below the airstrip in Robert Creek, three kilometres above the Mataura-Robert confluence, cross to the true-right. Follow up open flats on a good four-wheel drive track which continues up Ross Spur and provides the best access to Ross Hut. The eight bunk hut is inside the bush and not easy to find. With its dirt floor it has plenty of character. It is possible to follow the pack-horse track to Ross Hut which continues to the saddle below the Symmetry Peaks.

From the Robert Creek-Firewood Creek junction follow the four-wheel drive track for 20 minutes up Firewood Creek to where the two branches meet. The track climbs up the spur dividing the two branches to a large tarn. From the peak above the tarn good views are obtained of the head of the Long Burn and The Bowels of the Earth. To make a round trip the descent can be made on south side of Firewood Creek.

*Times:* *Robert Creek Carpark to Ross Hut, 4 hrs; Firewood Creek round trip, 6 hrs.*

## EYRE CREEK

Cars can be driven up Eyre Creek to beyond the homestead, but four-wheel drive vehicles are needed to drive to Shepherd Creek Hut, previously known as Windley Hut. The hut is owned by DoC and no vehicles are allowed past this point. Jane Peak at the head of the creek, the highest peak in the Eyre mountains, is normally climbed from the Gorge Burn in the Oreti catchment.

# Takitimu Mountains

The Takitimu Forest lies on and around the prominent range of mountains to the south-east of Te Anau, which rise to a height of 1700 metres. The bush consists mainly of open beech forest which becomes stunted with increasing altitude. Above the bushline there are subalpine scrub belts and tussock tops grading into scree and eroded tops. The area enjoys markedly better weather than Fiordland.

The area is well served by infrequently used tracks, huts and bivvies established by the defunct New Zealand Forest Service and all are currently in good condition. DoC is maintaining the tracks in the Aparima catchment, but little work has been done on most of the other tracks over the last six to seven years.

Travel on the tops, consisting mainly of scree and rock outcrops, is on the whole uncomplicated in summer. In winter the tops are snow covered and with good conditions offer, if anything, easier travel in a mild alpine environment. It is possible to cross from the heads of all of the valleys into adjacent valleys, making for interesting round trips. It is technically possible for a fit party to traverse the length of the Takitimu Mountains from north to south over a long weekend.

Formed legal access is limited to the Aparima River Track which starts at Pleasant Creek on the Dunrobin Valley Road and the road to the Princhester Hut. Providing they are asked first, adjoining land owners generally grant permission to cross their properties.

## APARIMA VALLEY

The track to the six bunk Aparima Hut is an easy tramp commencing at the bridge over Pleasant Creek on the Dunrobin Valley Road, just before the boundary of the farm owned by Pleasant Valley Partnership. The marked route is on the true-right of the Aparima River, passing through beech forest, red tussock and wire-rush peat bogs before emerging onto a four-wheel drive track. A swing bridge over the river, hidden in a clump of beech trees, is crossed five minutes down stream from the Aparima Hut. For at least part of the year four-wheel drive access is available through private land and then through the public conservation estate as far as the swing bridge. Check with DoC to confirm if it is open before starting.

The track to the upper Aparima and Spence Burn starts as an old bulldozer track behind the hut, which climbs up through a short neck of bush onto the open terrace overlooking the Waterloo Valley. Continue along this terrace for about half an hour until a prominent bend in the Aparima River is reached and a good, permalat marked track enters the forest shortly after, close to the edge

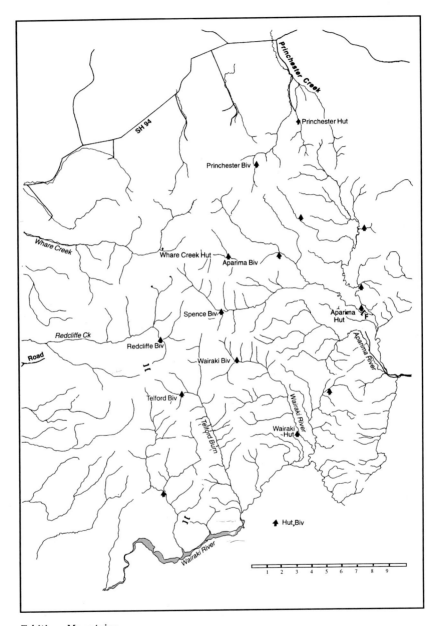

Takitimu Mountains

of the riverbank and high above the river. Initially the track is not well formed, but it soon becomes very distinctive and is easy to follow. A large peat bog is reached after another 20 minutes. Cross the toe of the bog to where the track to the Spence Burn starts.

From the track junction, follow the forest edge to the head of the bog and about ten minutes later a log over a small stream is crossed. After half an hour the track stops on the true-left of the main stream, down stream of the Aparima Forks. Cross the main stream and some small wet clearings. The two bunk Aparima Forks Bivvy is located on a terrace a short distance above the forks, on the true-right bank. From the bivvy there is easy travel to the heads of both branches of the Aparima.

To reach the Spence Hut descend to the river on the marked track at the toe of the bog mentioned above. Ford the Aparima River just below the confluence with the Spence Burn to find the track which climbs steeply at first and traverses the true-right side of the valley, on the whole well above the river, before emerging onto the lower of a series of tussock clearings. After 1$^1$/$_2$ -2 hours the track crosses to the true-left side which is followed until the two bunk Spence Hut is seen on the opposite side.

From the bivvy, both heads of the Spence can be reached: for the true-left head, travel up close to the stream. For the true-right head, climb up through a bush face between the two catchments to the open tops.

***Times:*** *Pleasant Creek bridge to Aparima Hut, 2 hrs; Aparima Hut to Aparima Forks Bivvy, 2 $^1$/$_4$ hrs; Aparima Hut to Spence Burn Track start, 1 hr; Aparima Hut to Spence Bivvy, 3 $^1$/$_2$ hrs.*

## PRINCHESTER VALLEY

Princhester Base Hut (six bunk) is sited at the end of a metal farm road which starts off State Highway 94, just before the Princhester Creek when approaching Te Anau. From behind the hut a marked track climbs gradually up the true-right of the Bog Burn catchment to a saddle to the Waterloo Burn. From here, the track bears left and downhill to the Waterloo Burn itself. Cross here and follow the route on the true-left bank to recross just before swampy open flats are reached. The travel from here on down to the Aparima River is straightforward although boggy in places, through open tussock flats. Becketts Hut (four bunks) is on the true-left about an hour down valley and as it is inside the forest edge is not able to be seen from the clearing. Note that S150 incorrectly marks it as being one clearing further south than its true location. Map D44 is correct.

The two bunk Princhester Hut is situated in the headwaters of the true-left branch of the Princhester Creek catchment. It is on the true-right bank of a high terrace where the forest and sub-alpine scrub combine. A short, steep track climbs from the bivvy to the tops. Owing to the broken nature of the banks, travel to the bivvy from down valley is best made up the creek bed.

*Times: Princhester road end to Princhester-Waterloo Saddle, 1 hour; Road end to Becketts Hut, 3 1/2 hrs; Becketts Hut to Aparima Hut, 1 1/2 hrs.*

## WATERLOO VALLEY

Becketts Hut (four bunks) is sited just inside the forest edge at the top of a small clearing on the true-left of the Waterloo Burn. See the notes in the Princhester section regarding this hut. The valley floor of the Waterloo Burn at this point is part of the Waterloo Station, over which there is no legal access other than the Queens Chain and the "paper" road up the first three kilometres of the Waterloo from the Aparima, which does not follow the four-wheel drive track.

Near the site of an old hut on the bush edge, Coal Creek emerges from the forest. The marked track follows near the stream, crossing several times and after about an hour's steady travel the track climbs steeply up the true-left face.

Takitimu Mountains. Freezing cloud leaves rime on the tussock on these tops in the Takitimu Mountains.

234

A small one-man bivvy is situated between the upper forest limits and tall subalpine scrub at approximately D44 166942.

*Times: Aparima Hut to Becketts Hut, 1 1/2 hrs; Coal Creek confluence to Coal Creek Bivvy, 2 hrs.*

## WAIRAKI VALLEY

Access to the four bunk Wairaki Hut is via Beaumont Station and permission must be obtained from the station beforehand. To travel to the Wairaki Bivvy from here, cross the river via a swing bridge where it emerges from the bush and climb onto a flat bush ridge. The marked, but rather overgrown track follows along this ridge for 3/4 hour before descending to the riverbank. This is followed for another two hours before climbing to the bivvy. The two bunk bivvy is situated in the last few trees before the subalpine scrub belt and tussock tops begin.

An alternative route to Wairaki Bivvy starts at Pleasant Creek in the Aparima Valley. As this route passes through Pleasant Valley Partnership property permission should be first obtained from Ian Grant of Castlerock, phone 0(3)248 7252. Follow up the four-wheel drive track through open tussock flats beside Pleasant Creek until the stream forks, just inside the start of the bush. Follow up the less inconsequential true-right branch on its true-right bank, sidling above minor gorges where they are encountered. About half an hour later another side stream coming in from the left is crossed. Carry on until it becomes clear that a route exists to a bush covered saddle. From the saddle, descend without difficulty into the Wairaki River, about 3/4 hour down stream of the bivvy.

Yet another alternative point of entry to the Wairaki Valley is through Mt Linton Station which has excellent farm roads throughout. Permission from Mt Linton Station is required to cross the station land. Take the road to Stone Hut, owned by Mt Linton Station, and depending on road conditions carry on until opposite the Telford Valley. From here, leave the vehicles and walk along the old four-wheel drive tracks to the Wairaki Hut on the bush edge.

The Cullers Crossing is an easy trip from the Wairaki Bivvy to the Spence Hut. Follow the stream immediately west of the bivvy and cross the ridge at D44 117866. From the col, make a bee line to the Spence Hut in the valley below.

An easy trip to the seldom used Telford Bivvy can be made from the Wairaki Bivvy. The open valley is followed to the low saddle at the head of Bull Basin. From here the upper Telford can be seen spread below. Drop down the steep bush face to the valley floor and follow the stream to the Telford Forks. Cross the Telford to the true-right bank and follow up this bank for about twenty minutes. The two bunk bivvy is situated amongst tall beech trees on the river terrace about 50 metres in from the river bank where there is a stone cairn.

From the Telford Bivvy, it is possible to cross to the Spence Hut with little difficulty. Descend the Telford to the forks and head up the north branch, choosing the best route that offers, to the col at the head of the valley. From the col it is a short, easy and rewarding climb to Spence Peak. Descend the other side of the col into a large basin which is crossed and from here it is best to keep to the spur on the true-left of the stream that joins the Spence just up stream of the hut. To avoid a scrubby sidle it is probably better to climb onto the spur earlier rather than later.

*Times: Wairaki Hut to Wairaki Bivvy, 3 hrs; Pleasant Stream bridge to Wairaki Bivvy, 5 hrs; Wairaki Bivvy to the Spence Hut, 2-3 hrs; Wairaki Bivvy to Telford Bivvy, 2 hrs; Telford Bivvy to Spence Hut, 4 hrs.*

## REDCLIFF CREEK TO APARIMA HUT VIA SPENCE BURN

Access to the upper reaches of Redcliff Creek is either up the open riverbed from the road bridge, or from a muddy forestry road leaving the Blackmount-Redcliff Road on the top of the hill overlooking the Redcliff and Windy Creeks. From the end of the forestry road, sidle around the base of the ridge leading up to the Chimney Peaks and down to the creek. Cross to the true-right, where there are deer-trails, as soon as the going on the other side looks less prickly than the current one.

The matagouri is soon left behind and it is a matter of sidling along the river bank through a series of gorges until the forks are reached. From here, follow the dogleg south branch to a bivvy near the bush edge. Carry on up the stream, northwards, through alpine meadows to climb onto the ridge to the east on loose scree. It is not critical where the ridge is met, but the descent on the other side is better down a prominent spur on the true-left of a creek joining the Spence just above Spence Hut. The track down the Spence is described in the Aparima Valley section.

As an alternative to travelling up Redcliff Creek, drop into Windy Creek from the forestry road end and continue up Windy Creek to cross the col at the head. A descent is then made into the south branch of Redcliff Stream. The going in the streambed is thick and rough and a sidle higher up on the east side is required. The little used Redcliff Bivvy is a welcome stop for the first night.

*Times: Reported times for parties travelling up Redcliff Creek vary considerably. It should be possible for a reasonably strong party to cross from the forestry road end to Aparima Hut in 10 hrs.*

## WHARE CREEK

A two bunk hut is situated in Whare Creek on the bush edge, 50 metres from the creek, just after the creek swings north. A good track on the true-left provides access from the road. From the hut there is easy access to the head of the creek where a scree saddle leads into the Aparima headwaters

## BLACKMOUNT TO DUNROBIN ROAD END VIA THE TOPS

This west to east route is a pleasant two to three day's trip following the ridges across the Brunel, Spence, Wairaki and McLean Peaks before dropping down into Pleasant Creek and meeting the Dunrobin road end. Being a high level route the trip requires good weather although there are good escape routes from most places on the tops into the valleys below where the numerous bivvies offer welcome havens and tracks to civilisation.

From the forestry road end above the Redcliff and Windy Creeks, drop into Windy Creek before climbing the first prominent spur leading to the ridge and the Brunel Peaks proper. The hut shown on S158 and D44 on this spur does not exist. The climb to the summit takes several hours.

From the top of the Brunels, the ridge leads on towards Windy River Col. It is mostly easy going except for a short steep and loose section where a rope can provide reassurance. Eventually the route drops to the saddle between Redcliff Creek and the Telford Burn before heading on towards Spence Peak. There is pleasant camping by some tarns at D44 088847.

The approach to and off Spence Peak is easy. Further on there is a gendarme on the ridge leading up to the Wairaki Peaks, but this can be sidled on the south side. From the Wairaki Peaks it is easier to drop into the basin on the south side to avoid a jagged section in the ridge before rejoining it further along.

The approach along the ridge to the McLean Peaks is obvious and fairly easy. Under the McLean Peaks there are some good camping places next to the tarns there. From here, the route drops directly into Pleasant Creek. Care should be taken not to be led down the obvious ridge into the Spence Burn. Once through the thick undergrowth on the bush line and into Pleasant Creek proper, easier travel is on the true-right where the old Cullers Track may be picked up from time to time. Once out of the bush the road end is another hour or so further.

# REFERENCE

# Glossary

| | |
|---|---|
| Bivvy | Either a small 2 bunk hut, or a bivouac rock boulder providing accommodation under its overhang. |
| Blaze | Bark chipped off a tree trunk to indicate a route or track. |
| Bluff | A small cliff face. |
| Board walk | A wooden platform for walking on, commonly used to protect fragile areas. |
| Boulder-hopping | Travel along bouldery riverbeds or moraine. |
| Burn | A stream or creek. |
| Bushline | Usually a sharp demarcation between the bush and open tussock tops. |
| Cairn | A pile of rocks balanced on top of each other to mark routes in riverbeds and on the tops. |
| Col | A low point in a mountain ridge. |
| Confluence | Joining of two rivers. |
| Corduroy track | A track consisting of sawn tree trunks laid crossways and used to traverse swampy terrain. |
| DoC | Department of Conservation. |
| DOSLI | Department of Survey and Land Information. |
| Exposure | (1) A common name for hypothermia; (2) Used to describe a precarious section of travel, high above the ground. |
| Fly | A sheet of nylon used to cover tents and people from the worst of the rain. |
| Flying fox | A one-person, manually propelled cable car. |
| Forest Service | Also known by its acronym, NZFS. A now defunct government department which used to administer most forest areas outside of national parks and provided deer control and huts. |
| Fresh | A rise in river level caused by heavy rain, but within the river's normal range of levels. |
| Gendarme | An unsurmountable rock prominence on a ridge. |

| | |
|---|---|
| Hanging valley | A side valley which is separated from the main valley by a steep drop. |
| Hughie | The fancied god of bad weather. |
| Hut book | Each hut contains a hut book in which parties enter their intentions and make comments of interest to others. Not to be abused. |
| Intentions book | Now often forms at Ranger Stations or road ends on which pertinent details of the party are written down for triggering Search and Rescue operations and providing valuable information for searchers should the party become overdue. |
| Leatherwood | *Olearia colensoi.* A stiffly branching subalpine shrub up to 4 m high. |
| Levee | An embankment running alongside a river. |
| Moraine | Rocks carried and/or deposited by glaciers. In this guide book, the glaciers have long gone and the moraine is often bush covered. |
| Mountain holly | *Olearia avicenniaefolia.* A subalpine shrub with tough prickly leaves. |
| Mountain radio | Small, lightweight HF SSB radio used by parties to pass messages and obtain weather forecasts. |
| MSC | Mountain Safety Council. A non-profit organisation that provides education and publishes books and pamphlets on safety in the mountains. |
| Nor'-wester | The worst weather comes with winds from the north-west in well defined weather patterns. |
| NZFS | New Zealand Forest Service. See Forest Service above. |
| Packing route | A route that can be reasonably expected to be followed by a party carrying full packs. |
| Pass | A low point in a mountain range, usually able to be negotiated. |
| Pepperwood | *Pseudowintera colorata.* An erect shrub or small tree with leaves very hot when chewed. |
| Permolat | 2.5 cm wide aluminium strips used for making venetian blinds and marking tracks. Usually red and/or white. |
| Public conservation estate | Includes national parks, reserves, conservation parks and marginal strips administered by DoC. |

| | |
|---|---|
| Radio sched | A radio contact made at a preset time. |
| Ribbonwood | *Hoheria lyallii.* A common, subalpine tree with white flowers and fresh green deciduous leaves. A poor wood fuel. |
| Road end | Where the road stops and the walking track starts. |
| Route | A general direction of travel, the details of which are left to the party following it. |
| Saddle | A low point between two rivers. |
| SAR | Search And Rescue. |
| Scrub | Sometimes also known as Monkey Scrub, consisting of subalpine bushes and makes for slow, difficult travel. |
| Scrubline | A sharp demarcation between the subalpine scrub and open tussock tops. |
| Sidle | To traverse obliquely across a hill or mountain face. |
| Slabs | Smooth, hard rock faces that can vary in inclination from flat to too steep to climb. |
| Spur | A ridge running off a range down to forks in a stream or river. A small version of a ridge. |
| Swing bridge | Commonly a bridge made of wire, capable of carrying a single person at a time. |
| Tarn | A small lake or pond, usually in a subalpine or alpine zone. |
| Three-wire bridge | A wire bridge comprising two cables for handrails and a single cable to walk along. |
| Tops | Above the bushline, usually tussock and snowgrass. |
| Track | A formed path, marked with blazes, tin disks, permolat markers, or plastic triangles. A track may be benched and major river crossings are usually bridged. |
| Trail | An unmarked path, usually formed by animals. |
| True-left | Left hand side of the river, looking down river. |
| True-right | Right hand side of the river, looking down river. |
| Walk wire | Another name for a two-wire bridge, comprising of a single wire to balance on and the other to hold on to. |
| Wapiti | Rocky mountain elk, *Cervus elaphus nelssoni.* The second largest deer species found in New Zealand, liberated at George Sound. |

# LIST OF CONTRIBUTORS

With the exceptions of the Kepler Track, Mavora Lakes and the Snowdon, Eyre and Takitimu Mountains, all sections are derived from previous editions of *Moir's Guide Book, Southern Section*. Those contributors have already been acknowledged in the appropriate editions. However, where contributors of up-to-date material from before 1986 are known to the present editor, these have been included. Where no contributors are listed the text can be taken as being materially unchanged from Gerard Hall-Jones' 1959 to 1985 editions.

Routeburn Track: *D Henson (95), DoC (92), R Peacock (94), I Thorne (94)*
Route Burn North Branch: *R McNeill (89)*
Routeburn Flats to Lake Mackenzie via Emily Pass: *R McNeill (87)*
Greenstone and Caples Valleys: *DoC (93)*
Mid Greenstone Hut to Lake Wakatipu: *R McNeill (86), D Henson (95)*
Lake Wakatipu to Upper Caples Hut via Caples Valley: *R McNeill (86)*
Upper Caples Hut to Mid Greenstone Hut via Steel Creek: *R McNeill (86)*
Divide to Key Summit and Lake Howden: *R McNeill (93), R Peacock (94), I Thorne (94), B Fraser (94)*
Falls Creek: *R McNeill (88), I Strang (88), B Fieldes (88)*
Monkey Creek: *S Lake (93)*
Gertrude Saddle: *R McNeill (90), R Kerr (94)*
Gertrude Saddle to Lake Adelaide via Gifford Crack: *B Fieldes (90)*
Homer Saddle: *R McNeill (88)*
Grave-Talbot Pass: *R McNeill (88)*
Milford Road to McPherson Hut site via Gulliver and Esperance Rivers: *R McNeill (89), BJ Smith (93)*
Cleddau Track: *B Fraser (94), KB*
Donne Valley: *B Fraser (94)*
Tutoko Valley up to Leader Creek: *R McNeill (94)*
Leader Creek to Turner's Bivvy: *R McNeill (94)*
Marian Valley: *R McNeill (92), I Thorne (94)*

Gunn's Camp to Mt Lyttle: *R McNeill (89), B Fraser (95), R Peacock (95)*
Hollyford to Phils Bivvy via Moraine Creek and Lake Adelaide: *R McNeill (89)*
Hollyford Track: *DoC (91)*
Road end to Alabaster Hut: *R McNeill (85), R Peacock (95), I Thorne(94), D Wilson (94)*
Alabaster Hut to Hokuri Hut: *I Thorne (94), D Wilson (94)*
Hokuri Hut to Martins Bay: *S Parry (93), I Thorne (94)*
Martin's Bay to Lake Alabaster via Pike River: *DoC (91), S Parry (93), Robynne Peacock(95), I Thorne (94)*
Martins Bay to Upper Kaipo Flats: *R McNeill (85), M Laternser (93), R Simpson (90)*
Upper Kaipo to Harrison Saddle via John O'Groats: *R McNeill (85), M Laternser (93), R Simpson (90)*
Harrison Saddle to Milford Sound: *R McNeill (85), R Thomson (93)*
Upper Kaipo Valley to Dale Point via John O'Groats: *V Thompson (94)*
The Milford Track: *R McNeill (88), DoC (93)*
Neale Burn: *R McNeill (90)*
North Branch of Clinton River: *R McNeill (86), C McFarlane (93)*
Epidote Cataract to Marshall Pass: *S McNeill (86)*
Joes River to Marshall Pass and North Branch of Clinton: *S McNeill (86), C McFarlane (93)*

Staircase Creek: *R McNeill (86)*, *R Buckingham(74)*
Green Valley: *R Buckingham(74)*
Diamond Creek: *R Buckingham(74)*
Diamond Creek to Poison Bay: *R Buckingham(74)*
Mackay Falls Creek: *R Buckingham(74)*
Poseidon Creek: *R Buckingham(74)*
Poseidon Cirque to Transit River: *R Buckingham(74)*, *R Wigley (86)*
Light River from Staircase Creek: *R McNeill (86)*
East Branch of Light River from Staircase Creek: *R McNeill (86)*
East Branch of Light River: *R McNeill (86)*
Light River to Poison Bay: *D Craw (80)*
Dark River to Mackinnon Pass: *M Laternser (93)*
Holdaway Memorial Hut to Worsley Forks: *BJ Smith (94)*, *T Broad (90)*
Castle River: *R McNeill (88)*, *BJ Smith (94)*
Terminus Creek: *M Laternser (93)*
Wild Natives Valley and Bernard Burn: *W Thorburn (90)*
Glaisnock Hut to The Forks: *R McNeill (88)*
Henderson Burn to Wapiti River: *B Horner (87)*
Nitz Creek: *G Souness (94)*
Taheke Creek to Worsley River: *R McNeill (88) to head of Taheke Ck*
Lugar Burn: *R McNeill (90)*
George Sound Track: *DoC (93)*
Lake Te Anau to Lake Hankinson: *R McNeill (94)*
Hankinson Hut to Lake Thomson: *R McNeill (94)*
Thomson Hut to Henry Saddle: *R McNeill (94)*
Henry Saddle to Lake Katherine: *R McNeill (90)*, *Robynne Peacock (94)*
Lake Katherine: *R McNeill (90)*,
Lake Katherine to George Sound: *R McNeill (90)*, *Robynne Peacock (94)*
Thomson Ridge: *R McNeill (92)*,
Mt Elwood Mica Mine: *R McNeill (90)*,

Henry Saddle to George Sound via Marguerite Peaks: *J Hall-Jones (90)*
George Sound Hut to Lake Alice: *R Kerr (94)*
Canyon Creek to Lugar Burn: *R McNeill (90)*, *R Buckingham(95)*
Canyon Creek to North-West Arm of Lake Te Anau: *R Buckingham(95)*
George River and Approaches: *R Suisted (93)*
Head of Stina Burn to Harrison Saddle: *S Collings (93)*
Whitewater River: *R Stokes (92,93)*
George Sound to Caswell Sound via Overlander Ridge and Stillwater Valley: *KB*
Stillwater River to Henry Pass: *R McNeill (94)*, *R Buckingham(95)*
South West Arm to Kiwi Flat: *R McNeill (94) to* Campbell Ck
Kiwi Flat to Lake Wapiti: *C McCallum (94)*
Campbell Creek to Lake Wapiti: *R McNeill (94)*, *B Horner (87)*
Lake Wapiti: *R McNeill (94)*, *B Horner (87)*
Lake Wapiti to Stillwater Valley via Twin Falls Creek: *R McNeill (94)*
Cozette Burn to Irene Valley: *R Buckingham (74)*, *C McCallum (93)*
Cozette Burn to Robin Saddle: *R Buckingham (74)*
Irene River to Windward River and Gold Arm, Charles Sound: *R Buckingham (74)*
Charles Sound to Nancy Sound: *R Buckingham (74)*
Irene Valley to Large Burn: *C McCallum (93)*
Emelius Arm, Charles Sound to Irene Valley: *R Buckingham (74)*
Large Burn to Kiwi Flat, Doon River: *C McCallum (93)*
Fowler Pass to Bradshaw Sound via Tuaraki Stream and Camelot River: *R McNeill (89) below Tuaraki Stream*
Lake Te Anau to Lake Eva and Macpherson Pass: *R McNeill (89)*
Lake Boomerang to Fowler Pass: *B Eaton (94)*

Freeman Burn Hut to Fowler Pass: *KB*
Steven Falls to Iris Burn via Lake Herries and Delta Burn: *R McNeill (89)*
Delta Burn: *G Nixon (90)*
Kepler Track: *R McNeill (89), DoC (92)*
Control Gates to Iris Burn Hut via Mt Luxmore: *D Wilson (94)*
Mica Burn: *R McNeill (93)*
Mica Burn Saddle to Oonah Saddle: *R McNeill (93), J Stevenson (94)*
Oonah Saddle to Awe Burn: *R McNeill (93)*
Awe Burn: *R McNeill (93)*
North Branch Awe Burn to Lake Annie: *R McNeill (93)* to L Annie
Lake Annie to Camelot River via Anehu Pass and Elaine Stream: *R Buckingham (74), H Renwick (95)*
Helena Falls Valley: *Robynne Peacock (94),I Thorne (94)*
Dagg Sound: *BJ Smith (94)*
Secretary Island: *I Thorne (94)*
Dusky Sound Track: *R McNeill (88), DoC (91), D Wilson (94), BJ Smith (94)*
Lake Roe Hut to Kintail Hut via Kintail Stream: *R Buckingham (74)*
Dingwall Mountains: *R Buckingham (74)*
Grebe Valley: *R McNeill (87)*
Percy Saddle: *D Humm (94)*
Florence Stream to Lake Roe, Southern Route: *R McNeill (87)* Florence *only*
Florence Stream to Lake Roe, Northern Route: *R Ferris (35)*
Florence Stream to Spey River via the tops: *G Nixon (94)*
Jaquiery River to Lake Roe: *R McNeill (87)* Jaquiery *only*
Lake Monowai and Borland Burn Area: *DoC (92)*
Carpark to Mt Cleughearn, Green Lake and the upper Grebe Valley: *R McNeill (87)*
Borland Valley: *R McNeill (89)*
Borland Saddle to Island Lake: *R McNeill (87)*
Hauroko Carpark to Teal Bay Hut: *S Parry (93)*

Te Waewae Bay to Teal Bay Hut via The Hump: *J Knight (93), C McFarlane (94)*
The Hump to Wairaurahiri Hut: *R McNeill (84)*
Lake Hauroko outlet to lower Lake Poteriteri via Rata Burn: *R Buckingham (74)*
Lake Hauroko outlet to head of Lake Poteriteri via Caroline Burn and Princess Mountains: *R Buckingham (74)*
Princess Mountains: *H Renwick (95)*
Lake Hauroko to head of Lake Poteriteri from Unknown Burn: *R Buckingham (74), M Copland (90)*
Lake Poteriteri to Lake Kakapo: *R Buckingham (74), S Brasch (93)*
Lake Roe to Head of Lake Poteriteri via Heath Mountains: *S Brasch (93)*
West of Lake Kakapo: *R Buckingham (74),*
Head of Lake Kakapo to the Richard Burn and Long Sound: *R Buckingham (74),*
Dunlop Stream: *R Buckingham (74),*
Long Burn: *R Buckingham (74),*
Preservation Inlet to Long Burn via Dark Cloud Range: *M Copland (90)*
Aan River to head of Lake Hakapoua: *R Buckingham (74),*
Big River: *R Buckingham (74),*
Cameron Mountains: *R Buckingham (74),*
Bluecliffs to Port Craig: *R McNeill (83), DoC (91), D Wilson (94)*
Port Craig to Wairaurahiri, Waitutu, and Big Rivers: *R McNeill (83), DoC (91), D Wilson (94)*
Big River to Hill E: *KB*
Hill E to Kisbee Bay, Preservation Inlet via the Inland Route: *KB*
Hill E to Puysegur Point via the Coastal Route: *P Craw (93), KB*
Eglinton East Branch to Cascade Creek and Greenstone Valley: *D Wilson (94)*
Eglinton Valley to Glade House via Dore Pass: *R McNeill (83), M Bourke (93), D Wilson (94)*
Hut Creek: *R McNeill (83), M Bourke (93)*
Hut Creek to Glade Burn via Glade Pass: *R McNeill (83), M Bourke (93)*

Mistake Creek to Hut Creek via U Pass: *R McNeill (84), S Lake (93), D Wilson (94)*
Melita Creek to Falls Creek: *I Thorne (94)*
Key Summit to Greenstone Valley via tops: *B Fraser (94)*
Mavora Lakes and Snowdon Forest: *NZFS (78)*
Mavora-Greenstone Walkway: *DoC (92), J Stevenson (94), S Parry (94)*
Mararoa River to Kiwi Burn Hut from Kiwi Burn swing bridge: *R McNeill (87)*
Kiwi Burn Swing bridge to Whitestone River via upper Kiwi Burn: *R McNeill (85)*
Tracks from the South Mavora Swing bridge: *R McNeill (87)*
Eyre Mountains: *NZFS (78), W Cooper (94,95), S Parry (94)*
Acton Hut to Cromel Branch Hut: *J Walton (93)*
Mt Bee Ridge: *W Cooper (95)*
Windley River: *J Stevenson (94)*
Mataura River to Billy Saddle and Eyre Peak: *M Spedon (93)*
Mataura River–Lochy River-Long Burn-Robert Creek: *M Spedon (93)*
Robert Creek: *M Spedon (93)*
Eyre Creek: *S Brabyn (94)*
Takitimu Mountains: *NZFS (78), DoC (93)*
Aparima Valley: *R McNeill (86)*
Princhester Valley: *R McNeill (86)*
Wairaki Valley: *J Walton (93)*
Redcliff Creek to Aparima Hut via Spence Burn: *S Parry (94), R McNeill (88)*
Whare Creek: *R McNeill (83), M Bourke (95)*
Blackmount to Dunrobin Road End via the tops: *J Rice (89)*

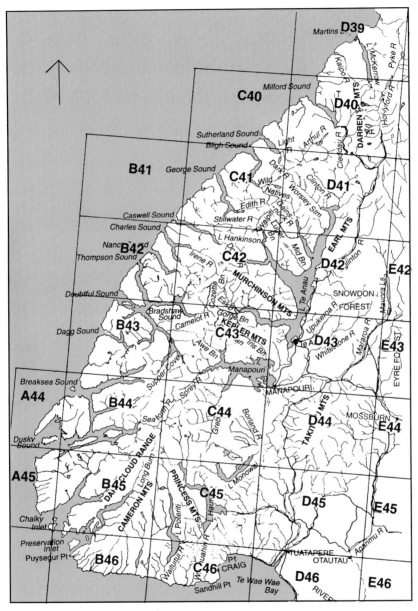

Fiordland Metric Topo Map Index

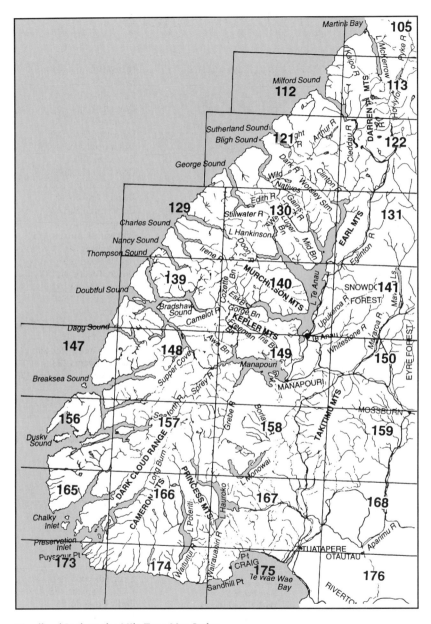

Fiordland Inch to the Mile Topo Map Index

# INDEX OF PLACES

# Some useful addresses

**Great Southern Lakes Press**  
PO Box 12-205, Christchurch  
www.thermocell.co.nz/gsl/

**Federated Mountain Clubs of New Zealand**  
PO Box 1604, Wellington  
www.fmc.org.nz

**New Zealand Alpine Club**  
PO Box 786, Christchurch  
www.nzalpine.org.nz

**New Zealand Deerstalkers' Association**  
PO Box 6514, Wellington  
www.deerstalkers.org.nz

**Mountain Safety Council**  
PO Box 6027, Wellington  
www.mountainsafety.org.nz

**Royal Forest & Bird Protection Society**  
PO Box 631, Wellington  
www.forest-bird.org.nz

**Department of Conservation**  
www.doc.govt.nz

Southland Conservancy Office — PO Box 743, Invercargill, phone (03)214 4589  
Te Anau Area Office — phone (03)249 7921  
Tuatapere Field Centre — phone (03)226 6607  
Safety Watch — Free phone 0800 999 005

**TerraLink maps**  
www.maps.co.nz

**Tourism and operators**  
Fiordland — www.fiordland.org.nz  
Southland — www.southland.org.nz

*Moir's Guide North*, the companion to this guide book, is edited by Geoff Spearpoint and published by the New Zealand Alpine Club. *Moir's Guide North* describes the routes from the Greenstone valley to the head of the Landsborough River, just south of Mt Cook.

A complete list of New Zealand tramping guide books can be found at the Federated Mountain Clubs' web site, **www.fmc.org.nz/book_and _map_sales.html/.** Guide books ordered from FMC are discounted for members of affiliated clubs.

# Mountain Radio Service

**CODAN PORTABLE SSB RADIO**

**Prices:**      $10.00 for two days
            $25.00 per seven day week
            $4.00 each subsequent day

**Weight:** 1 kilogram
**Radio schedules:**
            Daylight saving time: 8:00pm
            Standard time: 6:30pm

Mountain Radios are available from:

**Te Anau**      Southern Lakes Helicopters
            Phone: (03)249 7167, Fax: (03)249 7267
Return radios to Southern Lakes Helicopters on the Te Anau lakefront on
weekdays only between 8:30am-6:00pm, summer; 9:00am-5:00pm, winter.

**Invercargill**   Ray Phillips
            Mill Road South, RD 1.
            Phone/fax: (03)216 3751
            Phone (03)218 3305 (work)

Further details are on page 21.

# Intentions Books

Parties are strongly urged to complete their intentions in hut intentions books.
Not only do entries provide valuable clues should a search be activated, but
they provide hut-use statistics. These statistics are used by DoC to prioritize
maintenance funding. Filling in the intentions book is thus especially important for class 4 huts which receive minimal maintenance and are, at any rate,
free. Be assured that DoC does not check up on intentions books in order to
extricate outstanding hut fees from free-loaders.

Notwithstanding, parties contemplating free-loading on tracks that have hut
wardens should be aware that the wardens have methods to detect free-loaders. Those parties deliberately avoiding paying hut fees where there are wardens can usually expect Police attention.

# Changes and Damage to Structures

The following structures have been removed since this edition was first printed:

Stillwater walk-wire, p137
Glaisnock Falls bridge, p101
Borland Burn 3-wire bridges, p190.

DoC was still to decide if it would replace the Borland Burn 3-wire bridges at the time of this reprint (January 2000).

DoC has now constructed an emergency shelter adjacent to the Loch Maree 3-wire bridge (p170), on the opposite side of the river to Loch Maree Hut, as ponding of Loch Maree can result in the 3-wire bridge becoming uncrossable.

Parties should report any facility requiring urgent attention to the DoC Safety Watch free-phone, 0800 999 005.

Structures requiring general maintenance should be reported in writing to:

    The Conservator
    Department of Conservation
    PO Box 743
    Invercargill

DoC has insufficient funds to carry out more than infrequent visits to category 4 huts. Repairs to these huts and bivvies are generally carried out by DoC staff working on other projects in the area. As repeat trips are unlikely it is helpful to provide DoC with as much information as possible so that their staff can effect a repair on their first, and possibly only, visit. To this end, include suggested solutions to the problems, dimensions of broken window glass and suchlike.

# Amendments to this guidebook

This editor would very much appreciate contributions from users of this guidebook verifying route descriptions. Corrections to existing routes and descriptions of new routes are warmly welcomed. Please write to:

    Robin McNeill
    44 Duke St,
    Invercargill.
    **e-mail r.mcneill@ieee.org**

Ammendments to this guide book are posted at **www.thermocell.co.nz/gsl/.**

# Have you seen these?

The Southland Conservancy of the Department of Conservation maintains a number of species databases which contain records of bird, plant and other species sightings. If you see any of the species listed below, please record the species sighted, grid reference, date and observer's name and address. Send this information to the Information Management Section, Southland Conservancy, Department of Conservation, PO Box 743, Invercargill. Do not remove species from their habitats. However, a photograph of the species enclosed with your report is useful.

Sightings of birds which should be reported include yellowhead (mohua), kiwi, rock wren, robin, kaka and blue duck. Plants include mistletoes and other threatened species such as the alpine speargrass *Aciphylla leighii* (Darran Mountains only). Other species include weta, gecko, skink, beetle, snail and freshwater fish.

There are species experts at DoC offices who are able to assist with queries.

| Species: |
| --- |
| Region: |
| Locality: |
| Elevation: |
| Date: |
| Grid ref.: |

| Species: |
| --- |
| Region: |
| Locality: |
| Elevation: |
| Date: |
| Grid ref.: |

| Species: |
| --- |
| Region: |
| Locality: |
| Elevation: |
| Date: |
| Grid ref.: |

# Notes